Library of Congress Control Number: 2012943033

Designed by Justin Watkinson
Cover by John Cheek
Type set in Helvetica Neue LT Pro/Times New Roman

ISBN: 978-0-7643-4213-4
Printed in Hong Kong

Published by Schiffer Publishing, Ltd.
4880 Lower Valley Road
Atglen, PA 19310
Phone: (610) 593-1777; Fax: (610) 593-2002
E-mail: Info@schifferbooks.com

For the largest selection of fine reference books on this and related subjects,
please visit our website at **www.schifferbooks.com.** You may also write for a free catalog.

This book may be purchased from the publisher.
Please try your bookstore first.

We are always looking for people to write books on new and related subjects.
If you have an idea for a book, please contact us at
proposals@schifferbooks.com

Schiffer Books are available at special discounts for bulk purchases for sales promotions or premiums.
Special editions, including personalized covers, corporate imprints, and excerpts can be created in
large quantities for special needs. For more information contact the publisher.

In Europe, Schiffer books are distributed by
Bushwood Books
6 Marksbury Ave.
Kew Gardens
Surrey TW9 4JF England
Phone: 44 (0) 20 8392 8585; Fax: 44 (0) 20 8392 9876
E-mail: info@bushwoodbooks.co.uk
Website: www.bushwoodbooks.co.uk

J. Michael Mehltretter

PATEK PHILIPPE
CULT OBJECT AND INVESTMENT

With Contributions by Gisbert L. Brunner

and Photographs by Peter Milde

Schiffer Publishing Ltd

4880 Lower Valley Road • Atglen, PA 19310

1. Contents

Fig. 2 - Patek Philippe launched the first watch with a perpetual calendar and automatic movement in 1962, giving it the Reference number 3448. The design of the white gold case complements the annual calendar Ref. 5396 G in white gold, introduced in 2010. *Image Auktionen Dr. Crott/Patek Philippe.*

2. Preface

The unique watches made by Patek Philippe are among the beautiful things of this world. The significance of these watches is shown by their value and potential for value appreciation – the purpose of this book is to establish this connection. It will serve as a manual for watch collectors and investors.

In a time of collapsing banks, huge stock market losses, and growing concern about monetary reform, investors are fleeing into ever more tangible assets. These include property, precious metals, antique automobiles, and antiques.

In the search for crisis-resistant investments, acquiring vintage Patek Philippe wristwatches can be a new and still barely discussed path to take. During the recent world financial crisis in 2009 and 2010, these cult-status objects not only retained stable financial value, but also recorded astonishing increases.

In the chapter "Rarities and complications: Unprecedented record prices", we present some impressive examples. These include a chronograph, Reference 1463, with hand-wound movement and waterproof steel case, which, according to the 1961 German catalog, had cost DM 1350. This model was sold in Geneva on November 12, 2007, for CHF 529,000. The current record price was set on May 10, 2010, by a perpetual calendar with chronograph, Reference 1527, which achieved an incredible CHF 6,259,000. This collector's piece was manufactured in 1943 and sold on August 22, 1946.

This book has set itself an ambitious goal. That goal is to determine the important details necessary for secure identification of a watch, but have not previously been published. By years of research and through contact with insiders, it was possible find out astonishing things by evaluating many watches. These include:

- learning the secrets of the enameled dials
- explaining the design and inscription of the dials
- describing the inscription and identification marks on the watch case back
- how and when the Reference numbers were introduced
- itemizing names and histories of the watch case suppliers,
- exact information on the case dimensions

This has resulted in our being able to:

- illustrate the various case designs and surface finish patterns
- determine current prices for purchase and refurbishing of these watches
- compile a comprehensive checklist for buying a watch
- build a table of about 650 models (References), which were launched from 1935 to the beginning of the 1980s

This book could only be written because many watch enthusiasts and collectors made their valuable pieces available to us with their full trust. In selecting the models, the range stretched from the mid-1930s to the 1980s. We gave preference to those timepieces that have interesting technical features, broadly correspond to modern tastes, and are still affordable. Most of the watches presented have, in the course of years, been given a refurbishing by Patek Philippe. This not only established that they are original, but also makes it possible to conclude how vintage watches can be maintained and what this entails. In a summary at the end of book, all the References described are listed again in table form, so that the reader can find the desired watch immediately.

The description and valuation of a watch has a lot in common with a visit to the doctor. The doctor can only make a reliable diagnosis when he has the patient in front of him and can examine him. Using this concept, all the watches here illustrated were taken in hand, described most exactly, evaluated, and then photographed by Peter Milde. Over 200 unique composite images were created from the over 400 individual pictures. Further illustrations were made available by Patek Philippe and the auction houses.

Thanks to this book, it is now possible, for the first time, to identify a Patek Philippe wristwatch beyond question. Using multiple examples, extensive descriptions, and the elaborate photos, a reader can do the comparative analysis and make the evaluations that the previous literature did not make possible.

Watches from the current Patek Philippe collection are presented in Chapter 7. These timepieces were also photographed by Peter Milde. Here the reader will find the watches that he can buy at the nearest concessionaire without a long search. When comparing today's models with the classics, what becomes apparent is the distinctive continuity in design and technique that, over many decades, has become a mark of the products of this Geneva watchmaker. Old and new enhance each other so stylishly and perfectly that the excited watch enthusiast really does not have to make a decision: it will be the modern piece for everyday, the valuable collector's item for going to the opera and weekends.

The author is a graduate engineer and runs a medium-sized company; his métier includes development, design, and assembly. To write the account of Patek Philippe's highly eventful history, as well as the chapter on the new collection, we won the aid of the best watch historian we knew in Germany. Gisbert L. Brunner writes knowledgeably about the history of the Geneva watchmaker and reports on the new watches.

Together with the profound technical descriptions, the brilliant pictures by Peter Milde carry real conviction. His eye for technical details and the aesthetics of the micro-mechanical masterpieces enabled him to make sensational images.

Christian Pfeiffer-Belli, watch expert par excellence, edited the manuscript and provided additional valuable information.

Daniela Sygulla has earned heartfelt thanks. As the author's assistant, she took responsibility for the manuscript and made an essential contribution to the success of the publication.

For those who, after saving up for a long time, finally want to buy the watch of their dreams, this book is a must. The same goes for those who want to augment their portfolios with crisis-proof, tangible assets and want to acquire valuable collector's pieces from Patek Philippe – they will find the support they seek here. And, of course, the aesthete, who only wants to take delight in the design and beauty of the watches, should always have this lavishly illustrated book ready at hand.

Puchheim near Munich, Spring 2011

— J. Michael Mehltretter

3. On the history of the Geneva watch manufacturer Patek Philippe

Gisbert L. Brunner

3.1 PATEK PHILIPPE & CO., Geneva - a history that became legend

A certain Nicholas Paulovitch wanted to do nothing less than change the political world with his Poland policy. He is better known as Tsar Nicholas I, who ruled the Russian Empire from 1825 to 1855. His goal of making a new order actually succeeded, but lasted only relatively briefly.

But his absolutist actions had a long-term effect on the world of time-keeping. The founding of one of the most exclusive Swiss manufacturers dates back to the reign of Nicholas I – something completely unintended by the Tsar, of course.

This is how it happened. After the 1815 Congress of Vienna, which had grappled with the "Polish question", the former Poland was given to Russia. Only the former dukedom of Warsaw remained. Called "Congress Poland", it was conceded its own constitution and administration under the personal union reign of Russian Tsar Alexander I. "Congress Poland" also had an army for defending its interests. In the small "Congress Polish" village of Piaski, Joachim and Anna Patek de Prawdzik lived very modest and secluded lives, totally uninterested in the bewildering events of the time. Anna had given birth to her son Antoni Norbert on June 12, 1812.

Unfortunately – or fortunately for watch enthusiasts – the later political turmoil also affected the little Patek family. Nicholas I's profound decisions would have, above all, a lasting impact on the life of their son. At the age of 16, Antoni Norbert entered the first mounted riflemen cavalry company. Two years later, in 1830, the Polish cadets occupied the Belvedere Palace in Warsaw. On January 18, 1831, the Polish

Parliament resolved it would no longer recognize Russian rule. In response to this courageous step, Nicholas I sent in Russian troops. Heavy fighting followed, which Antoni Norbert joined as a freedom fighter against the superior Russian forces. By the turn of the year 1831-32, the revolution was suppressed and the hated result was merciless Russification. The only way for thousands of Poles, including most of the army, to save themselves, was flight from the furious Tsar's revenge and his brutal death squads.

Antoni Norbert also had to get far away, fast. At first he found political asylum in Paris. After a brief period working for a refugee committee in Bamberg, he eventually chose Geneva as his new home. He could not stay away from this famous city of watchmakers, since Antoine Norbert de Patek, as he called himself from then on, had caught the bug of measuring time.

At first, he bought high quality watch movements and had them set into cases under his personal supervision. He soon found this comparatively modest activity was not enough. On May 1, 1839, together with the ambitious watchmaker François Czapek, a Polish-Czech, Patek laid the cornerstone for his legendary life work: his own watch factory, Patek, Czapek & Co. The company, located in Geneva on the Quai des Bergues No. 29, would, with the aid of several employees, assemble around 200 high quality pocket watches a year.

In 1844, the young company displayed its products at an exhibition in Paris. It was there that Norbert Antoine de Patek first heard of a certain Jean Adrien Philippe, who had designed an astonishingly flat pocket watch, in which the movement and hands were wound and set without a key. Rather, both were

Fig. 3 - Complicated watches were previously assembled on the top floor of the original company headquarters. After a complete renovation, a very smart salon was created for private exhibits, and premiered at the new opening in 2006. Address: Patek Philippe Salons, 41 Rue du Rhône, 1204 Geneva. *Image Patek Philippe.*

easily facilitated by the crown, so that losing the key was no longer a concern, which fascinated Patek immensely. Quickly he offered the creative French watchmaker a partnership that would begin in 1845. This meant the end of the contract with Czapek. Due to serious differences about work ethics and orientation, the joint company of Patek & Czapek had no future. From this point, Monsieur Philippe would take over as technical director.

Chronology of the House of Patek Philippe's further historical development:

1845: Jean Adrien Philippe's acceptance of the offer led, on May 15, to the foundation of Patek & Co., with headquarters in Geneva, Quai des Bergues 15. Jean Adrien Philippe and Vincent Gostkowski were co-partners. Philippe's inventive powers brought Patek & Co. a range of innovative production machines, which made the most highly efficient and precise work possible.

1851: In order to make Jean Adrien Philippe's remarkable achievements known to the outside world, from January 1 the company was named Patek Philippe & Co.

1863: Jean Adrien Philippe's fundamental work on keyless pocket watches was made public in Geneva and Paris. He became the journalistic expert for all questions concerning any aspect of the pocket watch industry for the daily newspaper *Journal de Genève.*

1876: On Jan. 21, Vincent Gostkowski ended his partnership at Patek Philippe & Co. Three house staff took his place as co-partners: the Genevans Albert Cingria and Gabriel Marie Rouge, and the German Edouard Köhn.

1877: On March 1, Comte Antoine Norbert de Patek died in Geneva; Pope Pius IX had given him the title of Count for his merits as an active Catholic.

1890: Jean Adrien Philippe received the cross of the Legion of Honor of France for his merits.

1891: Edouard Köhn bought the company of the well known Swedish watchmaker Ekegrèn, ending his role as co-partner at Patek Philippe & Co. His life ended in 1908.

1894: On January 5, Jean Adrien Philippe died.

1901: On February 1, Patek Philippe & Co. became a joint-stock company incorporated with a capital of 1.6 million Swiss francs. Its name: "*Ancienne Manufacture d'Horlogerie Patek Philippe & Co. SA.*"

1932: Due to the 1929 world financial crisis and resulting collapse of high-quality watch sales in the United States, the company had to find a financially strong buyer for a majority of its shares.

The offer by Jacques David LeCoultre, a watch movement component manufacturer and supplier from Le Sentier in the Vallée de Joux, was not accepted. Taken instead, was the offer by the brothers Charles and Jean Stern. As proprietors of the watch dial factory "Fabrique de Cadrans Stern Frères", they had long had a close and very thriving business connection with Patek Philippe.

1933: The new company board chairman Jean Pfister, who until then had led the Geneva branch of the Tavannes Watch Co., in close association with Charles and Jean Stern, made the future-oriented decision that the company would from then on develop and manufacture its own watch components. Under Pfister's competent direction, the firm again was able to rapidly win ground, recover financially, and get new customers.

1934: The Henri Stern Watch Agency, New York, was founded and made responsible for Patek Philippe watches' immensely important American business. Henri Stern, born on May 25, 1911, son of Charles Stern, was the first director. The same year marked the debut of the legendary caliber 9'''-90. With dimensions of 18 x 25.6mm, the 3.65mm high shaped movement fitted exactly to the then-stylish rectangular case. It stayed in continuous production until 1967. From 1953 on, the "Gyromax" balance with free vibrating balance spring generated the timing interval.

Fig. 4 - Philippe Stern, born Nov. 10, 1938, standing before his company's collection of medallions. In the 1980s, he was still vice president and in 1993 followed his father Henri Stern as President. He remained in this position until the handover to his son Thierry Stern in 2009. *Image Patek Philippe*.

1935: The round counterpart followed, in the design of the 27mm 12'''-120. The four millimeter, hand-wound movement, with a small seconds hand, elegantly curved bridges and cocks, large screw balance, flat or Breguet spring, 2.5 hertz balance frequency, as well as attractive fine adjustment for the regulator, was impressive for its superior reliability and precision – the fine qualities naturally inherent in a Patek Philippe watch movement. This production cycle lasted until 1953. The first versions are found in the classic Reference 96.

1958: Henri Stern returned to Geneva to take over as chairman of the board from Jean Pfister.

1977: Philippe Stern, born in 1938, became general director of the company. As the third generation of the Stern family, he steered the firm's fortunes until the end of 2009.

2009: At the end of the year, Thierry Stern, after thorough training by his father, became President, taking over responsibility for directing Patek Philippe. The fourth generation of the Stern family should and will take the company well into the future.

3.2 The House of Patek Philippe's achievements in perfecting small watch technology

The wonderful microcosm of mechanical watch movements has received a whole range of decisive improvements since 1860, through the work of Jean Adrien Philippe and the House of Patek. It is no offhand statement to say that Jean Adrien Philippe's creation of the crown winding mechanism had groundbreaking importance for the genesis of the wristwatch. Without this highly functional and reliable way to wind and set the watch, the development of this revolutionizing time keeper would certainly have gone in a different direction. Everything that makes a the wristwatch eminently suitable for everyday life – being dust- and waterproof, its uncomplicated handling or sure functioning – would either not exist, or be only inadequately developed.

Fig. 5 - *All divisions of Patek Philippe are now united at the new factory in Plan-Les-Ouates. Earlier, the different specialty departments were scattered all over Geneva.* Image Patek Philippe.

The modern crown winding mechanism - a real stroke of genius

To see just what a groundbreaking development the crown winding and setting system was requires a brief analysis of what wearable watches were like before this discovery: Nothing worked without a small key. The watch was wound, as a rule, by opening the back cover of the case, and the hands set by opening the crystal. At the time, these procedures were no great evil. In the 17th, 18th, or early 19th centuries, the fortunate owners of their own timepieces still had enough time to dedicate for the necessary devotion to such special handling. The slogan of Benjamin Franklin, "Time is money", has only had its full impact in the course of the 20th century. The statement by sociologist Lewis Mumford concurs: "the wearable watch [is], more than the steam engine, the actual protagonist of the Industrial Revolution".

The real stumbling block was the inevitable key, which was so often, usually just when it was most urgently needed, not in the right place. Even before you could wind your watch, there was a search for the key. Creative watchmakers realized the urgent need for keyless alternatives for winding. It was this demand, and not the requirement for more convenience, that had already challenged Abraham Louis Perrelet. In 1770, this self-educated watch technician introduced new types of pocket watches, which were automatically wound by the body's natural movement.

We see that the search for a solution initially went in an entirely different direction than the one presumed. One of the two Perrelet models, which he called "percussion watch", had a pendulum that, impelled by the wearer's movements, moved rhythmically to and fro and so transformed kinetic energy into an energy potential. The future-oriented Perrelet equipped the other watch with a rotor. This spun continually and almost silently on its bearing shaft. These measures, however, hardly solved the problems. The self-winding mechanisms were full of glitches and only functioned satisfactorily with sufficient movement. After 1925, in the early years of automatic or self-winding wristwatches, watchmakers had to go through all these difficulties once more.

Other alternatives to self-winding were developed in the late 18th century to tighten a pocket watch's mainspring without a key. These included, for example, rotating bezels or "pump winders" that used a movable bow knob. None achieved lasting success. On March 25, 1838, the firm of the late Louis Audemars (1782-1833), based in Le Brassus, produced its first pocket watch with crown winder. Manipulation with a small pusher, made it also possible to set the watch hands by the crown. In the following years, Louis Audemar's sons tried to perfect this invention, which possibly dated back to Thomas Prest in 1820. Patek & Czapek also purchased incomplete ébauches or movement blanks with this crown winding mechanism

Charles Antoine LeCoultre (1803-1881) also used the crown. Around 1847, he introduced the most successful version of Prest's and Audemars' invention. At first, to set the watch hands with the crown, you had to use your fingernail to insert a small push piece at the same time. Later versions worked by pulling out the crown.

It was Jean Adrien Philippe who developed the recognized optimal system, still generally unaltered today. His creation was based on plans both from Breguet and Adolphe Nicole. After some 20 years of development work, on September 27, 1861, he was able to patent his well-nigh genius-like crown winding mechanism, which also made it possible to manufacture particularly flat movements. The only thing missing was the convenience of "empty" backwards hand winding of the crown. At long last, Adrien Philippe also solved this problem by adding a ratchet. The crown winder had attained a superlative level of perfection.

Yet, even with this, Philippe's inventive potential was certainly not yet exhausted. It is to his creative spirit and manual genius, that the watchmaker also owes thanks for:

– the so-called "free" mainspring, which prevents pulling off the mainspring when the watch is fully wound. This invention would later be very important for automatic movements.
– a fine mechanism to exactly adjust the regulator, which Jean Adrien Philippe patented in 1881.

Fig. 6 - In the Patek Philippe Museum, you can learn about the entire history of the firm and wonder at the many valuable pocket and wristwatches. Address: Patek Philippe Museum, Rue des Vieux-Grenadiers 7, 1205 Geneva. *Image Patek Philippe.*

A century later, Jean Adrien Philippe's successors were still intensely concerned with improving mechanical watches. That the primary focus of this work is on the wristwatch is completely understandable, given the unparalleled success of this type of timepiece.

The "Gyromax" balance, a decisive contribution to greater precision

Every deviation from an exact balance frequency causes the watch to malfunction. The watchmaker's art in fine tuning and regulating the watch movement also includes keeping it going as constantly as possible. Changes in temperature also work against this, by changing the steel coil spring's modulus of elasticity. Increasing temperatures cause the watch to run slowly; decreasing temperatures make it fast. The compensation balance created an equilibrium. In 1919, the metallurgical research of the physicist Charles-Edouard Guillaume led to auto-compensating coil springs, which made the expensive bimetallic balance wheel redundant. The "Nivarox" coil spring of 1933 worked even better. Combined with the "Glucydur" balance of beryllium bronze, introduced in 1935, the "Nivarox" spring represented an almost ideal regulator that is used in most mechanical wristwatches up to today. The rate can be controlled by shifting the regulator, whose backward fixed "key" acts on the active length of the coil spring. Sixty years ago, Patek Philippe recognized that eliminating the radially inserted grounding and adjusting screws of conventional Glucydur balance would mean increasing the diameter. This also meant an increase of the moment of inertia with approximately the same weight, creating the final result of an improved rate.

The new Gyromax balance, with its eight slotted, rotatable regulating elements set on axially arranged pins, was patented on December 31,1951. Initially, Patek Philippe also held on to the proven regulator mechanism with fine regulating device at the same time. First only used in combination with a fully free vibrating balance wheel spring, the advantages of the Gyromax came fully into effect somewhat later and up to the present. The latest version of the Gyromax has only four regulating weights. One pair allows a daily correction of +/–30 seconds, the other eleven. All in all, the rate can vary this way some 41 seconds. No wonder that the revolutionary silinvar "Spiromax" spring works best with the new Gyromax balance.

Finally, a brief calculation of a controversial and much-discussed topic: the accuracy of mechanical wristwatches. A timepiece with a daily rate deviation of plus 9 seconds fulfills the official chronometer norm. Calculated on the basis of the 86,400 seconds of an average day, the error rate is no more than 0.007 percent. Compared to a 40 ton truck, this would be about the same as the weight of a newborn baby. This is a highly respectable performance for a purely mechanical "machine". Modern Patek Philippe watches generally have notably better results. The groundbreaking, often emulated Gyromax balance made a significant contribution to this.

The stud fastener - not just for beauty

One feature of very fine watches is often a kidney-shaped small steel plate, under which the stud is held in a slit in the balance cock with two screws. The stud pins the outer end of the balance spring. Various interesting possibilities were devised to facilitate assembly and dismantling. Patek Philippe has protected four different variants of more manageable stud fasteners with a patent of August 31,1958.

Automatic winding - more than pure convenience

When Patek Philippe introduced its first automatic or self-wound wrist watch in 1953, competitors could already look back on decades of experience. Léon Leroy had already introduced the first self-winding wrist watch in 1922. Ten years later, Rolex was on the scene with rotor winding.

Patek Philippe wanted more than any just "me-too" product. Its innovation, patented on March 31, 1953, is distinguished not only by its specially designed accuracy, but also by the very effective installation of the rotary movement, to increase the energy of the mainspring. An important matter for the designers was the way power was transmitted from the rotor to the barrel. The usual change gear for polarizing the rotor movement caused significant losses due to friction and a considerable amount of idling. In contrast, the so-called offset reverser reduces the idling of the rotor, by changing rotational direction. The 18-karat gold guilloche rotor is an especially striking feature of Patek Philippe's first automatic caliber, known as 12'''-600 AT. Its high specific weight serves to increase efficiency. These movement are currently among the most beautiful and sought-after wristwatch calibers. Based on its special performance, this design, except for various detail improvements (i.e., ball bearing rotor), was kept until 1985, also in the successor caliber 27-400.

Wristwatches are very susceptible to style, and the watch industry always has to deal with this fact. As a result, Patek Philippe has also committed itself to keep developing flatter automatic calibers. This effort led finally to moving away from centrally mounted or centrally positioned rotors.

Fig. 7 - Double chronograph with hand winding mechanism (Rattrapante chronograph) Ref. 1563 with waterproof case (caliber 13''' Chrono Rattrapante, 25 jewels, movement no. 863,791, case no. 630,551). This watch was put up for auction on June 20, 1999 at Antiquorum in New York and sold for $673,500. Four years later it re-emerged on May 13, 2002, at Phillips in Geneva and sold for CHF. 2,533,500 Some years later, on Nov. 15, 2010, it appeared at Christie´s in Geneva and sold for CHF. 1,128,789 Instead of a healthy profit, this sale brought a considerable loss. *Image Phillips.*

Under the caliber designation 350 and – for the improved version – 1-350, Patek Philippe presented an automatic movement in 1969 in which the rotor mounting, a ball bearing, was relocated to the periphery of the movement. This artifice reduced the height considerably. This design required shifting the hand-set to the back side of the case. Above all, the improved caliber 1-350 could eliminate the very complicated switching device for polarizing the rotor, since the rotor moved only in one direction. This overall not very successful caliber group, was patented on September 30, 1964, and June 15, 1968.

An entirely different option to reduce the height was by integrating the rotor with winding mechanism at the factory level. This so-called planet rotor system had already been patented by Büren Watch in 1954. The caliber 1000 (height 4.2mm) started production in 1957. Eleven months later, Universal patented a similar design, the "Polerouter". Using this design principle led, in addition to the wanted reduction of the height, to decreased space for all the rest of the parts. Whether they liked it or not, Patek Philippe was also affected by this compromise in the 1970s. As Philippe Stern frankly admitted, at the beginning there was some skepticism as to whether a flat movement with unusual micro-rotor construction could legitimately meet the manufacturer's quality requirements.

Astonishing but true, and a real exception in the caliber canon of Patek Philippe, the entire development process, which would make history under the designation, needed no more than six months. The reason: amidst the quartz

crisis, the manufacturer had engaged a technician named Gérard Berret. He came from the micro-rotor warehouse and brought the required competence with him; knowing potential weaknesses, he could eliminate the negative features with his debut work in Patek Philippe's service. In the end, this meant indispensable perfection for Patek Philippe.

The caliber 240 then had two small disadvantages: a 31mm diameter is ideal today, but, in 1977, the possible applications were narrower, since larger cases were usually required. Also, there was no seconds hand. Traditionally, this had to be set either in the center or rotate by the "6". This did not go with the geometry of the 240. In 1992, Patek Philippe first ventured on a "breach of style", which spontaneously developed into a stroke of luck. In the caliber 240 PS, first installed in the immediately sold out Reference 5000, the seconds hand, unconventionally, rotates by the "5". Philippe Stern had finally shelved his original concerns. In contrast, he valued the 240, and the over 12 derivatives in between, beyond all measure. In any case, it has proven itself equally, in combination with a perpetual calendar as with a starry heaven or world time display. Had this merely 2.53mm high caliber classic not existed, it would have been developed 32 years after its premiere.

Patek Philippe's immensely versatile automatic best-seller has the designation 324. The 5.78mm high movement with one-way access central rotor joined the somewhat smaller and flatter 315 in 2004. And it appears to be destined to greatness, with the revolutionary new silicon components, such as the ultra-light escape wheel, the "Spiromax" balance and the innovative "Pulsomax" escapement, which all debuted in this exceptional caliber.

3.3 Wristwatches by Patek Philippe

The history of the wristwatch has certainly shaped that of manufacturer Patek Philippe & Co. along with it. This goes for both watch technology and appearance. Patek Philippe has patented an entire range of outstanding developments which also feature in wristwatches. Certainly there are many people who would like to be able to wear a "Patek" on their wrist, since that shows that the owner is a genuine connoisseur. For most, this wish will always remain a dream, because the watches by this classic Geneva manufacturer are costly, whether new or second hand.

Until the 1940s, wristwatch movements were made in three quality levels (first to third quality). The difference lay primarily in the execution of the oscillation and escapement systems (such as positioning the escape wheel pivots with or without cap jewels, Breguet or flat spring, the quality of the balance used, and so on). Even wristwatches with complications were also made with non-first-quality movements; however, for wristwatches with minute repeaters, only movements of the highest quality were used. Some of the Patek Philippe's outstanding achievements in manufacturing wristwatches are described in the following chronology. There can be some overlap between periods when the watch manufacturer introduced particular developments.

1850: Some five years after his split from Antoine Norbert de Patek, former co-partner François Czapek introduced a wristwatch in the form of a band with built-in watch movement.

Fig. 8 - Since 1853, Patek Philippe has resided in its current head building in the Rue du Rhône. This picture from 1860 shows the shipping then moving on Lake Geneva. The railroad was no alternative, since the stretch from Bern-Lausanne first opened in 1860 and the Gotthard railroad in 1882. *Image Patek Philippe.*

1868: The first jewelry watch with Baguette movement, in which the dial was set under a large, swing-up brilliant. Until the turn of the century, no more wristwatches are to be found in the archives.

1910: From this year, significant numbers of wristwatches are shown in the manufacturer's photo album. At first these were mostly jewelry watches, as ladies, as a matter of style, were especially taken with wearing a watch on the wrist. Somewhat later came models particularly designed for men, with round, rectangular, or barrel-shaped cases. Patek Philippe did not yet make wristwatches with calendars or striking mechanisms; these were reserved for pocket watches until the mid-1920s. It is possible that, in the beginning, Patek Philippe was not fully convinced of these new types of watches

1902: It is said that Brazilians held precision in high regard in the early 20th century, even though punctuality might not have been among their general virtues. Nevertheless, Patek Philippe took up the cause of accuracy and cooperated with their top customer in Rio de Janeiro, Gondolo & Labouriau, to make a timepiece specially designed for them between 1902 and 1927. Exactly how many were made is not known, but it must have been an impressive number, since between 1902 and 1935

this jeweler and watch specialist received some 22,264 Patek Philippe watches from Geneva, 177 of them with complications. What is sure, is that in addition to the classic three-hand "Gondolos" in different sizes, the watches also included pieces with 24-hour dials and chronographs. The ebauches or movement blanks came exclusively from LeCoultre and had an eye-pleasing square drive on the barrel arbor, gear wheels of 9-karat gold, a mustache lever with side wings, an eccentric fine adjustment for the regulator, and a Breguet balance spring. It is questionable whether Patek Philippe sent the watches for an official chronometer test, or the if the term "Chronometro" just became equated with the "Gondolo" wristwatches as they were sent to South America from about 1915.

1925: Patek Philippe modified an 1898 lady's pocket watch with perpetual calendar into a wristwatch. However, the no. 97,975 was not sold until October 13,1927. The under-dial work of the perpetual calendar featured jumping indicators. This highly sophisticated technology was not available again in later perpetual calendars models until 2009.

From 1925: Patek Philippe installed 11- and 12-line movements with minute repeaters in barrel- or pincushion-shaped wristwatch cases. These movements were first intended for ladies' pocket watches. These wristwatches, already extremely costly at the time, were sold only at such stores as Tiffany & Co, New York.

1926: Patek Philippe, working with its raw movement manufacturer Victorin Piguet & Co., developed an 11-line wristwatch caliber with basic perpetual calendar and moon-phase display. The calibers, with center date index and day and month window display, were first made in two qualities. The first piece, no. 198,063, was sold on May 22, 1928, to a U.S. customer for CHF 1000.

1927: Patek Philippe sold one of the very early wristwatch chronographs for CHF 2135. The 13-line ébauche came from Victorin Piguet. The crown was designed as a three-function push piece, for start, stop, and neutral. Utilizing 13-line ebauches from Louis-Elisée Piguet, Le Brassus, the first wristwatches with a double hand chronograph were developed.

1930: Patek Philippe watchmakers began work on movement no. 198,393, with double or rattrapante chronograph and perpetual calendar. Altogether Patek Philippe manufactured three such wristwatches between 1930 and 1938. The 11-line minute repeater movement no. 198,340 also achieved fame. In 1930 it was housed in a pincushion case. In 1939, it was completed with a perpetual calendar and set in a new, round platinum case.

1935 and **1936**: Patek Philippe delivered to the Goldsmiths & Silversmiths Co., London, two wristwatches with very special striking movements, a detachable "bell" repeater and self-striking "*Sonnerie de Bord*" (ship's bells). The method of announcing the time by chiming the ship's bell, comes from the period when hours were still measured with sand hour glasses, which had to be turned over every half hour. Each time the hour glass was turned, the ship's bell was rung. Each four-hour sea watch lasts eight "bells," each a half hour long. The first half hour was marked with one stroke, the second with a double stroke, and so forth. After eight bells, at 12, 4, and 8 o'clock, the watch ended. The movement diameter was 31.58mm x 36mm. The repeater striking mechanism was released with a push piece in the winding crown.

1936: Manufacture of no. 860,183, a wristwatch with perpetual calendar and special retrograde (recoiling) date display.

1937: In close cooperation with the genius Geneva watchmaker Louis Cottier, the first "*heure universelle*" wristwatches were made (Reference 96 HU, 515 HU and 542 HU). The dials simultaneously display the time in all the 24 time zones on earth, represented by well-known city names.

1940: Patek Philippe began work on the special order wristwatch no. 626,857, which has a centrally set hand to show the date. Days of the week and months are shown by drums on the watchband lugs. Work on this extraordinary watch took over two-and-a-half years, from April 1940 to December 1942.

1941: Serial production of wristwatches with perpetual calendars began with the Reference 1518 (13-line caliber with chronograph, case with rectangular push piece).

1942: Models with perpetual calendars and plain hand-wound movement were added, caliber 12'''-120 Q with small seconds hand. Patek Philippe made 210 of this Reference 1526 until 1952.

1944 until **1966:** Patek Philippe presented no fewer than 480 wrist- and very small pocket watch movements of simple design to the Geneva Observatory, where they participated in the annual precision competition. In 1944, 1946, 1948, 1954, 1956, 1957, 1959, 1960, and 1964, these movements carried away the prize in category D (diameter up to maximal 30mm or movement surface no bigger than 706.86mm²). Some of these movements were finally set in cases and sold with rate certificates. (These include the no. 923,822 – 923,827, caliber 12'''-120 with special balance, Calatrava case Ref. 96, sold in 1950 for CHF 850.)

1945: André Bornand made a 13 1/4-line pocket watch movement (diameter 30mm) with tourbillon and lever escapement (No. 861,115). It was only considered for chronometer competition category D, taking part in 1949, 1951, and 1953.

1948: Patek Philippe founded their own electronics division. It was later given the contract to develop a quartz caliber with analog time display as an alternative to mechanical movements.

1950: André Zibach and Eric Jaccard began work on a barrel-shaped wristwatch movement (caliber 34), with a surface of 702mm², again intended to compete in category D. It was finished in 1952. André Bornand constructed the lever-tourbillon for this movement. From 1958 till 1966, this tourbillon (caliber 34 T) participated in the Geneva Observatory competition with great success, with two of them taking the first two places in 1962.

1960: Patek Philippe models with independently adjustable hour hands came on the market. They were intended for world travelers, who wanted to easily adjust their watches to the local time when moving from one time zone to another. There were two different designs, with one or two hour hands. The latter model showed both home time and the local time (Ref. 2597 HS).

1962: Patek Philippe introduced, with Reference 3448, the first wristwatch in the world with automatic winding mechanism and perpetual calendar. It was based on the proven caliber 27-460 Q with central rotor of 18-karat gold. With 586 pieces, it became by 1982 the best seller of corresponding Patek Philippe models. The 1981 successor model 3450 also had a leap year display. There were 244 pieces made until production ended in 1985.

1985: After the ebauches for caliber 27-460 Q were used up and demand was shifting to a flatter perpetual calendar with automatic winding, Patek Philippe came up with the new caliber 240 Q. Its height, including under-dial work for the perpetual calendar, only 3.88mm.

1986: Patek Philippe showed the new version of a classic, the Reference 3970 with hand-wound chronograph, 30-minute counter, and perpetual calender. A 12-line chronograph ébauche by Lémania serves as the base for the CH 27.

Fig. 9 - The headquarters at the beginning of the 1990s. At that time the building still had two entrances, one on Quai General Guisan and the other at the rear from Rue du Rhône. After renovation, there is only one entrance from the latter side. *Image Patek Philippe.*

1989: The 150th anniversary of the firm. Patek Philippe again fulfilled its long tradition in the area of the repeater-wristwatch, and brought it new life. The company presented the Reference 3979 as its first wristwatch with automatic winding and minute repeater. This patented movement has a diameter of 28mm and height of 5.18mm. The April 9, 1989, Jubilee auction at Habsburg, Feldman in Geneva brought sensational prices for vintage Patek Philippe wristwatches.

3.4 Patek Philippe & Co.- Watchmaker *par excellence*

On to new pastures

Nowadays, no one likes to remember how things were at Patek Philippe before 1997. Administration, development, and production were scattered among several locations in Geneva. Daily work was done in very cramped conditions, and visitors, therefore, were not very welcome. In any case, at the time Patek Philippe was only manufacturing half of the its current production of time pieces.

Spring 1997 brought the shift to a nearly perfect situation and led to its becoming the manufacturer *par excellence*. Since then, all of Patek Philippe's production and administration facilities have been under one roof in the Geneva suburb Plan-les-Ouates, popularly known as the "Plan-les-Watches", because of the density of watch manufacturers there. Visitors approaching the distinctive building complex, with its much more than 155,000 square meters of space, generally do so with reverence. Most have high praise for the architecture, with its facades of white limestone (the production area for work components and cases) or pink natural stone (the watch factory and administration). When they reach the main entrance, visitors can have no more doubts about what is done inside. Here they see a gleaming stainless steel watch spring, almost as tall as a house and 82 meters long, designed by the Geneva sculptor André Bucher. Construction, which took 5000 hours, was done by a company in the space industry. A few steps further and the guests stand at the portal of the 20-meter high reception hall.

The first impression is enhanced when one enters the building. On the left side, a fascinating styrofoam relief, a huge white *opus technicus*, juts majestically upwards, inviting the visitor to linger and marvel. Interlocking "gears", "levers", and "springs" combine to depict a veritable switching mechanism. Fascinated visitors try to track the interconnections. Anyone unable to figure them out will get the desired solution from the friendly ladies at the imposing reception desk, set beneath a canopy made from a piece of the mast from former president and owner Philippe Stern's racing yacht. To the left of the entrance, as those seeking information will find, is a 16-meter high illustration by René Bittel of details of the legendary caliber 89 enlarged many times. Despite the information, non-experts will still find it hard to comprehend. This design, made of 1,782 components, is about the most complicated watch made today. It is capable of not fewer than 33 different functions. It took nine years to design, manufacture, assemble, and finish this masterwork. In 1989, the first example was sold at the spectacular Jubilee auction in Geneva for 5 million Swiss francs.

For normal watch enthusiasts, a visit to the fascinating world of keeping time ends here. Other than the some 1200 staff members who access the interior through a side entrance, the "Olympus" of the top-level watch manufacturer can only be entered by specially invited guests. Here, goods worth millions are regularly stored and future strategies and technical innovations are hatched in the respective departments. Every year some eight million components for around 40,000 watches emerge from the long hallways. Those working here do everything from smelting leftover gold to selling the products all over the world; from the noisy stamping out of the different ebauches to lovingly assembling the tiniest movement parts; from research and development using elaborate CAD programs to customer service for vintage watches. Until October 2009, all this was done in two building complexes, connected on every floor via bridges. Since then, "PP5" has been added, a building purchased and thoroughly renovated for Patek Philippe, where the "dirty" machining processes and the associated equipment are located. The bridges to the right and left are intended to bring the various professional branches and work fields closer together. Previously, administration and production were so far apart that hardly anyone knew anything about all the other work going on in the factory.

Things are totally different today. The staff now eat in two fine restaurants and drink coffee together on a terrace between two wings of the building. From there, one's eyes inevitably fall on the small palace, which the new building artistically shields from the main street. As a protected building from the 15th and 17th centuries, the "Chateau Blanc" had to be fully renovated in the course of the construction.

Philippe Stern and his son Thierry personally ensured that there is no anxiety about contact among all the various staff groups at Patek Philippe. They move through their watch empire naturally and totally informally, a friendly greeting here, an informed question there. And as long as there are no guests to entertain in the attached director's restaurant, they eat together with the employees in the canteen. People at Patek Philippe traditionally see themselves not only as a team, but also as a family. The Sterns have no inherent or inherited owner-conceit. To take over the prominent position of president, the son also had to earn his qualifications.

A Tour of the Company

A complete tour of Patek Philippe, at a normal pace, takes about a full working day. Except for a very few components, almost all watch parts are made in-house. Movement blanks or ebauches, in the usual sense of the word, do not exist anymore at Patek Philippe. More and more, the company produces watch components, finely crafted and assembled by qualified watchmakers. Using the most modern machinery, the manufacturer works precisely, with tolerances measured to the thousandth of a millimeter. The earlier contingent work, such as so called "*repassage*", is no longer necessary.

Everything begins with the research and development department, which is divided between movements and fittings (cases and watchbands). Among the most important tasks for the technicians, engineers, and watchmakers working there, is constantly seeking new procedures to increase reliability and precision, perfecting manufacturing methods, and, naturally, the creation of new products.

The areas of research activity include the discovery, evaluation, and testing of fundamental principles for the functioning of mechanical movements. The eternal fight against friction is especially important. The special nature of this challenge can be understood, when you visualize that friction accounts for around 80 percent of the energy loss in even an extremely high quality watch. The laboratory staff develops and tests new materials or technologies to reduce

friction. The best evidence of their successful creativity is the outstanding pioneering achievements using the material of which electronic dreams are made: silicon.

Working together with other manufacturers and specialists, Patek Philippe launched "silinvar". This manufactured raw material is light, anti-magnetic, especially smooth and thus creates low-friction surfaces. It had its debut in the limited Reference 5250 in a silinvar escape wheel, was used in the 5350 in the patented "Spiromax" silicon balance and culminated in the 5450, which also has the brand new "Pulsomax" escapement.

The development teams are engaged with the design and construction of new calibers as well as innovative mechanisms for other useful functions. From here emerged, for example, the future-oriented annual calendar, the functional "Travel Time" time zone mechanism, and the recently introduced chronograph caliber CH-29-535 PS. Patek Philippe has received more than 100 patents for its innovations.

A "simple" hand-wound mechanism, like the shaped caliber 25-21 REC for the "Gondolo" introduced in 2009, has to be ready for production in one to two years, while an automatic may take two to three years and a complicated mechanism, such as the chronograph caliber CH 29-535, may require as much as a full five years.

Of course, superfast graphic computers dominate the development offices. With their help, even the functioning of complicated mechanisms can be simulated. The mechanics for the prototype producers are also regularly involved in the work groups. These craftsmen can give the technicians on one side valuable advice, and, when their ideas are too high-flying, they sometimes bring the theoreticians back to earth. For logistical reasons, the prototype manufacturing is in the immediate vicinity. The group leaders and their mechanics have the most modern equipment available to them, such as computer-driven manufacturing centers and spark-erosion machines. If, against all expectations, this considerable machine park is not sufficient, the part manufacturing for complicated watches is also helpfully located right there. Short distances and close personal contacts are generally conducive to product development.

However, this principle is not always kept. Despite the expensive new building, which cost some 125 million Swiss francs, Patek Philippe has also a small, gracious building in the Vallée de Joux. Here, in the former workplace of Victorin Piguet, a gifted cadraturier, the valley dwellers are devotedly at work on the complications. Philippe Stein's offer to move them to the new buildings was given a friendly "no" by the "Combiers". Had a move been enforced, they would have renounced their demanding jobs with the world famous Genevan brand. True "Joux Vallee dwellers" just can't cope with the lively city atmosphere; in fact, it wears them down. Only in the quiet seclusion of the high valley, 50 km from the Rhône metropolis, can these contemporaries, with their penchant for tinkering, breathe freely. This gives them the necessary quiet and inspiration for such outstanding watchmakers' achievements as the legendary caliber 89.

Fig. 10 - Chronograph Ref. 130 with suspension-style gold bracelet, in its original packaging. Underneath is the guarantee certificate, issued on Sept. 22, 1948. *Image Antiquorum Geneva.*

Flexibility writ large

The principle of absolute flexibility reigns in the various production divisions of Patek Philippe. To eliminate costly stock levels, production must, if possible, react to market demands. As required, production can be converted to another caliber within a week. The high volume production levels that typify the industry are naturally and absolutely an alien concept.

For technical reasons, Patek Philippe produces the plates for the movements with minute repeaters in series of one hundred. The approximately 60 combined manufacturing processes per plate, which – as for everything – must be made accurate to the thousandth of a millimeter, take up to two months. As a result, each raw plate represents a substantial equivalent value of about 700 Swiss francs. When it comes to the mechanics of watchmaking, Patek Philippe has only one standard and that requires the best of all possible solutions.

Production technology starts out with all the "normal movements", the plates, bridges, and wheels. Here only the latest and most modern machines are used and more than 200 such machines are needed to produce all the required components. Some were developed out of close cooperation between Patek Philippe and competent machine manufacturers, as the only way to meet the specific requirements of such demanding manufacturing. The new "PP5" plate-making facility alone holds double-digit millions' worth of highly technical, mostly electronically driven, equipment. With all technical perfection, there are further manufacturing processes, which the humming robots, shining with oil, cannot perform, even with all their drilling and cutting heads. These include attaching the oil sink for the barrel arbor bush or the milled grooves for barrel and escapement. Here, each part must be clamped by hand several times in preparation for the appropriate manufacturing process; no machines can do the tedious burring work. Only skilled hands and well-nigh antiquated sounding tools can be used.

The manufacturing of wheels and pinions is as it was in bygone days. While pinion movement blanks are made with the aid of renowned, cam-controlled machines, further finishing processes are generally completed by hand. Including finishing, a wheel set (pivot, staff, gear drive and gear wheel) requires about 40 separate operations. Most impressive, for example, is making the small stars for the day of the week control. Next to normal polishing for the tooth flanks, Patek standards require an indentation to better contain the oil. Overall this task takes just less than 10 minutes.

In this way, the work expended to make the parts of a mechanical caliber adds up significantly. Anyone who has seen these workrooms has no trouble understanding the price of a Patek Philippe watch movement. On the long path from a raw brass part to the ticking movements, there is no point where any compromise is tolerated. These high standards are shown by the fact that since November 2009, without exception, all Patek Philippe calibers bear the notation, "of our own manufacture". Another criteria of quality is the Geneva Seal, gradually going out of use, which, since spring 2009, the manufacturer has been replacing with its own, even more exclusive *poinçon*, or hallmark.

About the small components

The plate is the supporting part in every movement, on which the bridges, cocks, and other parts are mounted. In this sense, the plate holds everything together. At Patek Philippe, these plates are made of brass or nickel silver, alloyed with copper, zinc, and nickel. Depending on the caliber, producing a plate takes 30 to 50 different work steps and, for complicated movements, it can be many more. Galvanic rhodium plating makes a silvery surface and protects it from corrosion.

To reduce work time, the plate milling workshop functions, like the other work places, as a so-called manufacturing island. This means nothing more than that the raw materials enter on one side and are sent on from the other.

Bridges and cocks are small brass or nickel silver plates, in whose – often jeweled – bores at least one mobile pivot rotates. Cocks are screwed to the plate at one end, bridges on both sides. Their names come from their functions, such as balance cocks, barrel bridges, train wheel bridges, and so on. A "simple" hand-wound movement generally requires four such pieces; complicated calibers seven or eight. Each piece needs 25 to 45 separate manufacturing steps, including manual burring, manual counter drilling to remove burrs and sharp corners on bore holes, and the insertion of dowel pins, jewels, or small guide tubes. The watchmaker uses small metal scrapers and pneumatic press staves to accomplish the task. The final work is done by hand, so that there is no damage to the components.

To please the eye, all cocks, bridges and plates get an elaborate finish, a big contribution to the great beauty of a deluxe movement à la Patek Philippe. Affixing the Geneva Seal and/or the circular graining is of course done by hand. The oblong *Côtes de Genève* is inscribed by hand, using a small boxwood wheel with grinding paste. The recipe for the paste is a secret of Patek Philippe. The small, circular graining served earlier to deal with the dust which had penetrated the case. Today they are mainly decorative. These *"Kringel"* or whorls, are also created by hand, using a cratex, a stick of hardened emery. The craftsman's art and experience is displayed in a very consistent arrangement.

The turning shop produces mainly round pieces: wheels, pinions, shafts, and barrel drums. To manage having everything ready "in time", the precision machines run 24 hours a day.

The gear wheels and steel pinions are made in the milling department. The preparatory and follow-up work is also performed here, such as stamping, planing, beveling, and grooving. Gilding protects the brass wheels from corrosion. In contrast to the gear wheels, the pinions have only a few teeth. They are milled from steel, then hardened and polished. After this, a special turning shop makes the shaft pivots. The pivots are rolled out, pre-polished, their faces rounded, and finally, again, highly polished. Only then are the wheels grouted with the pinions.

Patek Philippe produces one million gear wheels annually, in a range of some 300 types. As with bridges, cocks, and other components, the number of gears needed for a movement depends on the complexity of the caliber. At the end of its manufacturing, each gear wheel has 40 to 60 work processes behind it – and only then is the Patek Philippe standard achieved. Of the 42 steps needed to make a third wheel for the round caliber 215, only 33 percent are necessary for functioning. Another 24 percent are required to meet the Geneva Seal regulations and, even if no longer verified by this hallmark, they will continue to be an absolute requirement for the Patek Philippe *poinçon*. The remaining processes, 43 percent, are due to self-imposed quality criteria.

Trust is good, control is better

It should be obvious that, after every production step, all the individual parts must undergo a strict quality control. There are specialized workshops for this delicate work, equipped with ultra precise measuring instruments. Using these "Statistical Process and Quality Control" procedures, parts are examined many times in the course of the manufacturing process. The first test is made by whomever produced the piece. Next, the inspection team makes sample tests and, finally, there is a further, minute checking of the movement part. These time-consuming controls have another purpose in the production process: in this way, technicians can recognize eventual deviations from the norm early and optimize the manufacturing process. Altogether, the time expended for checking all the components in a movement series, during production and assembly, is 500 to 600 hours.

The final process

At the conclusion of all these procedures, the watchmakers in the pink building take over. They and their skilled hands create that unity that is known to be more than the sum of its parts. That the ultimate school of the watchmakers' art reigns here, that all steel parts are bevelled and polished many times over, is obvious from just a glance at a Patek Philippe watch movement.

Fine core, fine case

Without the protective and ornamental watch case, even the finest movement is only of limited value. Knowing this, Patek Philippe now also produces its own cases. In the responsible workshops, the same strict measures apply as for making the movements. Modern and older techniques go hand in hand, to create, step by step, a treasured artwork of our time.

The Reference 3919, the elegant Calatrava with its hobnail pattern bezel, for example, simply could not be manufactured without the applied craftsmanship of an experienced *guillocheur*. His studio is a small room, where the tone is set by two technical "fossils" from 1905 and 1913. One of these, more complicated since it makes a variety of ornamentations, behaves "like a diva". On many days, whatever you do, you achieve nothing, just because this complex mechanism is not pleased. This often means taking long hours to discover whatever might be the tricky problem with the machine's functioning – a really tedious business. Back to the hobnail-patterned bezel: at most 40 pieces can be made a day, using one of the *guillochier* machines and incessant hand motions reminiscent of Charlie Chaplin's *Modern Times*.

Since qualified *guillocheure* are rare, Patek Philippe opportunely sets aside the most gifted apprentices for the masters of their expertise, and not just here. This is the only this way the manufacturer can make a future for traditional craftsmanship. Taking care of the up-and-coming generation is one of this manufacturer's most important policies. A firm still strongly characterized by its craftsmanship – despite the most modern machinery park – survives based on the commitment that traditional techniques should be handed down from one generation to the next, from father to son, from master to journeyman. This reality and a very small personnel changeover ensure continuity, which is so important to Philippe and Thierry Stern and their family firm. A Patek Philippe automatic wristwatch, ready for sale in its final packaging, represents 1212 production steps that have taken over a year to complete. In this process, all movement components are repeatedly subjected to very time-consuming controls. During assembly alone, checking and observation takes about 160 hours. Any further commentary is superfluous. Philippe and Thierry Stern hate complaints; such things are simply not appropriate for the image of Patek Philippe.

Worth every effort: the watch "face"

Conscientious designers, as part of their professional work, reflect on just about everything. This includes the design and appearance of watches. The dial, as clever brains realize, is itself responsible for a good eighty percent of the watch's appearance. In other words, creating the disc on which the hands keep turning their circles, which is the first thing most people see, enjoys a high, if not the highest priority, for Patek Philippe wristwatches. It is well known that the first impression distinguishes one item from the others within seconds. Something else we cannot ignore is that, in the course of a day, men and women look at their watch dials more often than they look in the mirror.

It is no wonder, then, that at Patek Philippe and at Flückiger, its daughter firm which manufactures watch dials on the outskirts of the small city of St. Imier, Jura canton, these important components get all kinds of attention. Color, surface design, indices, and printing are all given full consideration, so that, with this myriad of details, the final product creates a coherent impression of the entire ensemble, whether consciously or unconsciously.

Everything begins with the design or many designs, to be exact. Along the long, tedious journey from the first prototype sketches to the finally approved product, signs reading "trial and error" crop up again and again. What looks good on paper, is not necessarily as good as a finished product, especially when combined with the watch case made of one of many different materials, the hands, and the various kinds of watch bands.

Every detail is carefully considered and oriented towards everything else. At Flückiger, the creative and manufacturing processes have been combined for generations, bringing together high grade technological and artistic know-how. For Patek Philippe watches, the starting point for making dials is often solid gold. The blanks, including the holes for the center arbor or pin and the window for the digital indices, are made by conventional stamping – using some very martial-looking equipment – or with aid of electronically controlled production centers. This is how Flückiger makes the sometimes microscopically small appliqués.

Embossing, etching, brushing, and satin-finishing are all used for the all-important surface design. Dials for Patek Philippe chronographs or the many other complicated timepieces require more manufacturing processes. These include making indentations for secondary dials or milling cut-outs on the back for the control mechanism. All this work is done with the highest precision; even a deviation to the three- or four-hundredth of a millimeter is unacceptable.

If the dial should display hand-riveted indices, each of these requires at least two tiny holes with a diameter of just three decimillimeters. All must be drilled with greatest accuracy, and that on a material thickness of usually just 0.4mm. The dial is then fastened to the movement, using a cylindrical pin, known in technical language as a "foot". This is made of copper and is electrically soldered to the holes in the plate. Extremely exact work is essential here, so that the dial fits perfectly.

After these preparatory procedures and many cleanings, the dial blanks are sent to the grinding and polishing department, where they get a perfect surface for later design processes.

First comes a single galvanic surface tempering. This also applies to "high-end" products such as dials made by Flückiger for Patek Philippe that are subsequently lacquered. The expenditure on lacquering, which must be done in absolutely dust-free areas, is no less high. Up to 15 layers of enamel are applied, one atop the other. After each spraying, the dial is kiln dried at 60 degrees C, ground and polished. After the final step of this fine work, at least 11 to 12 layers of lacquer remain. Galvanized, i.e., gilded, rhodium-plated, or silver-plated surfaces are carefully sanded and then painted with colorless cellulose lacquer.

The next work at Flückiger is printing the various scales, index markers – unless they are applied by hand – signatures, and inscriptions. The work is primarily done by hand, using the so-called pad-transfer method, with special rubber ball. The writing or inscriptions are photo-technically etched in a steel plate and the printers to fill the resulting indentations with paint using a putty knife. After removing the excess material, they apply the rubber stamp to the plate; the stamp takes up the paint and transfers the printing to the dial, with a hundred percent accuracy. Multicolored printing requires a corresponding number of steps. It takes a specialist to apply luminous materials.

The dial makers also put a lot of emphasis on quality control. Every piece, without exception, is examined meticulously under a magnifying glass. Any rough edges, imprecise centering, or other blemishes mean it is rejected.

The sky is the limit as far as dial making at Flückiger is concerned. For complicated pieces, manufacture can involve 65 steps or more. Glittering diamonds or colored stones get their own chapter.

Forward planning is essential in the manufacture of watch dials. A prototype can be made relatively quickly, but producing the series of dials can take months. High end manufacturers such as Patek Philippe and its Jura daughter firm Flückiger, think ever further into the future for dial making. To provide for all eventualities and be able to guarantee perfect service later, production always exceeds immediate requirements, so that the Geneva manufacturer can supply a dial, even years later. There is no question that the "face" of a Patek is worth every effort.

Patek Philippe and its own *poinçon*

Of course, Philippe Stern has nothing against the traditional *Poinçon de Genève*. How could he? For centuries, Patek Philippe has helped it earn its international reputation. Yet, the manufacturer has relinquished this tried and true quality seal after a long internal discussion. The company will continue to fulfill the relevant quality criteria. In the future, however, it will be Patek Philippe's own seal, developed over many years, that attests to the watchmaker's extremely high quality standards in all areas. The seal encompasses all the criteria of design, technical realization, the quality of handcrafted execution, and the indisputable precision of a high-quality watch movement. For the latter, the Geneva Seal is no longer relevant. Patek Philippe has also integrated other components, such as cases, dials, hands, and band lugs in its broad manufacturing range. According to the Sterns, both father and son, "a modern quality label must be good for the entire watch. It must define all responsibilities and distinguishing qualities, which are relevant for Patek Philippe – manufacturing, precision, and long-term maintenance of the watch. Furthermore, adequate consideration must be given to the aesthetic and functional aspects of the finished timepiece".

In addition, Patek Philippe guarantees its customers lifetime service for its noble time products.

Fig. 11 - World time watch Ref. 2523 HU (*Heures Universelles*) with yellow gold case and two crowns (caliber 12'''-400, movement no. 722,706, case no. 306,205). One such model was auctioned on April 2, 2006 at Antiquorum in Geneva for CHF 2,250,500 (movement no. 722,708, case no. 306,210). *Image Antiquorum Geneva.*

Fig. 12 - The first watch with automatic winding mechanism was launched in 1953 and has the Reference Number 2526. The attached gold band is of D-type *guilloché* and cost, according to the 1961 catalog, exactly DM 1285 extra. The supplier was the firm Gay Frères of Annemasse in the Savoy Alps, which started in 1835, (Caliber 12'''-600 AT, movement no. 760,951, case no. 683,698). *Image Antiquorum Geneva*.

In this way, the Patek Philippe makes a promise of quality, much greater than that encompassed by the Geneva seal. These stated assurances naturally apply also to watches that will soon come on the market or are still just on the computer. Chronometry is the dominant factor in creating watches and implies the best possible readability for all indicators. Beyond this, the family concern values timeless elegance in relation to all current style trends, which is realized through the flattest possible design of the watch movement and an equitable case diameter.

Every step taken in this regard can be found in the detailed set of criteria, since all employees must know exactly just what is to be done, observed, and, also, omitted at every station in the development, manufacture, regulation, and quality control of a watch.

Making the components of a automatic movement requires, for example, no less than 1200 manufacturing steps. The quality control process (control of the parts at the work places, statistical examination, end-control) takes many hundred hours altogether. The finished, mounted sub-assemblies also have to undergo incoming controls. The finished watch movements, according to complexity, have been subjected to examinations that can take up to thirty days. Then, the finished watch must of course again undergo testing. Various checks, precision measurements, wearing simulations, and function control require up to 20 days. There is also a scrupulous accuracy check. For this, the manufacturer distinguishes, on technical grounds, between small watch movements and larger ones of more than 20mm diameter. Tolerance for the first is between -5 and +4 seconds per day; the latter are required to be within the narrow spectrum between -3 and +2 seconds per day. These rates must be achieved without exception, while the movement is housed in its protective case.

This is certainly not all new. Patek Philippe already held to these quality standards before introducing their own seal. They have created their own committee to ensure consistent maintenance of these standards, as of course was done earlier by Philippe Stern and, today, by his son Thierry, who not only have a name, but also a reputation, to lose.

Retrospective: the "*Poinçon de Genève*"

At first glance, the hallmark of Geneva is rather unimpressive. Its origins go back to 1886, when, on December 6, the first law for voluntary quality control of wristwatches by the Geneva Observatory came into effect. It set the legal basis for usage of the so called "Geneva Seal". As of April 5, 1957, this regulation was strictly tightened. From then on, the *Poinçon de Genève* set eleven different quality requirements. The accuracy was also examined. A strict, full 18-day control program became mandatory for wristwatches with a movement diameter of maximum 30mm. The quality controller would grant the hallmark only after all criteria were met.

The most recent version dates from December 22, 1994. It includes every quality control check, which Patek Philippe had already imposed for decades. For this process, the numbered movements were submitted to the Genevan Watchmaking School, where the "Office for Voluntary Control of Geneva Watches", with its official certification staff, is located. They must all be Swiss citizens and have no conflicts of interest. Previously, they accepted only mechanical movement watches which had been assembled and regulated in the Canton of Geneva. Regulation included twelve guidelines for the quality level of all components and their processing. These focus on the steel parts or the screw heads, jewels, gear wheels, shafts, and pivots. Further guidelines address how the balance spring is mounted, technical execution of the oscillation and escapement systems, the craftsmanship of the design of the winding and hand setting mechanisms, as well as the amount of effort required to create other movement parts. Only accuracy is no longer in question. Here, Patek Philippe traditionally sets the highest standards, meeting the official chronometry examination without any problem.

Caliber, caliber

Caliber goes with watch making as salt goes with soup. At Patek Philippe, the chapter of manufacturing their own movements began in 1932, when the Stern family became the new owners. Charles and Jean Stern, who were not watchmakers themselves, immediately engaged Jean Pfistger, an experienced craftsman. The mission was to give watch manufacturing at Patek Philippe a modern face and create an interesting spectrum of their own movements using modern machinery; the new technical director immediately tackled the job. In 1934, Patek Philippe presented the new design caliber 9'''-90, which at 18 x 25.6mm, exactly suited the growing trend for rectangular cases. Its production continued unbroken until 1967. The 27mm 12'''-120 came in 1935. This hand-wound movement, manufactured until 1953, had a small seconds hand, elegantly curved bridges and cocks, larger screw balance, flat or Breguet springs, 2.5 hertz balance frequency, and attractive fine regulation for the regulator pointer. It made a great impression with its superior reliability and precision. The successor designs, the 12'''-400, the 27 SC and the smaller 23-300 (diameter 22.7, height 3mm) created the bridge to the modern spectrum of manual winding mechanisms, which left nothing to be desired. It ranged from the 21.9mm small 215 for ladies' wristwatches up to the ultra complex, 686 parts R TO 27 QR SID LU CL, which gives gently ticking life to the immensely fascinating Sky Moon Tourbillon.

The latest members of the caliber family include the 25 21 REC with manual winding. The three letters indicate a shaped movement. It measures 24.6 x 21.5 x 2.57mm, has over 44 hours power reserve, 130 parts, and is considered the legitimate successor to the legendary caliber 9'''-90, which has already been discussed.

Pretty complicated

Patek Philippe is considered the manufacturer of mechanical complications. In the R 27, the R stands for minute repeater, which is the costliest way of telling time. Already the understatement – caliber R 27 PS with self-winding and small seconds hand, represents a beguiling delicacy. The really sophisticated caliber R TO 27 PS QI also has minute repetition, along with perpetual calendar, jump indicators, and tourbillon. Anyone wearing the 686-component R TO 27 QR SID LU CL on their wrist, has the "Sky Moon Tourbillon". Here, the functional interplay of wheels, levers, and other components, presents the mean solar time, a perpetual calendar with recessed date hand, the leap year cycle, and the phases of the moon.

Time recorders

Patek Philippe introduced the first wristwatch chronographs in the 1920s. With their own calibers, of course, they next moved to their own caliber notations. This 13 line piece, considered by informed watchmakers as the finest ébauche made in Savonnette- or Lépine-style, was supplied by the appropriately experienced specialist Victorin Piguet, from the Vallée de Joux. The difference is shown by the position of the permanent seconds hand and 30 minute counters. In a hunter calibre, the seconds hand is situated at a right angle to the winding stem; in a Lépine calibre, it is mounted in line with the winding stem.

The equally well known and treasured Reference debuted in 1934, equipped with the Valjoux-Caliber 23VZ. That year, the 13 line, 5.85mm high movement with classic intermediate wheel control, had already reached its maturity. In spite of its high quality, Patek Philippe submitted it to a complete reworking. This included installing the lever, seconds, and carrier wheels under separate cocks, a regulator pointer with swan-neck fine regulation, the individual design of the chrono-bridge, a cap for the intermediate wheel, and a complete redesign of the clutch wheel and its installation concentric to the second wheel shaft.

For the next 52 years, chronographs all came under the banner of this fine watch movement. In its purest form, it inspired the References 130, 530, 533, 1463, 1506, 1554, 1561 und 1579. Reference 146 has split seconds; 1518 and 2499 have, besides the chronographs, perpetual calendars. The three versions of the top Reference 2571 can boast a drag pointer and perpetual calendar. Since Valjoux ceased selling the 23VZ in 1982, Patek Philippe had to find an adequate replacement. The manufacturer found it in the manual caliber 2320, the Nouvelle Lémania (earlier Lémania CH 27), equipped again with intermediate wheel control and horizontal wheel coupling.

From 1986, the movement blank produced in the Vallée Joux supplied the basic components. Patek Philippe modified the design of the lever and seconds wheel cogs, the chronograph bridge, the form and installation of the clutch wheel and the intermediate wheel with cover plate, and optimized the torque by modifying the gear wheel profiles. A new gear transmission ratio resulted in 60-hour power reserve, a good ten hours more than for the original. Also not to be missed is the Gyromax balance with free oscillating Breguet spring.

The CH 27-70 Q came on the market in 1986 in the Reference 3970 with perpetual calendar. The 5970 with a larger case came in 2004. The caliber CH 27-70/150 has a split seconds indicator; it ticks in the Reference 5004 of 1997. In 1998, the purist Reference 5070 was finally born. But, since autumn 2009, the glorious Lémania chapter has become history. The future meant 100 percent manufacturing, including hand-wound chronographs.

The chronograph itself

The prologue to Patek Philippe's own chronograph movements for wristwatches had already begun in 1998. Philippe Stern personally gave the order for developing the 28-520 IRM QA 24H with automatic winding. The president's specifications included that they be unconditional suitable for larger series. Otherwise required were such traditional features as an intermediate wheel, meeting all the criteria for the Geneva Seal, eighth of a second stop accuracy, thanks to four Hertz balance frequency, 55 hour power reserve, power-saving friction clutch, 12 hour counter, permanent neutral position, also called "flyback", and an annual calendar. The execution had to be innovative, incorporating not only all traditional features, but also the best possible readability for all the indicators. For such a proverbial squaring of the circle, there were a lot of pitfalls to be avoided. To complete the first prototypes in 2003, there were extensive tryouts and 30 versions with special cases were given the horological "acid test" at the independent examination institution, Chronofiable. In 2006, Reference 5960 went to the specialist trade. Due to the friction clutch and flyback function, the caliber CH 28-520 did not require a permanently moving seconds hand; the function control directly took over for the chronograph hand. It required no additional energy from the movement and could therefore turn continually. The chronographs started by activating the zero position setter by the "4".

Manufacturing hand-wound chronographs

In 2005, Patek Philippe created a stir with the split seconds Reference 5959. The installed CH R 27-525 PS measured only 5.25mm high. A look into the thick archive books, in the pages for 1903, shows a 5.9mm high movement number 124,824. This historic caliber, with an ébauche from what is now the Patek Philippe daughter firm, Victorin Piguet, was the inspiration for the flattest split seconds chronographs of all time, executed with all the features of traditional watchmakers' artistry. These included two intermediate wheels for chronograph and flyback hand. It may be that this marked the establishment of a "*haute horlogerie*", or high quality watch making department, with a small workshop, where five to six master craftsmen concentrate on one complication, working hand in hand, like watchmakers of former times.

Serial production is an alien concept. All movements are unique pieces, with all the components individually filed, chamfered, polished, justified and finished. The ultra-flat construction is made possible by the special design of the continuously running 60 minute counter. But that is hardly the only innovation of this caliber. A new patented tooth profile for the chronograph mechanism wheels ensure the light, barely vibrating movement of the chronograph hands. A balance stop lever ensures exact setting of the time to the second. The Gyromax balance including Breuget spring is typical for Patek Philippe, and, of course, the Geneva Seal.

New, exclusive, classic, yet different: the CH 29-535

The genesis of the newest of all Patek Philippe calibers began in 2004, as the finale for the CH 27-20 was already approaching. The six member development team around watch engineer Pierre Maurice Rochat faced the challenge: the new CH 29-535 PS could not to be too similar to its predecessor, but still had to keep all the classic features and have a power reserve which would function through the weekend. Precision and reliability were musts. Unconventional paths were open for the technicians and watchmakers and, here and there, they actually took them.

At first glance, the complex, 269-part "Opus Technicus" appears fully conventional. A chronograph, hand-wound classic required an intermediate wheel as well as a horizontal clutch wheel, which connected movement and chronograph at the touch of a button. This is the only thing providing complete insight into the interconnected functions, since the force-fitted vertical variant always made the connection secretly.

In the CH 29-535, the clutch wheels have the rolling gears, already proven in the CH R 27-525 PS. It also minimizes the feared start jump from the meshing of the gears. Anyone who has eyes to see, quickly recognizes the separated cocks for the chrono-central wheel and the 30 minute counter. Until now, these made a v-pattern here.

Then comes the turn of the totalizer, which counts up to 30 circuits of the central chronograph hand. Here, practically everything is new. The engineers devised a sophisticated, lightning quick, jumping design. The spring triggers a fusee on the shaft of the chronographer hand. A lever and a coil spring allow the small counter hand by the "3", with minimal time tolerance, exactly one quick step forward when the rotating chronograph hand reaches the "12".

Forced synchronization and other refinements

When the chronograph is stopped, to be able to read the arrested time-interval, the hands must remain in absolutely the last position. This is taken care of by blocking levers, which work like brake pads on the chronograph wheels, after the stop button is pushed. Here the CH 29-535 shines, with its intelligent positive control by means of a swiveling clutch lever. Its free end is lifted to disengage from the eight prongs of the pivoted intermediate wheel. However, at starting it always falls between two prongs. This requires an exact definition

of the depth of engagement. Here the traditional cover cap for the first time gets an active function as a feature of the finest chronographs: minimal eccentricity allows sensitive regulation of the clutch lever movement angle. Traditionally this job is done by a less finely adjustable eccentric screw in the plate.

Complex procedures

There remains the chronograph zero reset/flyback. The watchmakers gave this lever, whose two ends press on the heart piece, an equally stable and smooth running ruby bearing. In the CH 29-535, the V-shaped object has two parts. When the flyback push piece is pressed, the left one turns the central chronograph hand "northwards". After a brief delay, the right one activates the minute counter linked arm. The narrowly flexible fastening and use of separate flyback springs for each end, allows the precision desired by Philippe Stern without individual adjustment and alignment. The function-oriented geometry is always retained.

Apart from this, the flyback is a ticklish issue with chronographs. Due to their length alone, enormous pressure is put on the resetting chronograph hand; the hand tip recoils like a whip. Pictures taken with a high speed camera prove what the eye cannot see. The deflection can reach up to 60 degrees. The unfortunate result: in extreme cases the hand comes off its shaft, and it can bend or even break. Patek Philippe has prevented all this with the CH 29-535. The already mentioned totalizer fusee has an inlet on its rung, with a depth conforming to the stated 60 degrees. At zero reset, the ingenious tip of the minute counter lever dips into this recess, so that the zero-set chronograph hand moves as a whole, and without any wagging into the "readiness position".

Homage to the ladies

With all his modesty, Philippe Stern does not wish to hide his pride in this new movement. "Besides, this is the first, we have developed with regard to our own Patek Philippe quality seal". The gentle sex explicitly was able to enjoy the first pieces, which were christened "Ladies First" by Patek Philippe, due to the watch band which belonged to it. The Reference 5070 for men followed in 2010.

New subjectivity at Patek Philippe

There is no doubt about it: staying still means retreat. Astonishingly, this is nothing new for the oh-so conservative mechanical watches, which can proudly look back on more than 700 years of very diverse history.

So the 21st century offensive in materials, in which Patek Philippe is appropriately very involved, is not especially surprising. The magic word is silicon. In monochrystalline form, this material, of which electronic chips are made, has the same crystal structure as diamonds. This means that it is very hard, 60 percent harder than steel, yet very light, 70 percent lighter than steel. Silicon is non-magnetic, corrosion-resistant, and, without elaborate post-processing has an extremely smooth surface that significantly reduces friction.

That makes oil superfluous. Silicon is also elastic, but not malleable, which caused some headaches for potential users. To solve the problem, Patek Philippe, Rolex, and the Swatch Group cooperated with the Center for Electronics and Microtechnology (CSEM) and the Institute for Microtechnology of the University of Neuchâtel. In 2005, they reached their goal. Patek Philippe introduced a classic lever-escapement with silicon lever, installed in just 100 Reference 5250 pieces with the annual calendar-automatic caliber 324 QA. In 2006, the "Spiromax", a patented "silinvar" balance spring, with unaltered length, self-centering balance spring collet to fasten it the balance shaft, and integrated balance spring stud fastening, was installed in the same movement. Due to its ingenious geometry with thicker segments on the outer ends, it swings in the flatter version, as precisely as a Breguet spring. Just 300 associated Reference 5350s were made.

Special class escapement

Patek Philippe called the third ignition step of the ambitious Advanced Research Innovation Program quite simply 5450. As with 5250 and 5350, it was based on positive experiences with the patented silicon material "Silinvar". In contrast to components of pure silicon, this offsets temperature fluctuations. Also, Silinvar needs no surface coating. The "Pulsomax" escapement, launched in 2008, with Silinvar escape wheel and lever, was just a logical consequence. In contrast to other escapement concepts, Patek Philippe remained true to the principle of the good old Swiss lever escapement. At the same time Pulsomax brings three remarkable innovations with it:

1. The lever is a mono-block structure without inlaid ruby pallets. Adjusting the depth of penetration into the escape wheel is superfluous. Both pallets are optimally shaped to maximize the energy flow, a new geometry which Patek Philippe has patented.

2. The second "Pulsomax" innovation refers to the built-in limitations of the lever for its angular motion. The wall inset in the small pivot or the plate, can be omitted. Here, Patek Philippe consciously broke from the stated rules of the Geneva Seal, which until then adorned all the manufacturer's movements.

3. The function of the security pin set between the lever forks, which prevents the parallel fork swinging off, is retained. Pulsomax has this protective device in the form of a small bridge set on a second horizontal level between the two fork ends of the anchor. Patek Philippe has also patented this technical detail.

To increase efficiency, the engineers increased the size of the lever pallet area. This required a modified silinvar escape wheel with 16 instead of the until-now required 20 teeth. The approximate 15 percent increase in energy throughput, brings 30 percent more power autonomy with it. As a result of this increase, Patek Philippe has newly conceptualized the wheels of the entire automatic caliber 324 S IRM QA LU, with a four hertz balance frequency. This finally means oil-free functioning, giving a longer life to this 356 component movement. Production was again limited to 300 pieces.

Innovation Epilogue

Philippe and Thierry Stern confirmed in unison that silicon has a future at Patek Philippe. The total of 700 silicon timepieces 5250, 5350, and 5450 have shown no problems. The quality of the watches' timekeeping is, according to customer response, more than positive. The best evidence for the great perspectives for this material is the construction of a new factory building between La Chaux-de-Fonds and Le Locle. From 2010, the tradition-rich manufacturer will work with the new subjectivity of mechanical luxury watches. After more than 170 years, things are still exciting at Patek Philippe. And that is what creates the fascination of this family manufacturer.

4. What collectors and investors should know about vintage watches

4.1 First entry – beginning is always a challenge

Based on the statistics alone, every first step into the wide world of small watches is much the same. In the first fire of a new passion, you buy some watches here and there, because they have taken your fancy and do not cost too much. With this approach – without consideration of principles, time periods, or brands – you acquire not only your first practical experience, but also basic knowledge of the disciplines of technique and design. It is the all-important watch dial which catches your eye, not only as a first impression, but also in daily wearing of a watch.

Next, you learn to differentiate between a manual and automatic winding mechanism. Further on, you learn to recognize the design and construction of the case and the difference between "splash-proof" and "waterproof". Other points include how a case is made and put together, with the distinction between a snap or screw back. The third level, is learning to recognize the different materials used to make the case and to distinguish between steel and various precious metals. Often the big price differences will quickly identify which material was used for the case and inhibit further purchase plans.

Once you have dealt with "the externals" and technology of a wristwatch, the next step takes on the various functions of a timepiece. Is a simple manual winding mechanism recommended or do you already start with an automatic? For a three-hand watch, do you also want a date display, or to have even more index markers on the dial?

The biggest help in making decisions is often your personal budget, since the vintage watch market is on a cash basis; partial or installment payments are rarely accepted.

The first piece of good advice: Take time, save your money, and make your purchase only when you know exactly what your dream watch looks like and find one that meets all your other requirements. It should also be clear to you, what your criteria for beginning a small collection are, including how the purchase price is in keeping with investment value.

The second piece of good advice: You can buy your longed-for dream watch quickly, but selling it later on can be difficult and costly. Overall the issue is that your purchase decision can be affected by some personal ideals that might not be relevant for the next potential buyer. If you do not have self-discipline, you will soon have a small collection of watches, which are, according to taste, pretty, that pays no attention to being systematic or considering investment value.

This book provides sufficient tangible examples, leads, and advice, which make it possible for you to purchase a vintage watch and avoid the risk of making the wrong decisions. Considering the size of the investment, you need to be much more thorough and deliberate about making such a purchase. The following discusses what to look for in detail.

4.2 The wristwatch in all its variations

Wristwatches were being made by the first decade of the 20th century, but in small numbers in comparison to the then-common pocket watch. We begin with our focus on the 1930s, when Patek Philippe again produced its own calibers and thus stopped using ebauches (movement blanks) made by Jaeger-LeCoultre of Le Sentier. The initiative to take this step towards future independence came from then-president Jean Pfister, who assumed that post in 1933. We have already learned the historical details of this development from Gisbert L. Brunner in Chapter 3.

In 1934, the first shaped movement, caliber 9'''-90, was launched, and production continued, with modifications, until 1967. In the same year, came the round caliber 12'''-120, initially made with a small seconds hand, but since 1938 manufactured as the caliber 12'''SC with sweep seconds hand. Both rectangular and round cases can be used with these hand-wound movements. The first model of the Reference 96 used caliber 12'''-120. This timepiece was produced in many versions. The author knows of more than twenty-six versions with a small seconds hand, and more than eight with a sweep seconds hand. Models with calendars and perpetual calendars next to retrograde date displays and moon-phases were produced in smaller numbers. You can admire a piece with a platinum case in the Patek Philippe Museum in Geneva at the same time Patek Philippe introduced its first chronograph as Reference 130, manufactured in many versions. For this model, a caliber made by another manufacturer (Valjoux 23) was used.

With time came many other models, always equipped with the already noted hand-wound calibers. The References 541 and 542 are distinctive pieces. The first has indicators for day, month, date, and moon-phase display; the latter has the first world time indicator. We can propose the Reference 565 as a modern cult status watch, which then had a dust cover and screw back (see Fig. 40). For the 2006 celebrations of the re-opening of the fully renovated head office on Quai du Rhône, just 300 pieces of this Reference, with a new number 5565, were made. Today, you have to pay up to €30,000 for this rarity.

There are some special watches among the large number of models launched in the 1940s and 1950s. These include the split seconds chronograph, Reference 1436, the simple chronograph, 1463 (see Fig. 176), and the chronograph with perpetual calendar, Reference 1518 (see Figs. 174 & 175). All of these rare models represent the highest level of a watchmaker's artistry and today are only to be had for the highest prices. On the same level are the split seconds chronograph Reference 1563 and the models with perpetual calendar, Reference 1526 and 1591. Other highlights are the models with perpetual calendar, References 2438 (see Fig. 172) and 2497. A crowning achievement of the Geneva watchmaker is the Reference 2499, a chronograph with perpetual calendar (see Fig. 173), with a price that has reached astronomical heights. There are also rarities which are still affordable today. One favorite is the Reference 2526, which is not only the first with automatic movement, but also had an enameled dial (see Figs. 70 & 71).

In Chapter 5, we will review the entire spectrum of our Geneva manufacturer's earlier watches.

4.3 The dial - the watch's face

A watch dial does not have as many ways to communicate as a person's face, but still this most evident watch part can create a very engaging effect.

The motion of the hands shows us the passage of time and the steady advance of the seconds hand reminds us of the transience of our existence. A gleaming silver-plated dial set with tapered index markers (appliques) and Dauphine hands, creates both respect and enjoyment. When you look at your watch, you not only see the exact time, but also can appreciate a small micro-mechanical work of art. An artistic watch enthusiast's heart will beat even faster when he sees an enameled dial. These were customary in most versions of the famous Reference 2526, Patek Philippe's first automatic. Most examples of the successor model Reference 3428 were also make with enameled dials.

Finally, we mention that special watch enthusiast, the "Sunday watch wearer", who goes to his bank's safe deposit on Friday afternoon to get his "Perpetual Calendar" for the weekend. A glance at the face of the Reference 3940 or 5140, with secondary dials and moon-phase (see Fig. 186), or the even finer dial of the very rare Reference 2438 (see Fig. 172) awakes such happy feelings in the owner that they can only be surpassed by an unexpected smile from a beautiful woman.

Technique and design

Now we turn to the technique and design for the different dials.

A dial is principally made up of the base metal (sheet), the surface coating, various imprints, the index markers (appliques), and the company's inscription. Then comes the central boring for the hands and one for the small seconds hand, if there is to be one. A window is punched for the day of the month and, for more complicated versions, more windows for the weekday and month display and the opening for the moon-phase (see Figs. 186-188).

To make the dial, sheet metal of steel, copper, brass, silver and – although not often – gold is used. We will take a look at the manufacturing process to make such a dial. First, the blank parts are stamped from a rolled out flat ribbon (called a semi-finished part in the industry). If it is to get a curved shape, this is die-stamped. The next step is to bore the holes for the hands and stamp the above-mentioned openings. After all the holes, openings, and edges are deburred, two cylinder pins are soldered on the back side to hold the movement. After quality control for measurements and function, the dial side gets a fine sanding and is ready for the next step. Now it is decided whether the dial will be enameled, gilded, or silver-plated. If the latter, it often gets a surface finish, such as a sunray or other polished decoration.

If the dial is to gleam with enamel, first a basic enameling is done. As required, the dial gets a fine sanding in between application of one or more enamel layers. The next step is printing the minute and second index markers. Chronographs often get more, often multi-colored, imprints for the sub-dials, speedometer, and other indicators. Following this is the company insignia and the notation "SWISS". All the work steps are carried out using the pad-printing process. In this printing technique, a sharp edged printing plate with engraved image, also called the stamp, is filled with paint, wiped exactly and then, using a pad, transferred 1:1 to the dial. The elastic pad makes it possible to also to print on bumps and in depressions, exactly and without error.

Finally, the dial gets another layer of clear lacquer (cellulous lacquer), which protects it from oxidation. Only then, are the index markers (appliques), counters, and hands with the tiny cylinder pins set into the holes provided and riveted from behind. After another control for appearance and measurements, quality assurance gives the okay to mount the dial.

Fig. 13 - Detail of an enameled dial of Reference 2526 Version 3. This style has glued on index markers. To display these, the dial maker carefully removed the mark for the "9." On the back side is the identification 93 133. "93" was the Patek Philippe customer number at the dial producer CADRANS STERN SA, "133" was the running production number.

Fig. 14 - Detail of an enameled dial of Reference 2526 Version 1. This dial has riveted index markers. The index markers are set in their holes using two small cylinder pins. To use this marker, the number "6" was removed. On the rear side, the identification 93 165 was printed. "93" stands for Patek Philippe; "165" for the running production number.

At Patek Philippe they also employ another technique, which was used for many of the watches shown in this book. Instead of the minutes, seconds, and firm name being printed, they are marked with baked enamel. For this process, the minute and seconds markers and the firm insignia are milled in, filled with enamel powder and then fired. This creates lucent lettering and markings which are raised well above the dial level. Even the lettering "SWISS" was sometimes done using this process, beneath the "6". Only after this elaborate preparatory work is the dial lacquered many times and the index markers (appliques) and numbers applied and riveted. Because this lacquer is affected by gravity, it drains off the raised enamel lettering and only stays on the dial surface. In Fig. 64, we see a detail of the dial of a Reference 2508 with enameled lettering and lacquered surface. Opposite this, in Fig. 63, is a silver-plated dial that is only printed.

The enameled dial

In addition to dials made by the two processes described above, the royal class of Patek Philippe dials is the enameled dial.

Such masterpieces take first place among the dream watches; they were launched in 1953 with the era of the automatic winding mechanism. The Reference 2526 was produced from 1953 to 1959, in cases of yellow gold, pink gold, white gold, and platinum. With few exceptions, the watches left the Geneva factory with cream-colored enamel. Only 20 timepieces were fitted with black enameled dials, as a long-deceased employee revealed to the author many years ago.

But why so much secrecy about these enameled dials? The author got to the bottom of this matter, by speaking with retired employees of the firm CADRAN STERN SA, the former supplier, and visiting many Swiss companies, which today still make dials with enamel faces. In this way, the author learned of some of the methods used to make these enameled dials in the 1950s.

As far as the actual enameling of the dial is concerned, the three variations of the process began in the same way: the two holes for the hand movement are bored in the semi-finished dial parts and the two cylinder pins soldered on, the edges deburred, and the dial side finely sanded. In the first variation, the twenty-six 0.2mm diameter holes needed for the 13 index markers (11 single, 2 at the 12) are then made with a boring jig. In the next step, the indentations for the minute interval marks, the lines for the seconds, and lettering are milled, filled with enamel powder before the final firing, and then fired. In these earlier steps, up to five enamel layers were applied and fired.

Often, uneven stress levels in the enamel layers could cause a layer to crack during cooling, spoiling the dial. A second challenge was boring the holes for the pins for the index markers (appliques). During firing, the liquid enamel will have leaked into these holes, reducing their diameter. After the enamel layer was finished, diamond drills had to be used in the holes, to restore the needed diameter. Then, in a final work process, the index markers (appliques) were set in the holes with their pins and riveted. The enameled dial was finished.

In a second method, the holes for the index markers were not cut before the enameling, but afterwards, in the fired enamel layer, using a boring jig and diamond cutter for all 26 holes. The remaining work is done as already described.

In a third process, no holes were cut; after the enamel layers were finished, all index markers were applied to the dial using a stencil and then glued to the dial. Even today, there are versions of the Reference 2526, which have a dial made this way. Because they lacked knowledge of the various processes, some experts assumed that these dials were fakes.

Whoever has once held an enameled dial in their hands, would notice that the back side is also enameled. These mostly russet colored coatings are called counter-enamel (*contre-émail*). This second enamel layer is applied to the back side to prevent warping or bending of the dial during baking (stress-equalization).

For the non-expert, we can note at the end that only flat dials can be enameled. If a dial is curved, the enamel will flow down during firing and not stay where intended. Enameled dials are very rarely found in contemporary watches. The model Reference 5078 P, a minute repeater with automatic caliber R 27 PS and platinum case, has the imprint "ENAMEL" on the dial over the "6". The Roman numerals, the minute and second interval marks are enameled, but lucent index markers (applique), as seen on the Reference 2526, were omitted.

Fig. 15 - Detail of a replacement dial for Reference 2526. The surface is only lacquered, the minute interval points and the seconds marks only printed. Under the "6" is the imprint "0 SWISS 0," the identification for gold index markers. The steel sheet dial is stamped 93 ★ 2526 on the back.

Fig. 16 - Detail of a replacement dial for Reference 3445. This dial has yellow gold index markers and belongs to a yellow gold case. The dial sheet is of 750 yellow gold.

Special dial features

The imprint "SWISS" is always found by the "6" on the original dials. Until the mid-1960s, all watches had the origin notation "SWISS". From 1968, another distinction was begun, by which all watches with gold cases and index markers (appliques) had the imprint "0 SWISS 0". Figure 172, is a picture of a Reference 2509 in pink gold, which according to the Patek Philippe archive extract, was made with a black dial. At a later time, during a servicing, the dial was exchanged and the new one displayed the new regulation. A comparable case is shown at the right in Fig. 69. Here one of the famous automatics, Reference 2526, was given in exchange for the costly enameled dial, a plain, simply lacquered dial, but also with the imprint "0 SWISS 0".

Summing up the most important facts:

1. All dials produced in the period under consideration were given the imprint SWISS under the "6" by the dial-suppliers. If this is missing, the reason must be determined. Often the issue is a replacement dial, where the supplier had not printed "SWISS." Today, if a Patek Philippe watch is handed in and the customer wants the dial replaced, this request can only be met when there is a replacement dial in stock. These dials have the "SWISS" or "0 SWISS 0" imprints.

2. Should the sought-after dial no longer be available, Patek Philippe will offer to restore the existing dial and also offers a picture of the dial with it. Should this, contrary to expectations, not have the SWISS imprint, the customer can complain and have it altered. According to the dial type, a restoration costs about €400-€600.

3. To exactly evaluate a dial, it has to be disassembled. The case back must be removed, the winding shaft taken out and the dial and movement removed. The dial sits on the surface of the movement (dial side) and positioned exactly by two cylinder pins, which go into the bores in the movement and are held by set screws.

We can see a certain logic – although with difficulty – in the analysis of watch dials presented here. The pink gold Reference 570, Fig. 41, has a sheet steel dial with the identification 93 429. "93" was the customer number of Patek Philippe at the dial maker CADRANS STERN SA in Geneva. Whether the "429" was the running number or type number for the Reference 570 cannot be determined.

Several dials were made for the Reference 2526. The dial is made of a copper alloy and silver-plated. The dial on the Reference 2526 shown in Fig. 71, has the ID 93 133 on the back side. In this case, "93" is the customer number, "133" the serial number. Other dials of this model examined, have the ID 93 165, 93 321, and 93 571, the latter as highest production count encountered.

For the replacement dials produced later for Reference 2526, which had lacquered surfaces instead of the enamel layer, the ID 93★2526 was chosen (see Fig. 15). The "93" stands for the customer number, "★" for CADRANS STERN SA and "2526" for the Reference.

In the Reference group 3400, all watches have, in addition to gold cases and automatic winding, dials of yellow, pink, or white gold. The dials of two Reference 3445 watches in white gold had the ID 2 301927 and 2 303355 and the purity notation "18K/0,750", augmented with two small five pointed stars (★) of the firm CADRANS STERN SA. Patek Philippe had begun a cost-saving program for the successor models at the end of the 1960s and even dials for gold watches were sometimes made from steel sheets. An example is the dial in Fig. 108. Here, the separately pictured dial has the ID "93Y3514A". The "93" is the Patek Philippe customer number, "3514" stands for the Reference 3514 (Fig. 125).

The dial on the Reference 3558 shown in Fig. 135, with yellow gold case, has a yellow gold dial printed with the ID "93G3558" and purity notation "18K/0,750". The imprint "SWISS" under the "6" tells us that this is an original dial from 1967.

4. The imprint "SWISS MADE" was never used by Patek Philippe in the period discussed here. This imprint was first used in the third millennium, and it is on most new models. Exceptions include References 5120 (Fig. 179), 5134 (Fig. 182) and 5196 (Fig. 192).

Fig. 17 - Screw back inside of a Reference 3445 6. From the top are imprinted the "small Helvetia," purity notation, company name, case and Reference numbers and the casemaker's mark.

Fig. 18 - The case of Reference 3445 from the rear with screw back. To open it correctly, a 29mm decagonal key is needed. The label is from its latest servicing by Patek Philippe.

5. The history of the company imprint "Patek Philippe, Genève" is also important for investors and collectors. To present the necessary information exactly and aptly, we will discuss this using the respective watches in Chapter 5.

4.4 The case - Impressions of shape and design

The most important criteria to define a watch case are the shape, the structural design, the material, and the manufacturing methods. Among the basic shapes are the round, square, rectangular and barrel (tonneau) cases. Patek Philippe also has used other designs, such as the ellipse, the Nautilus, and the Aquanaut. As to the size of the case, note that in the 1930s and following decades the cases had more modest dimensions than are used today. For the 1930s Reference 96 (see Fig. 39), a diameter of 30.5mm sufficed, whereas the current model Reference 5196 is an impressive 37mm.

The watch structure design has three parts: the bezel, the middle section, and the back. The bezel is the upper section of a watch and holds the crystal securely. Generally the bezel is snapped on. Professional sports watches have screwed down bezels.

The middle section of the case encloses the movement and dial and has lugs to attach the watch bands, to keep the watch securely on the wrist. The back closes the underside of the case securely. Previously, a snap back was generally used, such as for the Reference 96. A case of this design is only splash-proof. With the launch of Reference 565 (see Fig. 40) in 1938, Patek Philippe put a waterproof watch on the market. The design solution was made by connecting the case middle and back using fine threads, with the internal threading in the case and the external threading in the back. To screw the back on straight and flat, both threads must be aligned very accurately and exactly.

There is an alternative to the fine thread of the screw back, where the case and back are put together with a cylindrical fitting and fastened with six inset cylinder head screws. Technically, this design is a more limited solution than the one described above, but can significantly lower production costs. This simpler design was never considered at Patek Philippe.

Before we move on to the manufacturing methods, we should also look at the materials. Patek Philippe uses only three materials: stainless steel, 75% gold, and 95% platinum. Patek Philippe never made cases of 14-karat gold.

Case construction

For a high quality watch, you can expect special manufacturing processes. By the 1930s, these were already very precise, even without modern production centers. In our computer-dominated world, it is hard to imagine that excellent designs of highest exactitude could be as accurately and successfully derived from the drawing board, as those made today with modern CAD systems.

Already in the 1930s, intricate work pieces were serially produced on lathes using copying templates. The middle sections of the cases were first stamped out from flat ribbons and shaped on a lathe. With screw backs, the last work step was making the complicated grooves for the fine threads for the screw back. The appropriate screw back was first cut from a round mold and turned. If the screw back required six notches, these were shaped by die-stamping. The next step is fine turning and inserting the external thread. The thread of the finished screw back is checked with a case gauge for fitting and function. Finally the required numbers and hallmarks are struck and the back fastened to the case.

Two-part cases are easier to make and less costly. Patek Philippe often uses two-part cases, independent of back design. Even the famous Reference 2526 (see Figs. 70 & 71), the first automatic, has a two-part, albeit very elaborately designed, case with an intricate screw back. The simpler and less costly technique combines the one piece case with a snap back. Case and back were attached with a cylindrical fitting. Since the pressure closing is only splash-proof, the wearer should take off the watch when washing his hands.

A snap back has a small notch, into which the case opener tool fits Usually this small slit is at 9 o'clock or by the crown. To securely close the case with a snap back, it must have sufficiently thick walls for stability, meaning that there can be no sparing of material. Patek Philippe has never used false economy and its cases and backs are always sturdy.

Overall, the screwed case, especially those with a fine thread fastening, represents a better system. This is not just for waterproofing, but also the stability of the whole case. In terms of technical mechanics, the case housing and screw back create a force-fit and positively locked connection.

The watch band lugs, which fasten on the band to both sides of the case via spring bars, are manufactured in two ways. In the first, the case housing and lugs are stamped as one flat piece, then die-stamped, milled, and turned. In the second, the case is first made as a turned piece and, at the end, the four lugs are soldered on. When soldering, a gauge ensures the exact fit of the band lugs. Gold lugs were generally made by die casting and machined to fit the connection exactly, before they were soldered on. Steel cases generally are made using just the first, one piece, process.

Finishing the surface

The last production step is adding the desired surface finishes. Here, we use the terms diamondizing, satin finishing, smoothing, polishing, and turning.

Diamondizing is the manufacturing technique of turning a round object using a diamond-edged lathe tool. This creates the most precise and highly polished surfaces. The jewelry industry often does not require such high standards. There, diamondizing is considered machine engraving with special steel cutting tools. The result is a highly polished surface pattern with a diamond-like shine.

Satin finishing is created using a corundum (aluminum oxide)-embedded steel polishing disk. Non-technicians also call this brush-polishing.

Smoothing and polishing is done on the polishing machine. The smoothed effect comes from the grinding wheels, covered with special cloth or paper. The work piece, in this case a watch case, is put on a spindle and clamped. With this spindle, the case can be precisely positioned in three dimensions, so that all desired areas are smoothed. With exact correlation of wheel and work piece, very exact and repeatable designs can be made.

The fourth surface finish is done with normal **turning** on a lathe, making deliberate grooves which contrast the smoothed or diamondized surfaces (see Fig. 127).

To the connoisseur of expensive watches, it is clear that all these methods for surface finishing are more or less "machine methods". And who can tell how often a 40- or 50-year-old watch has already undergone such a procedure, done more or less expertly? If the once well-defined edges of a watch case are rounded and the various surfaces are no longer even, do not buy the watch. When many generations of watchmakers have left their traces on a piece, it helps sometimes to use plastic calipers to measure it. Patek Philippe always noted the exact case diameter in its catalogs. If the diameter measurements deviate even one or two tenths of a millimeter, it can no longer be asserted that the watch is in mint condition.

Hallmarks and Helvetia

The condition of the imprinted hallmark, the "small Helvetia", can also give important indications of many attempts at polishing. The Helvetia hallmark shows a woman's head with a tiara, looking to the left. This hallmark is official and stands for gold with a minimal purity of 750/1000. Under the Helvetia head is the letter for the office where the watch was given the mark. Sixty years ago, Switzerland had 13 examination offices, as follows: Biel/Bienne (B), La Chaux de Fonds (C), Délémont (D), Fleurier (F), Genève (G), Granges (g), Le Locle (L), Neuenburg/Neuchâtel (N), Le Noirmont (n), Porrentruy (P), St. Imier (I), Schaffhausen/Schaffhouse (S), Tramelan (T). The board of directors of the Swiss examination office was in Bern (mark +). [Excerpt from the *Journal of the Jewelers, Gold and Silver Workers,* Prague, 1937]

On Patek Philippe watches with gold cases, the small Helvetia was printed at various places and several times. The central case housing bore the hallmark above the "4" or the "9". This mark can also often be found on the outside of the band lugs; other models have it printed on the underside of the band lugs. Finally there are also gold watches with no hallmark.

The hallmarks can be made two to three tenths of a millimeter deep. Concrete details will be provided with the detailed descriptions of the watches and sometimes also in the picture captions (see Figs. 92 & 93).

To sum up, check the watch case with your own eyes for well-defined edges and original surface finishes. Do not be confused by gleaming cases that were just polished. Be convinced by the depth of the hallmarks. If these are just below the level of the case surface, it is an indication that a good deal of material has already been removed. Finally, take your plastic calipers in hand and measure the actual diameter of this watch. If a seller, claiming a risk of scratching, refuses to allow such measurements, politely say goodbye. Should, however, the selling price appear so interesting that a full refurbishing, including restoration of the case, could balance things out, you should resume the discussion about buying the watch.

4.5 The watch movement – miracle of micro-mechanics

Before we start considering individual watch movements, we shall look briefly at how a hand-wound movement runs. If a fully wound spring has a running time (power reserve) of 40 hours, you know the performance characteristic of this drive. Performance means the work accomplished in a set time. First, we shall trace the path of the torque, from barrel to time display, of a three-hand watch. In the classical arrangement, with minute and hour hands at the center and the small seconds hand at the "6", the torque is carried directly from barrel to escapement. The gear ring and gear wheel of the barrel drives a cog (pivot) whose staff (arbor) turns once a minute. The arbor with the minute hand is at the upper end of this staff. A second cog (pivot) on this staff takes the torque over a reduction gear, made of the minute and hour wheels, back to the center, to the hour indicator. The hour arbor bearing is designed as a tube, in which the minute arbor runs.

Train wheel with Great wheel

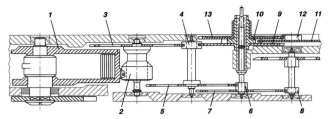

Train wheel with Center wheel

1 Barrel	6 Second wheel pivot	11 Minute wheel
2 Great wheel pivot	7 Second wheel	12 Minute wheel pivot
3 Great wheel	8 Escapement wheel pivot	13 Hour wheel
4 Third wheel pivot	9 Carrier wheel	
5 Third wheel	10 Minute pivot	

1 Barrel	5 Third wheel	9 Minute pivot
2 Center wheel pivot	6 Second wheel pivot	10 Minute wheel
3 Center wheel	7 Second wheel	11 Minute wheel pivot
4 Third wheel pivot	8 Escapement wheel pivot	12 Hour wheel

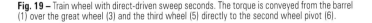

Fig. 19 – Train wheel with direct-driven sweep seconds. The torque is conveyed from the barrel (1) over the great wheel (3) and the third wheel (5) directly to the second wheel pivot (6).

Fig. 20 – Train wheel with small seconds. From the barrel (1) the torque is conveyed via the central wheel (3) and third wheel (5) to the second wheel pivot (6) *Both images FET, Le Locle.*

At the lower end of the central wheel is a gear wheel (central wheel) which, over two further reduction gears (third wheel pivot–third wheel–second pivot), drives the arbor of the seconds hand. From this seconds hand arbor, a further reduction gear leads to the arbor of the escape wheel, meaning the watch movement escapement. This escapement consists of the escape wheel, lever, and balance, with spring, which gives our watch its beat.

For a sweep seconds hand, there can be either direct and indirect drive. With a direct second drive, the hands move in a direct torque band (train with great wheel). On the arbor, whose cog (pivot) is driven by the barrel gear ring, the great wheel sits above a gear wheel. This gear wheel meshes with the next staff via a cog (pivot). On the other side is a gear wheel (carrier wheel) which drives the minute pivot at an equal speed. Another reduction gear from the minute pinion drives the hour pivot, on which the hour wheel is set. The staff above the third wheel has beneath it a further gear wheel (third wheel), which functions as reduction gear for the second pivot in the center. The hollow minute pinion drives the seconds hand pivot staff. On the same staff as the second pivot, the torque is conveyed over a further gear wheel (fourth wheel) via a reduction gear to the escape wheel staff. With indirect drive, the torque band is carried indirectly via the third wheel.

After so much technical mechanics, we now want to move on to the various hand-wound movements that were exclusively used in Patek Philippe timepieces until the introduction of the first automatic movement in 1953.

On hand-wound movements

Until the 1930s, the Geneva watch manufacturer used the movement blanks (ebauches) of other manufacturers, such as Jaeger-LeCoultre of Le Sentier. Jean Pfister's future-oriented decision in 1933 that they would manufacture their own watch movements, brought the Geneva brand its great breakthrough. We begin the following array of the hand-wound movements from that decisive epoch.

12'''-120 (12-120)

The wristwatches produced in 1935 are interesting for collectors, since the first hand-wound calibers 12'''-120 ticked in them. With a 26.75mm (12''') outer diameter, 4.00mm height, 18 jewels, 18,000 vibrations/h, and about 40 hours power reserve, it was produced in four series and remained in production until 1953. The following compiles the four series:

Fig. 21 - Manual movement caliber 12'''-120 with small seconds This movement has no caliber designation (movement-ø 26.75mm, height 4.00mm, 18,000 vph, 18 jewels).

1. Production series: movement nos. 826,892 to 829,999 (3108 movements, 1935 to 1940)
2. Production series: movement nos. 920,000 to 929,999 (10,000 movements, 1940 to 1950)
3. Production series: movement nos. 938,000 to 939,079 (1080 movements, 1952 to 1953)
4. Production series: movement nos. 960,000 to 969,999 (10,000 movements, 1947 to 1952)

The caliber 12'''-120 powered the first "Calatrava" men's wristwatches with Reference 96, launched in 1932. At first, the new Reference 96 had a caliber 12''' with 15 jewels, bimetallic balance, and flat coil, which was supplied as an ébauche by Jaeger-LeCoultre.

Comparing the particular overall number of movements, 24,188 caliber 12'''-120 versus 13,358 caliber 12'''SC, we can conclude that watches with small seconds hands were in much greater demand at this time. In the course of the production periods, both calibers were altered in many ways, including replacing the flat spring with a Breguet spring.

Fig. 22 - Manual movement caliber 12''' SC with sweep seconds hand, reconstruction of the caliber 12'''-120 for sweep seconds hand. *Image Auktionen Dr. Crott.*

Fig. 23 - Manual movement caliber 10'''- 200 with small seconds (movement-ø 22.70mm, height 3.65mm, 19,800 vph, 18 jewels).

12'''SC (12 SC)

Three years after the basic caliber 12'''-120, the version with an indirectly driven sweep seconds followed. This got the caliber-designation 12'''SC and was manufactured in five series.

1. Production series: movement nos. 828,812 to 828,835 (24 movements, 1938 to 1939)
2. Production series: movement nos. 828,920 to 828,943 (24 movements, 1939)
3. Production series: movement nos. 829,238 to 829,261 (10,024 movements, 1939 to 1940)
4. Production series: movement nos. 861,704 to 863,995 (2292 movements, 1939 to 1948)
5. Production series: movement nos. 864,002 to 864,994 (994 movements, 1948 to 1950)

The movement 12'''SC has an additional, intricate design for the indirect second pivot, which came from the firm Victorin Piguet. Via an altered train wheel bridge and a smaller capping bridge, three additional gear wheels take the pulse for the seconds hand from the small seconds position to the center.

10'''-200 (10-200)

With the manual movement launched in 1946, it became possible to equip smaller men's watches with modern movements. With a 22.7mm diameter and a height of 3.65mm, it could be manufactured with and without a small second. The caliber 10'''-200 had 18 jewels and a Breguet spring, and worked with 19,800 oscillations per hour. There were two series and production continued until 1965.

1. Production series: movement nos. 950,000 to 959,999 (10,000 movements, 1946 to 1953)
2. Production series: movement nos. 740,000 to 751,199 (11,200 movements, 1953 to 1965)

In square or rectangular watch cases, there was a special mount for the caliber 10'''-200 in the form of a brass ring set and soldered on sheet brass. This mount was finished with a protective coating of rhodium.

Fig. 24 - Manual movement caliber 12'''-400, successor to the caliber 12'''-120, with the same technical features.

12'''-400

The successor to the caliber 12'''-120 was the manual movement 12'''-400, which appeared in 1950. With 26.75mm diameter and a height of 4.00mm, it had the same external measurements as its predecessor. It was produced in only one series and was in production for 11 years.

Movement nos. 720,000 to 729,999 (10,000 movements, 1950 to 1961).

Fig. 25 - Manual movement caliber 27 SC with sweep seconds (*seconde central*), successor to the caliber 12''' SC (movement-ø 26.75mm, height 4.95mm, 18,000 vph, 18 jewels).

27 SC

The replacement caliber for 12'''SC appeared in 1949 with the designation 27 SC. It had same diameter of 26.75mm and height set at 4.5mm. The caliber 27 SC was produced in two series and stayed in production until 1970:

1. Production series: movement nos. 700,000 to 712,699 (12,700 movements, 1949 to 1970)
2. Production series: movement nos. 888,000 to 888,178 (179 movements, 1953 to 1965)

The two calibers can be easily differentiated visually. The 12''' SC has an added, elaborate design for the indirect seconds pivot, made by Victorin Piguet. The caliber 27 SC shows its own, cleanly structured design, with the seconds wheel being elegantly set under the train wheel bridge. The barrel bridge was thus made smaller and the crown wheel bridge set separately.

Fig. 26 - Manual movement caliber 27-AM 400 with small second. AM stands for "amagnetic" (movement-ø 26.75mm, height 4.00mm, 19,800 vph 18 jewels).

27-AM 400

For watches that need to withstand the risk of magnetic fields, the 27-AM 400 version was developed from the caliber 12'''-400. This was fitted with the Gyromax balance and Breguet spring, in which balance, lever, and other components were made from "amagnetic" (Swiss for anti-magnetic) materials. The number of beats was increased from 18,000 to 19,800 oscillations/h. The ID numbers of the two series are:

1. Production series: movement nos. 730,000 to 735,239 (5240 movements, from 1958)
2. Production series: movement nos. 739,700 to 739,799 (100 movements)

The difference between the two series lies, first, in the diameter of the balance spring collet, which was 0.55mm in the earlier series, then 0.45mm. From movement number 732,700 on, the height of the balance wheel was reduced from 0.70mm to 0.50mm. This caliber was mostly produced in the model "Amagnetic" as References 2570/1 (1958), 3417 (1960, see also Fig. 94) and 3460 (1962). They were also made in other models, such as References 3420, 3418 and 3419 (see also Figs. 96 & 100).

23-300

For especially flat wristwatches, the caliber 23-300 was introduced in 1956. With a 22.70mm diameter and a height of 3.00mm, it was available with and without small seconds. Planned with 18 jewels and 19,800 oscillations/h, this caliber, despite its lower height, was equipped with both a Breguet spring and a Gyromax balance from the beginning. From movement number 1,148,400 on, another adjustable stud support was installed. This allowed a very compact design that could deliver an astonishingly good performance. The caliber 23-300 remained in production until 1977 and was produced in the following series:

1. Production series: movement nos. 780,000 to 799,999 (20,000 movements, 1956 to 1966)
2. Production series: movement nos. 1,140,000 to 1,159,999 (20,000 movements, 1966 to 1971)
3. Production series: movement nos. 1,210,000 to 1,228,549 (18,550 movements, 1971 to 1977)

A comparison to the total production of the previously described manual movements lets us cite the caliber 23-300, with a total of 58,550 movements, as Patek Philippe's most-produced hand-wound movement. Due to its smaller dimensions it was made as a jewelry watch and in models with square or rectangular cases. Just three pieces were made with a module for a perpetual calendar and they are here designated as caliber 23-300 Q. This movement was installed in the Reference 3449 in 1961.

9'''- 90

Finally we come to the 9'''-90 shaped movement, which was in production for 34 years. Its width x length measurement was 18mm x 26.60mm; the height 3.65mm. The movement had 18 jewels and 19,800 oscillations/h; those produced from 1954 on had a Breguet spring with a Gyromax balance. The two series were:

1. Production series: movement nos. 830,000 to 839,999 (10,000 movements, 1934 to 1950)
2. Production series: movement nos. 970,000 to 977,889 (7890 movements, 1947 to 1967)

This caliber came in various luxury watches with rectangular cases. The best-known models included the Reference 2441 (also called "*Tour Eiffel*" or "Eiffel Tower") and the Reference 2469 (see Fig. 55).

Fig. 27 - Manual shaped movement caliber 9'''-90 with small seconds (Measurements 26.20 x 18.70mm, height 3.65mm, 19,800 vph, 18 jewels).

In this chapter, we have only described the hand-wound movements from Patek Philippe that are relevant for collectors and omitted the calibers 10'''-105 and 10'''-110. Due to their diameters of 21.78mm, they were only used in models with very small watch cases and are not in so much demand today from collectors.

On automatic watch movements

Compared to other watch manufacturers, the era of automatic watches began relatively late at Patek Philippe. It was only in April 1953 that the Geneva company presented its "famous automatic watch" at the 24th Swiss Watch Fair in Basel, as we can read in the sales brochure. The Swiss Watch Fair was then quite manageable, as an offshoot of the Swiss Industrial Fair. In 1953, the Fair was held from April 11-21. The new automatic caliber, named 12'''-600 AT, though arriving later than those of the other renowned brands, such as IWC, Jaeger-LeCoultre, Rolex, and Vacheron & Constantin, had so many technical and innovative new features that it immediately replaced all the before-named competitors. Why did this masterpiece appear so late? For one thing, developing the first self-winding movement required several years. Also, at that time, manual movement Patek Philippe wristwatches were so much in demand, that the firm saw no need to manufacture automatic watches. In the first seven years of automatic wristwatch production, only 7100 were made and cased. This means that self-winding watches accounted for only some 20% of total production.

Fig. 28 - Caliber 12'''-600 AT with automatic winding mechanism (Movement-ø 27.00mm, height 5.40mm, 19,800 vph, 30 jewels).

12'''-600 AT

Patek Philippe introduced the era of automatic watches in 1953 with this masterpiece. The movement had technical features such as Breguet springs, Gyromax balances, micrometer fine regulation with swan's neck fine adjustment, winding by an eccentric cam mounted in ball bearings, guilloched gold rotor, and much more. Together, all these features made this a unique movement. The digit and letter caliber designation 12'''-600 AT – this goes for most Patek Philippe movement – reveals at a glance the most important data on diameter, height, and functions: 12''' means 12 lines, an old French length measure used in watchmaking, which indicates the movement diameter (1 = 2.223mm, 12mm x 2.223 = 26.676mm). The figure 600 stands for the (approximate) height of 6mm. In reality, the movement diameter is exactly 27.00mm and the height is 5.40mm. "AT" means an automatic winding mechanism.

There are two assembly groups for automatic movements: The essential watch movement (basic movement) and the generally used automatic assembly group. The basic movement has a two-shanked Gyromax balance with eight Masselotte weights, Breguet spring, Super-Shock shock absorber, an offset ball bearing winder for both-sided winding, and 30 jewels; it performs at 19,800 oscillations/h. The guilloched gold rotor, *Côtes de Genève* stripes, beveled edges, and the Geneva Seal emphasize the high level of horology that created this masterpiece (see also Figs. 86 & 90).

Even though it had been conceptualized to meet the highest standards, the caliber 12'''-600 AT was improved in various ways, which served to increase precision and performance. From the movement numbered 760,300, the beryllium balance screw was replaced by Patek Philippe's patented Gyromax balance. Up to movement number 760,950, ten further relevant alterations were made altogether. These include a strengthened rotor shaft, a modified rotor fastening,

replacement of the offset wheel cam with a ball bearing, and increasing the movement fasteners from two to three screws. From movement number 760,951, all the stated improvements were incorporated in manufacturing. The Patek Philippe movements up to number 760,950 were converted to the newest design standard whenever they were sent to Geneva for refurbishing.

Then-Production Director Françoise Cart had overall responsibility for the development and production of this masterly movement. Even today, the caliber 12'''-600 AT is one of the most beautiful and best automatic movements ever manufactured. It included movement numbers 760,000 to 767,099 (7100 movements, 1953 to 1960).

As a retired Patek Philippe employee reported, another 31 pieces were made as replacement parts.

Patek Philippe's first automatic wristwatch, the caliber 12'''-600 AT, was also the first version of the sought-after Reference 2526 with an enameled dial. The movement was number 760,000, case number 674,938. It was first produced in March 1953 and, according to the exclusive U.S. concessionaire, the Henri Stern Watch Agency, Inc. in New York, it was delivered on July 27 that year to the American J. B. Champion in Dallas, Texas.

The often-mentioned Patek Philippe Gyromax balance requires fuller description. In contrast with the previous screw balance, this design needs neither regulator nor other devices for precision adjustment This bifurcated balance usually has eight cylindrical weights on its rim, with a hole in the middle and slots on one side. These weights are rotatable and set on pins in recesses perpendicular to the balance wheel. If you turn the slots in the weights, also known as Masselotte-weights, to the center of the balance, the balance moment of inertia (GD2) increases and the watch goes more slowly. If you turn the slots outwards, this reduces the moment of inertia and the watch goes faster. This regulation is done in fine increments and without altering the balance mass or functional length of the spring. This maintains the symmetry of the vibration system, made up of spring, balance, lever, and escape wheel.

The Gyromax balance is a Patek Philippe discovery, and is protected by many patents. The first and basic Gyromax patent is number 261,431, granted on March 26, 1947, and was published August 16, 1949, by the official Swiss office for intellectual property. A further patent with number 280,067 was applied for on August 18, 1949, and published on April 1, 1952, including various further design improvements on the balance wheel and the Masselotte weights.

27-460 and 27-460 M

Despite breakthrough success for the caliber 12'''-600 AT, there were two new trends for wristwatches at the end of the 1950s: one was the trend for a flatter overall design and the other was watches with date indicators. Patek Philippe also went in these directions and, in 1960, brought out the successor caliber 27-460. One year later, the 27-460 M version with date display was launched, the M standing for "monodate". By using the modified automatic assembly group, the almost unchanged basic watch movement, with diameter of 27.00mm and 19,800 oscillations/h, could be reduced to an overall height of 4.60mm (with date display 5.30mm).

Fig. 29 - Caliber 27-460 with automatic winding mechanism, successor to the caliber 12'''- 600 AT (Movement-ø 27.00mm, height 4.600mm, 19,800 vph, 37 jewels).

Externally, the two successor calibers can be distinguished from their predecessors in that they do not have the guilloched gold rotor with sliding bearings, but a solid gold rotor set in a ball bearing and *Côtes de Genève* stripes (see also Figs. 110 & 116). The second difference is in the execution without fine adjustment by micrometer screw and swan-neck spring. The number of jewels was increased from 30 to 37 rubies.

During the production period, the movement of this caliber family was also modified. From movement number 1,116,899, caliber 27-460 was fitted with an altered Gyromax balance of beryllium bronze. The Masselotte weights, previously set at the middle of the balance wheel, were arranged on the inner side of this wheel (see Figs. 90 & 116). The last version of the caliber 27-460 M was fitted with an adjustable mobile stud support and the designation 27-460 M PM (PM stands for "*piton mobile*", in English "adjustable mobile stud support") and was produced until 1975. The movement numbers were:

1. Caliber 27-460, movement nos.1,110,000 to 1,116,899 (6900 movements, 1960 to 1970)
2. Caliber 27-460 M, movement nos.1,120,000 to 1,129,999 (10,000 movements, 1961 to 1970)
3. Caliber 27-460 M, movement nos.1,116,900 to 1,119,999 (3100 movements, 1970 to 1986)
4. Caliber 27-460 M PM, movement nos.1,230,000 to 1,234,999 (5000 movements, 1970 to 1975)

The caliber 27-460 M was generally produced with a small seconds, but sometimes without. The caliber 27-460, in version 27-460 Q, had a module for a perpetual calendar and installed in References 3448 and 3450. The last named Reference can be recognized by the leap year indicator by the "3".

For the third series, they returned in 1970 to the number groups of the 27-460 and used these from the movement numbers 1,116,900 to 1,119,999. For the caliber 27-460

M PM, the number group was one originally reserved for a pocket watch movement, of which 35 pieces had already been made. Though the numbers 1,230,000 to 1,230,034 were already given out, the double usage of these numbers presented no problems, since it is easy to distinguish a pocket watch movement from that for a wristwatch.

Fig. 30 - Caliber 350 with automatic winding mechanism, a new design with rotor set outside (Movement-ø 28.00mm, height 3.50mm, 21,600 vph, 28 jewels).

Fig. 31 - Caliber 1-350 with automatic winding mechanism, a re-worked version of caliber 350. In addition to the changed caliber designation on the barrel bridge you can see the difference in the gold segment of the outer rotor. For the caliber 350, a less costly version of heavy metal was used.

350 and 1-350

With emergence of quartz technology in the 1960s, wristwatch design and construction changed decisively. The trend went clearly to ever-flatter models and reduced the prices for the previously made higher automatic movements. Patek Philippe was not spared this change and by the mid-1960s, began developing a new automatic movement. This work, under the Technical Director Eric Jaccard, led to the introduction of caliber 350 in 1969. The movement diameter was set at 28.00mm and the height at 3.50mm. The balance worked with 21,600 oscillations/h and the movement had over 28 jewels. To fulfill the requirement for even lower height, a completely new design was chosen. Instead of the central rotor used previously, the watch now was wound by an outer rotor with ball bearing and gear ring. The watch movement is set inside. The earlier crown was omitted; manual winding and setting was henceforth done with a flat crown set in the screw back case, using generally the system of the Jaeger-LeCoultre "Futurematic". The elimination of the crown by the 3 made it possible for the designers to create interesting, attractive case designs, which, in the beginning, were particularly well received in the United States. Just about everyone there could get a Jaeger-LeCoultre "Futurematic", but only a few could buy a Patek Philippe.

After an apparently good start, the caliber 350 did not get the hoped-for success. The ball bearing of the rotating ring was prone to interference; the reverser for the winding mechanism in both directions of the rotor was sluggish and gave the watch a very low power reserve. The market response, coupled with the response at the Patek Philippe Service Department, made further development of this caliber essential. In 1979, the new version appeared with designation 1-350. In place of the heavy metal weight there was now an 18-karat gold piece. A new bearing, the removal of the reverser, and improvement of the manual winding and setting systems not only benefitted the user, but also the Service Department. However, no one was ever fully pleased with this caliber and production ended in 1985. It also had the drawback that the design would not allow a date display.

The series numbers are:

1. Production series, movement nos.1,180,000 to 1,189,999 (10,000 movements, 1969 to 1979)
2. Production series, movement nos.1,490,000 to 1,499,999 (10,000 movements, 1979 to 1985)

Models with this caliber were already known as the "Backwinder" in the U.S. René Schwarz, today Service head at Richemont in Munich, was with Patek Philippe in New York for 12 years. He knew, like no one else, the problems of these two calibers. According to him, there were so many complaints, that Patek simply took back the watches and exchanged them for other models.

Calibers 28-255 and 28-255 C

In 1976, Patek Philippe launched its new model, the Nautilus, on the market. There was no reliable automatic movement available for this new steel sports watch, designed by Gerald Genta. There was no question of using the caliber 1-350; it was not sturdy enough and had no date indicator. A solution was found in cooperation with the movement supplier Jaeger-LeCoultre. This automatic movement, equipped at Patek Philippe in caliber 28-255 without calendar and in 28-255 C with calendar, had demonstrated its worth since 1972 in the high-quality brand Audemars Piguet's Royal Oak sports watches, and later also for Vacheron & Constantin in the Reference 222.

Fig. 32 - Caliber 28 255 C with automatic winding mechanism, a super flat movement with external rotor ring (Movement-ø 28.00mm, height 3.15mm, 19,800 vph, 36 jewels).

When it appeared in 1967, this caliber was the world's flattest automatic movement. With 28mm diameter, height of 2.45mm and 19,800 oscillations/h, this ébauche bridged the gap for the period when Patek Philippe still had no reliable automatic caliber of its own. The design of the caliber 28-255 is clear and service-friendly. The 22-karat gold weight rotor moves in both directions, run by a copper-beryllium wheel with four ruby bearings. The 22-karat gold swing weight fastened on the outside of the rotor reinforces the winding mechanism power. The excellent design solution for the reverser, not only allows using the winding mechanism in both rotor directions, but also has a very short switching time and is, thus, very efficient. The watch is wound after just a few hours of wear. The few alterations made during a decade of production, which included change to an adjustable mobile stud support and a date indicator (height 3.05mm), proves just how well-engineered this movement was.

As already noted, this Jaeger-LeCoultre caliber was a movement blank for Vacheron & Constantin and Audemars Piguet. The caliber dimensions were 2.45mm without date display and 3.05mm with date display, making it the world's flattest automatic movement. It is often written in the literature, that this caliber was provided only to the companies Audemars Piguet and Vacheron & Constantin, and was a reserved movement blank (ébauche). At first, this reservation for Audemars Piguet and Vacheron & Constantin prevented a business arrangement with Patek Philippe. But, as a retired movement maker told the author, a colleague of his had the notable idea of making the swing weight 0.1mm thicker, changing the height to 2.55mm without calendar and to 3.15mm with calendar. This alteration gave the supplier Jaeger-LeCoultre an elegant way out of their contract commitment to only supply the world's flattest automatic movement to the previously named firms. The altered movement was always a tenth of a millimeter higher than those for Audemars Piguet and Vacheron & Constantin, but performed just as well. The caliber versions have the following production numbers:

1. Caliber without date display, movement nos.1,280,000 to 1,299,999 (20,000 movements, 1970 to 1980)
2. Version with date, movement nos.1,300,000 to 1,319,999 (20,000 movements, 1970 to 1980)

Both of these calibers have proven themselves at Patek Philippe and still represent a reliable value investment today. In 1999, Audemars Piguet bought all rights to this caliber from Jaeger-LeCoultre, with the plans and tools for it, and launched its own new production in 2005. The first watches with this new movement were on the market the same year.

4.6 About case number s

No logical plan for setting up the case numbers at Patek Philippe can be established. In the 1930s and 1940s, case numbers had six digits, but in the mid-1950s seven-digit numbers came into use. These were tied to ordering procedures at the case suppliers. If Patek Philippe ordered a new case for

Fig. 33 - Screw back of a Reference 3541 from 1968 with case number 320,933. The inner area is bead blasted, the inscription on the vertical axis clearly visible.

Fig. 34 - Back of the 1984 Reference 3563 3, also called the "Backwinder," with case number 2,698,334. On the back edge you can see the two notches which must fit exactly with their opposites on the case. To the right, the through hole for the winding stem and crown on the back exterior.

a stated Reference in a series, the delegated casemaker had to deliver these according to exact standards, complete with numbering and hallmark. The Reference 2526 pictured in Fig. 70 can serve as an example: It has movement number 763,637 and case number 696,013, both of which come from the production year 1956. An identical model made the following year has the movement number 764,962, but the case number 2,604,085. Watches assembled over 10 years later again have six-digit case number s, as seen with the References 3541 and 3542 shown in Figs. 128 & 132.

In summary, the case numbers are six or seven digits and always stamped on the inside back. Engraved, i.e. machine cut, numbers were not used on Patek Philippe cases. An example of a case back which has been tampered with, is shown in Fig. 200.

References 3439/1 and 3561 watches have sapphire crystal inserts. We shall see how the case number was inscribed in these models with the Reference 3561 in Fig. 142.

Fig. 35 - Watch cases are closed with screw or snap backs. The back inside inscriptions have changed significantly over the decades. At right the snap back of a Reference 96 in pink gold (see Fig. 39); the watch was made in 1942. At the top of the back, is inscribed the notation 4/10 for the material thickness 0.4. The Reference number 96 is missing; only the case number 297,660 is there. At the bottom is the slot for opening the snap back, always set by the crown.
Left above, the screw back of a Reference 2509 from 1952, (see Fig. 65); the inscriptions on the inside back has changed from the case at right. This also goes for the surface. The left back is circularly grained, the right bead blasted.

4.7 On the Reference numbers

The Reference number should be considered the watch's model designation ID. It is not so easy to determine today just when a systematic identification system for wristwatches was introduced at Patek Philippe. The fact is, that watches made at the beginning of the 1940s, which have a struck Reference number, are the exceptions.

The following information came from a Patek Philippe worker, long-deceased. After a caliber was introduced, the lists of Reference numbers were written by hand and were identical with the photo number, i.e. the respective picture of the watch. This registration is still done today in the Patek Philippe archives, even if data has been computerized for a long time. Some of the watches pictured in this book show that the Reference numbers were only struck on the case back in a planned manner beginning in 1948. One example is the Reference 96, which includes watches both with and without a Reference number (see Fig. 39). After Reference 96, came the three-digit Reference numbers ordered in 100, 400, and 500 groups. Four-digit Reference numbers were introduced subsequently. During the next year, these were the Reference groups 1400, 1500, 2400, 2500, 3400 and 3500. Examples are shown in Fig. 40 & 42, where the Reference numbers 565 and 570 can be distinctly seen on the backs. On the steel watch shown

in Fig. 44, made in 1939, you will look in vain for the Reference number 592.

Only the watches with complications had, at least in part, Reference numbers stamped in the case back before 1948. In the table, Fig. 36, are some examples, produced with or without Reference numbers.

In Fig. 112, since the watch is opened, we can see the complete numbering and hallmarking on the inside of the back. For Reference 3445-6, the "6" means the sixth and last version of this model.

In summary: When production of wristwatches began, the watches were listed internally under the particular Reference number, with some noted exceptions, but the identification marks were first die-stamped on the case back at the factory beginning in 1948. The Reference number is always struck on the inside back, never on the outside.

With older watches, it sometimes can be that a back was damaged and a new back had to be specially made. Even if the original watch was made before 1948, it will have a Reference number struck on the back.

In Chapter 11, all the References are compiled with associated information.

Reference	Complications	Year	Movement No.	Case No.	Reference Record
1436	Double chronograph	1942	862,420	630,552	no
1436	Double chronograph	1943	863,057	646,703	yes
1463	Chronograph (Walser Wald)	1946	863,724	640,561	no
130	Chronograph	1948	867,454	655,062	yes
1527	Chronograph with perpetual calendar (see also Fig. 171)	1943	863,247	634,687	no
1518	Chronograph with perpetual calendar	1943	863,195	633,139	no
1518	Chronograph with perpetual calendar	1947	867,243	646,599	no
1518	Chronograph with perpetual calendar	1951	868,004	663,680	yes
1526	Perpetual calendar with moon-phase	1942	864,271	652,371	yes
1526	Perpetual calendar with moon-phase	1948	963,263	657,232	yes
1415	World time watch	1945	929,694	647,130	yes

Fig. 36 - At Patek Philippe, all models were given Reference numbers, but these were only regularly inscribed on the inside back from 1948 on. Watches with complications had these identifying inscriptions earlier, in part, but this was not done with any discernible logic. This table shows some interesting examples of the, at times, inconsistent handling of Reference numbers.

4.8 Other identification - Marks, hallmarks, and stamps

If you want to purchase a watch not only as a presentable piece of jewelry, but also as a potential investment, you should carefully examine all the documentation on the inside of the case back. In addition to important notations from the manufacturer, there are also stamped hallmarks, which state the purity of the precious metals used.

Switzerland has 13 examination offices, directed by Bern, to supervise the authenticity of the materials used. The "Helvetia", a woman's head looking left and wearing a tiara, stands for the lowest gold purity of 750/1000. The Helvetia is an artistic national symbol of the Swiss confederation, comparable to Germany's "Germania". There are both small and large Helvetia. The small Helvetia hallmark is found mostly on the outside of a watch case; the larger on the inside back.

We show the insides of the watch backs in this book, so the reader can see the many versions of identifying marks that are stamped in this place. In Fig. 79, we see the relevant information on the inside back of a pink gold automatic Reference 2540 (production year 1957). On the upper part of the case are, in three rows under each other, the lettering "PATEK-PHILIPPE & Cᵒ", "–GENEVE–", and "SWISS". Here we find no accent

on the "E" in GENEVE, but a dash to the right and left. The inscription SWISS has no period at the end.

On the lower third of the back, we see at left the hallmark of the casemaker, in the middle the official stamp for "18 K/0.750" purity, and at right the large Helvetia. Underneath is the case number "699 844" and finally the Reference designation, stamped as "RÉF. 2540". The É has an acute accent, and the F has a period.

There is another version of the lettering on the inside of the automatic Reference 3445 (production year 1970) in Fig. 108. At the top is the large Helvetia, underneath the official notation of "18 K/0.750". Below follow in three rows, "PATEK, PHILIPPE & Co", "≡GENEVE≡", and "SWISS.". Under this in three rows are case number 328637, Reference designation 3445 and the casemaker's mark. The following differences can be established: Between the names PATEK and PHILIPPE there is no hyphen as before, but a comma. The "Cᵒ" in the first case is replaced with a "Co". The location, "≡GENEVE≡" now has three dashes on each side. The national origin, "SWISS.", here has the final period. Finally, the Reference designation is without the previous "RÉF". In this book, we will note and describe even more versions in this area.

Watches with 950 platinum cases have an hallmark, a right-looking chamois head with an oval frame. As with the Helvetia, there are two different sizes. The smaller mark is generally stamped outside; the larger only inside.

The Geneva hallmark, also called the Geneva Seal, is a guarantee of origin, highest precision, durability and watchmaking expertise. Only a few watchmakers are among those chosen to bear this good quality seal.

The three basic requirements for this seal are:

— The caliber must first be approved and recognized by eight official members of the city examination office of Geneva.
— The exclusively mechanical watch movement must at least be assembled and regulated in the Canton of Geneva.
— Every caliber must fulfill 12 technical regulation criteria, for development, features, production quality and finishing.

Fig. 37 - The 1972 Vienna Convention hallmarks for gold (left) and platinum (right).

To make trade and production of precious metal products easier, the then EFTA (European Free Trade Association) nations reached an international agreement on examination and identification of precious metals in 1972 (the Vienna Convention). This set a common hallmark for gold and platinum. For 18-karat gold, it is a symbolized balance scale with the number 750 at the center and framed with a double circle. For 950 platinum, the scale is inside a rhombus and has the number 950.

In newer Patek Philippe watches, these marks are imprinted on the inside back and outside (see Fig. 165).

On August 1, 1995, Switzerland introduced a new metal purity control law (EMKG) for trade in precious metals and their products. The new official stamp, a St. Bernard's head, affectionately known as "Bello", replaced the Helvetia.

In summary: The Patek Philippe watch brand uses only two precious metals for its cases: 750 gold or 950 platinum. A hallmark is omitted on steel cases, but the other information is identical. When buying an old or new watch of this brand, examine and check all the identification very carefully. In case of any doubt, the German subsidiary in Munich or central office in Geneva can provide assistance.

4.9 Precious metal or stainless steel – A short note on materials

There is yellow, pink or red, and white 750 gold. Yellow gold, as 750/1000 gold, is made from the addition of silver (125/1000) and copper (125/1000). For red gold the same metals are added but in different proportions: silver (45/1000) and copper (205/1000). For white gold, silver (200/1000) and nickel (50/1000) are used. Often, gold is also alloyed with platinum, especially because nickel can cause skin sensitivity.

In very special cases, Patek Philippe also makes platinum cases. Platinum can only get the hallmark with a minimum purity of 950/1000. To maintain this purity, platinum can be alloyed at most with 50/1000 parts of copper, gold, rhodium, iridium, and palladium. The most important physical properties of all described metals are noted in a table (Fig. 38).

Next to platinum, stainless steel, a steel alloyed with chrome and, therefore, rust free, has the best qualifications for making watch cases. It is not for nothing that steel watches are especially valued today. The processing times for steel, for machining such as turning, milling, and grinding, are some eight times higher than for gold. Like stainless steel, platinum is hard to work with. In an overall calculation it must be noted that platinum costs about 40% more than gold.

If vanity or budget are not the main issues when buying a new Patek Philippe, watches with stainless steel or platinum cases are the best choice.

Material	Specific Weight kg/dm3	Elasticity modulus E kg/mm2	Melting temperature °C
Gold (Au)	19.32	7,900	1063
Copper (Cu)	8.96	12,500	1083
Platinum (Pt)	21.45	17,320	1774
Silver (Ag)	10.49	8,160	960
Steel X 10 Cr 13	7.75	22,000	1500

Fig. 38 - Table of the most important data on metals used for watch cases.

5. The Patek Philippe Classics
More than just a secure investment

There are few investments you can make with double élan. On one side, you can always take pride in the timeless design and perfect technology of a wristwatch made by Patek Philippe. On the other, you are buying a timepiece which, as a rule, will only increase in mid- to long-term value, independent of what happens on the financial markets. In addition, even a new investor can acquire the expertise necessary to enter this arena, even if it was previously unknown to them, as we shall discuss further, using the wristwatches presented in this book. As already noted at the beginning, the respective owners of these rarities made them available to the author so he could compile this documentation.

Leafing through the out-of-print book *Patek Philippe Genève* by Martin Huber and Alan Banbery, 1998, you will find well over 200 different wristwatches pictured. The many different watch cases not only show the taste current at the time, but also indicate the limited numbers of models produced. Since less can often mean more, we have concentrated on just some 90 watches, in the selection of the watches illustrated here. They include interesting technical features, broadly meeting current tastes, and are often still affordable. In broadening the scope of the existing literature, we have provided such detailed descriptions for these time pieces, so that a previously uncertain investor can decide to make a substantial investment in a valuable Patek Philippe.

The descriptions of the watches below generally follow the same idea. First, we list the movement number s, then describe the dial, case, and movement. We give a lot of importance to the inscriptions and hallmarks on the case and inside the watch back.

The history of the particular watch follows, with information on purchase price and refurbishing costs. Finally, we list the results and prices these watches attained in sales or auctions. We highlight the watches' Reference numbers as a heading, so that the reader can easily locate them and quickly find the information wanted.

It is certainly the case that the following expert texts are not always easy to read. But when a lot of money is at stake, the reader would be served neither by a flowery text nor an exciting style. Technical watch descriptions and financial market reports have a lot in common. These are not exercises in rhetoric, but the exact and indicative expert statements that an investor or speculator requires, to be able to carefully plan and successfully carry through the purchase they have in mind. The following descriptions were collated with these goals in mind.

So that novices, watch collectors, and investors can get recommendations that, while not legally binding, reflect the current trends, the watches presented here will be identified based on three criteria: "To Wear", "To Collect", and "For Investment". These three categories will be evaluated as "good" (+), "very good" (++), or "excellent" (+++). Of course, there can be different opinions about all three criteria, but what is important is that readers develop their own individual criteria and can make their investment decision on that basis. Despite all opinions and discussions, one thing can be certain: As a rule, a Patek Philippe wristwatch is a safe investment. This goes for most of the vintage and many of the modern models. Purchasing watches as capital investment also raises the decisive question about what will be to the taste of the next generation of people interested in buying a beautiful watch. In this area, the author can help with his more than 20 years of experience and contribute to a successful selection.

Fig. 39 - The men's wristwatch Ref. 96 shown here was launched at the end of 1934 (officially 1935). This was the first "Calatrava," with the manufacturer's own manual caliber 12'''-120. The version at top, with pink gold case and black dial, was made in the production year 1942 (movement no. 922,367, case no. 997,660). The Reference ID was omitted on the inside back. The yellow gold model was made in 1951. Stamped on the inside back is the Reference no. 96 (movement no. 968,921, case no.303,990).

5.1 From the 1930s to the 1950s – Beautiful, but still manually wound (Reference range 96 to 2499)

Reference 96 "Calatrava" (Fig. 39)

The first men's wristwatch that Patek Philippe put on the market in large numbers was manufactured in 1932 with the designation "CALATRAVA". It was given the first Reference number, 96, and was initially equipped with a 12''' manual winding mechanism from Jaeger-LeCoultre. Only at the end of 1934 (officially from 1935) did Patek Philippe install its own caliber 12'''-120. The latter can be easily distinguished from the first. Jaeger-LeCoultre movements lack the fine adjustment for the regulator, with a micrometer screw and

swan's neck spring and the ruby bearing for the center wheel. What is still missing is the small plate above the escape wheel pinion, as is the Geneva stripe pattern on all bridges and cocks. Finally, the Jaeger-LeCoultre 12''' caliber had only 15 jewels; the Patek Philippe 12'''-120 has 18.

The Reference 96 was manufactured with many different dials. The author knows of more than 26 different versions with caliber 12'''-120 with small seconds hands.

In 1938, a caliber 12'''-120 with sweep seconds hand also came on the market. This version, with indirectly powered sweep seconds hand, has a Victorin Piguet-made intermediate gear, which connects to the second wheel via an intermediate

Fig. 40 - In 1938, Patek Philippe put its second waterproof watch on the market. Our picture composition shows this sought-after collector's item from the front and opened back. To the right are the dust-proof cover and screw back, the latter from outside and inside. The watch shown here was made in 1952. The installed caliber 12‴-120 has two Geneva Seals, one on the plate next to the balance and one on the barrel bridge by the movement-retainer ring with inscription "METAL" (movement no. 938,562, case no. 667,674).

wheel, newly centrally-installed (see also Fig. 49). A technically trained eye comparing this caliber with the successor 27 SC, will recognize that this is an inelegant, contrived design. Nonetheless, it stayed in production for over 11 years.

The Reference 96 version with sweep seconds hand also found its fans. The author has encountered more than eight different dial styles. Despite its relatively small case diameter of just 30.5mm (earlier versions had to make do with 30.0mm) the Reference 96 remained in production for 30 years and was finally replaced by the successor Reference 3796. Even today, there are plenty of admirers for these classic CALATRAVAs, including the version now produced under Reference 5196 with a case that has grown to a substantial diameter of 37mm. Today you can also get the Reference no. 5296 with automatic winder.

Even in the 1930s, there were a limited number of other versions of the Reference 96 on the market. These had full calendars with moon-phase by the "12" or a perpetual calendar with retrograde date indicator, small seconds hand, and moon-phase by the "6". Today, you can see a collection in platinum cases in the Patek Philippe Museum in Geneva.

But now to the gems of this book: two versions of the Reference 96. According to the Patek Philippe central archives, the first time piece, in pink gold, was made in 1942, the second, in yellow gold, in 1951. The Reference 96 case has three parts and is made of snap-on bezel, the case housing, and a snap back. The case housing is stamped from one piece and made to include the four band lugs. Holes were made for the spring bars and are, thus, visible from the outside.

Many look at the dial as the face of the watch, and this is right. You can only make the assumption that the dial of the pink gold watch has been restored, if you know the original inscriptions used each time when the watches were manufactured. Up to 1952, both watches read "PATEK, PHILIPPE & Co". The shorter form was first used during 1952 and the previous information "& Co" omitted. The accent grave on the second "È" of the origin notation, "GENÈVE" and the imprint "SWISS" under the "6" were retained. With this timely information, it must still be noted that Patek Philippe then only made 400 to 500 watches a month and the dials were always prepared in advance. So it could be, that for one of the models made in lower numbers, there would be enough dials already in the storehouse to last several years. The production year of a watch and that of a dial can differ by one or more years.

When both watches were refurbished, the dial of the pink gold Reference 96 was refurbished by the Causemann Company in Frechen, Germany, and printed as for post-1952. The dial of the yellow gold Reference 96 still corresponds to the original version, but has certainly suffered over time. After the refurbishing, both caliber 12'''-120s look close to new. The respective movement numbers 922,367 and 968,921 indicate a production year between 1942 and 1951 (see also Chapter 4.5).

The "small Helvetia" is on the case housing outside by the "4" on the pink gold Reference 96; on the yellow gold watch it is on the underside of the band lugs by the "11". Inside the watch backs, we see notable differences. For the pink gold piece, the older version with case number 997,660, we find the material thickness information 4/10, for 0.4mm gold sheet thickness and the framed company hallmark "PP. C°". The Reference number is missing. For the yellow gold piece, with case number 303,990, the same company information is on the lower area, but also the figure 96 for the Reference. The right dash was forgotten on the origin notation "–GENÈVE–", but the national information "SWISS." has a period in both cases.

Looking at the opened caliber, you recognize another small difference. In the pink gold version, the Geneva stripe is done at a 60° angle on the arbor crown-center wheel; for the yellow gold, it is a 30° angle. Could the polisher, lacking more precise specifications, have been using his own discretion here?

Conclusion: with its case diameter of 30.5mm, the Reference 96 no longer meets current tastes. The high quality of the movement and case still set standards. On the wrist of a pretty lady, this piece of jewelry can still outclass the current models of many competitors.

Reference 96 watches in yellow gold with Breguet numerals (see also Fig. 44) rarely come on the market, and would not be offered for less than €10,000. Models with steel cases are still sought-after and are offered at between €10,000-€30,000. The four yellow gold versions shown in Fig. 39 were acquired in 2008 by a collector for $4650 (about. €2982,87) in the United States; the collector then invested another €1650.53 for refurbishing at Patek Philippe. The separate case renovations cost another €150. Patek Philippe in Munich charged €75.40 for mounting a new hand mechanism. The owner swapped the pink gold model in spring 2009 at the Munich Watch Technology Fair for €4500, despite its dilapidated condition.

To refurbish the movement and the case, experts in Pforzheim charged a total of €480. The German firm Causemann refreshed the dial using exact specifications and charged €201.70.

All in all, both watch owners can be happy with the overall cost. There are few Reference 96 watches in such excellent condition on the market. In both instances, this can be considered a secure investment. Even in more difficult economic times, a well-maintained Reference 96 will always find a new admirer.

To Wear: + To Collect: + For Investment: +

Between the References

We should mention a few more of the many models that ranged between the Reference 96 and its successor, Reference 565. In first place is the chronograph Reference 130. With just 33mm case diameter and three-part case including snap back, it no longer meets modern tastes. The manufacturer Valjoux gave the movement the caliber designation 23; the chronograph control is via two rectangular flat push pieces. The cases were made in steel, yellow, and pink gold, as well as in a combination of steel and red gold. The author knows of more than 33 different versions. This watch, launched in 1938, was still in the product line until 1961. At the time, the price for the yellow gold piece was exactly DM 1710. The successor model Reference 530, also launched in 1938, is still offered today. With 37mm case diameter, 20mm width between the band lugs, and flat push piece, this model's appearance almost matches the new chronograph Reference 5170 launched in 2010 (see Fig. 178). This chronograph was also made in steel, yellow gold, and red gold. The author knows six different styles.

Reference 565 (Fig. 40)

In 1938, Patek-Philippe launched its second waterproof watch. It was given the Reference number 565. A then-opulent case diameter of almost 35mm (exactly 34.8mm), an inner dust cover, and a solid screw back helped this new product give a masculine, sporty impression. Even though it is more than 70 years old, this classic has not lost its attractive appearance and remains a real eye-catcher. The first waterproof watch, given the Reference number 438, was launched in 1935. The author knows three dial variations for this watch.

The watch discussed here belongs to the very rare styles that had an original black dial. The imprint runs "PATEK PHILIPPE & Co"; at the "6" is the notation "SWISS". According to the archive extract, this timepiece, with movement number 938,562 and case number 667,674, was manufactured in 1952 and sold on December 2 of that year. The two-part case is made of a housing with integrated bezel and a screw back. The housing was stamped from one piece, die-stamped, milled, and turned.

Most surfaces are diamondized; a dust cover ensures additional protection. The screw back closes with a fine thread and decagonal closure. The small Helvetia was imprinted on the case housing by the "4" and on the band lug below by the "11". Next to the patent information are, under each

Fig. 41 - The Reference 570A is cult status watch with high sustained value. The first pieces, with small seconds hands, were made in 1938; the model with sweep second a year later. The watch shown here has a pink gold case with a diameter of just 35.30mm. The original measure must have been 35.60mm. The "small Helvetia" inscribed on the case housing by the "4," is barely recognizable and indicates that subsequent work has been done on the case. This watch has the manual caliber 12'''-400 (movement no. 723,856, case no. 306,726).

other, the entries "PATEK-PHILIPPE & Co", "-GENÈVE-", and "SWISS", here without a period. Next to the gold purity notation, the large Helvetia, and hallmarks from casemaker (collective trademark no. 5, key no. 11, manufacturer Taubert, Geneva, closed in 1974), can be seen the Reference and case number s. The "REF." has another period, but no acute accent. The inside back has circular graining. The dust cover has left its marks there as it was screwed closed.

The caliber 12'''-120 is in nearly mint condition. The balance staff has no shock absorber. The Geneva Seal is printed on the plate near the balance and on the barrel bridge. This rarity was auctioned at Sotheby's in New York on October 17, 2003, as lot number 316. The estimated price in the catalog was $7000 - $8000. An German buyer on the telephone got the piece for $7500. Including the 20% premium, the entire price came to $9000. With shipping and import sales tax, the buyer paid €7891.30. This rare watch was sent to Patek Philippe for refurbishing. Of the total charges of €2172.68 (invoice of August 6, 2004), the restoration, at €1437 was the biggest item. Two gold spring bars cost €66; the archive extract cost €86.50.

As a "cult status watch", the Reference 565 is among the most sought-after collectors' pieces. With yellow gold case, these rose in value between $15,000 and $25,000; with

steel case, they often doubled in price. A piece comparable to our watch, in pink gold with black dial, was offered on November 16, 2009, at Christie's in Geneva and was sold for CHF 62,500, or about $62,202 (sold by Freccero, movement number 938,728, case number 667,705). At the same auction, a steel version, with Breguet numerals, sweep seconds hand, and a steel band, was offered and sold for CHF 93,000, about $92,557 (movement number 700,276, case number 662,276). Another steel version with two-toned dial and vendor signature "GÜBELIN" was offered at Antiquorum in New York on June 14, 2006, and sold for $82,000.

At the re-opening of Patek Philippe's renovated central office on the Quai du Rhône in Geneva in 2006 a reproduction Reference 565 was made in steel. This was given the Reference no. 5565 and limited to 300 pieces. These collector's pieces sold out immediately and appeared at auctions in the following year, attaining high prices. At Antiquorum in New York on June 14, 2007, a Reference 5565 piece was sold for $45,600 (movement number 3,559,510, case number 4,409,445). At the same auction house, on October 16, 2008, another watch was sold for $49,200.

To Wear: ++ To Collect: ++ For Investment: ++

Fig. 42 - Reference 570 with sweep seconds hand and manually wound movement caliber 27 SC. The Reference 570 always has a case with snap back and is, thus, only splash-proof. Both snap backs deserve a special note. The front one is of gold and made by sand casting procedure, with hand finishing. The other back was made as a turned part and is the official replacement back (movement no. 708,105, false case no. 708,105, corrected case no. 4,178,999).

Reference 570 with small and sweep seconds hands
(Figs. 41, 42, & 43)

Another highly popular cult-status watch is the Reference 570. It was made with either small or sweep seconds hand. The case diameter varies, and can range between 35 and 35.8mm. The Patek Philippe catalog listed a diameter of 35mm. When both the watches described here were measured, the results were 35.3mm for the pink gold watch and 35.6mm for the yellow gold. The pink gold watch is powered by a caliber 12'''-400 and has a small seconds hand. The balance staff has an early Jaeger-LeCoultre shock absorber. The movement number is 723,856; the case number is 306,726. The case is three-part, including snap-on bezel, a case housing made in one piece, and snap back. The "small Helvetia" hallmark is by the "4" on the case housing, and below the left upper case lug.

The yellow gold version, with caliber 27 SC (Fig. 43), is of a more recent date. The movement number is 708,105; that of the case first was 708,105, and later 4,178,999. A servicing in Geneva revealed that the back with the latter number was from another manufacturer and was replaced by a newly made back. The new case number is also noted in the archive extract.

The markings on both snap backs are of interest to the expert. The back of our pink gold watch was made as a die-stamped piece, that was shaped under high pressure. The faulty back of the yellow gold piece was turned from a cast body. You recognize this by the "surface streaking" resulting from basic sanding, which could not be concealed, despite the surface polishing outside and circularly grained on the inside. The new replacement back, turned from one piece, has a wall thickness of exactly 0.5mm; the one by the other manufacturer measured just 0.4mm. The inside inscriptions on the latter are almost perfectly imitated, but the obligatory "large Helvetia" was forgotten. The hallmarks on the inside back of our pink gold Reference 570 are done correctly, but on the "–GENÈVE" the right dash was again forgotten.

There is also a repair entry with "Cm 26831 6/61". Finally, we look at both dials. That of the pink gold case has enameled lettering and was then lacquered. The dial of the other watch is silver-plated and has a light-ray design. The lettering is also enamel. The manufacturing technique must have been almost miraculous, unless the light-ray design was applied with a polishing brush. The fine steel wires of this brush could hardly do anything to the hard enamel.

The yellow gold watch was bought by a German collector on July 15, 2002, for $7000 (about €7000). With shipping costs and import sales tax, the total investment for this watch

Fig.43 - The manual caliber 27 SC of the Reference 570 with sweep seconds hand, presented Fig. 42. At the front of the picture you see the screw balance with Breguet spring and "KIF" shock absorber, balance cock, and regulator with fine adjustment via micro-meter screw and swan's neck spring (caliber description on page 34).

was about €8200. The refurbishment done by Patek Philippe in Munich cost another €2898.26 (invoice of July 29, 2003). The restoration of the movement at €1376 and the newly made back from Geneva at €1010, were the most costly items in this invoice.

The seller of this watch, a Korean construction engineer from Marina del Rey, near Los Angeles, California, USA, was not, however, happy with the back made by the other manufacturer and paid for a new back, which reduced the servicing costs by about €1171.60 to €1726.66 .

The pink gold Reference 570 with small seconds hand, was sold on April 29, 2009, for $6766 (about €5100). The antique dealer, Rocky's Gold & Silver in Weyers Cave, Virginia, USA, had inadvertently offered this watch with the notation "yellow gold" and with a very indifferent photo on eBay.

The response was correspondingly small, limited to just three bidders. For this valuable collector's piece, the new owner had only to invest €6135,89 including shipping and import sales tax. At our editorial deadline, it was not decided if the watch would get a refurbishing by Patek Philippe.

Fig. 44 - The Reference 592 in stainless steel with dial and Breguet numerals is a rare collector's item. This model was made in 1938. The version in the picture belongs to production year 1939. Compared to the previous Reference 96, the case diameter is 32.5mm, not 30.5mm (caliber 12'''-120 with movement no. 829,746, case no. 506,760).

Reference 570 watches are always in great demand at auctions. A pink gold watch was sold at Sotheby's in Geneva for CHF 19,200; one in white gold at Antiquorum for CHF 34,220. At Christie's in New York on April 12, 2000, a Reference 570 of pink gold, with Breguet numerals was sold for $14,100. The record breaker, however, was a steel case model auctioned at Sotheby's in Geneva on May 17, 2005, for CHF 110,400.

To Wear: ++ To Collect: ++ For Investment: ++

Reference 592 (Fig. 44)

One of the small sensations of our watch selection is the steel version of the Reference 592. With a distinctly larger case diameter than the standard model Reference 96, Breguet numerals, and small seconds hand, this model is very rare and the author has seen it only once. The caliber 12'''-120 has the number 829,746, the case 506,760. The Reference number 592 is missing on the snap back, since the watch, according to the archive extract, was made in 1939 and sold on April 19,1941. The steel case is made of a housing, including bezel and a snap back. The case diameter is exactly 32.5mm. The case housing was initially made as a turned part. Four grooves were then milled, into which the band lugs were soldered. It is hard to set a price for this rarity, in part because this version has not yet been offered at auction. Due to its larger diameter, the price will be more than that of the steel version Reference 96.

The watch shown here was purchased by a European collector from the antique watch dealer FGW (Feel Good Watches) in Scottsdale, Arizona, USA, for $7000. It was then sent to Patek Philippe in Geneva for refurbishing. The overall costs came to €1213,36 with the movement refurbishing for €383.50 and dial restoration for €545 being the largest amounts

Fig. 45 - The Reference 1450, also known as the "Top Hat", was among the most popular men's wristwatches of the brand in the 1940s and 1950s. This model was launched in 1940 and was immediately in great demand in the United States. The model has the shaped movement 9'''-90. The case has a snap back. The crystal has a peculiar shape and is cut from one piece (movement no. 970,304, case no. 651,174).

(invoice of October 8, 2002). At Antiquorum in New York, a steel Reference 592 was offered on September 17, 2009; it sold for $19,200. This watch has a black dial with Arabic numerals (movement number 921,243, case number 507,497).

To Wear: + To Collect: ++ For Investment: ++

Between the References

Some other very special watches were manufactured between Reference 592 and the next watch, although in very small numbers. These include the Reference 1415-1 HU, a world-time watch with chronograph functions. The normal, but very rare Reference 1415 HU, with world time display, was made with platinum, pink, and yellow gold cases. Another rarity was manufactured as a split seconds chronograph, with the Reference number 1436. The author knows of 17 different versions. The yellow gold version of the Reference 1436 was still in the program in 1961, and, according to the catalog of the time, could be had for DM 2660. A steel version with movement number 863,056 and case number 630,772, attained a price of CHF 1,244,800 at Antiquorum, Geneva, on March 10, 2009. An excellent investment.

Reference 1450 (Fig. 45)

Although it was introduced as a lady's watch, the men's Reference 1450 watch was one of Patek's most successful models in the 1950s. With its nickname, "Top Hat", many men found this creation pleasing and, at the time, were not bothered by the modest dimensions (25.1 x 37.0mm). Today, this model is a chic lady's watch. The yellow gold "Top Hat", shown here, has the dial inscription "GÜBELIN". The caliber 9'''-90 has number 970,304, the case the number 651,174. There is no Geneva Seal on the movement. The case has a snap back and intricate case housing. The hallmarks are different from those of other models. It is not, as with other watches, laid out from top to bottom, but rather from side to side. It begins with the purity notation "0.750" and large Helvetia. Then come the marks of the casemaker, the lettering "PATEK, PATEK PHILIPPE & Cº", "GENEVE", and "SWISS". Finally, the case and Reference numbers are listed. Six repair notations indicate the intense wear of this watch, but also that servicing at Patek Philippe was too expensive for the cost the various owners.

A small Helvetia was imprinted on the right side of the case.

A collector from Munich acquired this watch for €4750. As of our editorial deadline, he had not yet decided on a final refurbishment for this beautiful timepiece. Styles in yellow and red gold and platinum were produced. One rare piece had a platinum case and bracelet, and a dial with diamond-studded index markers. At the Geneva Antiquorum on November 14, 2004, a model in pink gold with a "*Klötzli*" bracelet was offered and sold for CHF 19,200. On March 16, 2006, a platinum model with platinum bracelet was offered at the same auction house and sold for CHF 23,400.

To Wear: + To Collect: + For Investment: +

Reference 1491 with small seconds hand (Figs. 46 & 47)

The author can recount an interesting history about the next wristwatch. A watch enthusiast acquired this rare collector's piece, Reference 1491, in pink gold at the London branch of Sotheby's, paying some €5000. With caliber 12'''-120 (Fig. 46), movement number 968,379, and case number 664,108, this timepiece was registered and known in Geneva. After the sale, our watch enthusiast wrote to Patek Philippe in Geneva and inquired after an archive extract of the newly acquired collector's piece. The answer soon arrived. The watch was registered as stolen and the former owner was immediately informed of the reappearance of this precious piece and of the inquiry from the new owner and his address. A lawyer must still determine whether the legal regulations of protection had been correctly observed here. In any case, after a short time, a letter in excellent German arrived, confidently demanding the uncompensated return of this allegedly stolen watch. After a brief interchange in writing, both parties got in contact by telephone and discussed the case. The previous owner, who said he was a high-level administrative official in Tel Aviv, demanded the watch back, since it was inherited from his father and was stolen during a burglary.

After longer discussions, the details were confirmed. It emerged further that a police report had been made and the matter was registered with the insurance company in question, which had allowed an insurance payment of $10,000. The watch enthusiast informed the robbed Israeli about English law, which states, among other things, that allegedly stolen goods can be legally purchased in good faith at a public auction.

There is no answer yet to a written offer to return this heirloom after the incurred costs were paid. Apparently, the initial interest to regain the beloved paternal inheritance suddenly disappeared, when it was clear that it could not be done for free.

The renovation established that the outside of the snap back had been refinished, and about 1/10mm of material filed away. The back was then competently re-turned. It is possible that an inscription was removed, something an earlier owner could have had done.

At the time, both versions of the Reference 1491, with small and sweep seconds hands, were very popular and much in demand. The two-part case (diameter 34mm) consists of the housing, including the bezel and a snap back. The band lugs are especially striking; these are made in one piece and spirally rolled. On the version at hand, the lettering, the interval marks for small seconds hand, and the imprint "SWISS" are enameled, and the dial itself is lacquered. The inscriptions on the back also reveal interesting information. They start at the top with the lettering "PATEK, PHILIPPE & Co", with the "Co" now lacking the previous dash under the "o". The place of origin, "≡GENÈVE≡", is framed right and left with three dashes. Finally there is the type notation "REF: 1491", here without acute accent, but with a colon.

These noble Reference 1491 timepieces do not come up for auction very often. Prices have fluctuated in recent years between 10,000 and CHF 28,000, depending on design, condition, and provenance. Since recently ladies have also begun wearing men's watches, a Reference 1491 on the wrist of a pretty woman would be a really special piece of jewelry.

Fig. 47 - The Reference 1491 is a watch with a striking case design. The band lugs are made in one piece and rolled outwards. That these band lugs were soldered with yellow gold on a pink gold case, did not bother the then-quality control. The Reference 1491 was made with both small and sweep seconds hands. The model shown here with pink gold case and small seconds has a remarkable history (movement no. 968,379, case no. 664,108).

Fig. 46 - Detail of the manual movement caliber 12'''-120, which powers the Reference 1491 shown at right. All the parts, such as balance cocks, screw balance, Breguet spring, and fine adjustment are distinctly recognizable. At left is the small cap jewel with end piece and the setting for the escape wheel staff. The balance has no shock absorber. Below can be seen a distinct scratch, which likely resulted from the slip of a screwdriver. There was still no stamped caliber designation on the caliber 12'''-120.

At Antiquorum in Geneva a pink gold model was auctioned on October 15, 1989, for CHF 10,800. Eleven years later, on October 16, 2008, a yellow gold version was offered at Antiquorum in New York and sold for $12,000. On May 14, 2007, at Christie's in Geneva, a yellow gold watch sold for CHF 16,800 ($13,835).

To Wear: ++ To Collect: ++ For Investment: ++

Reference 1491 with sweep seconds hand (Figs. 48 & 49)

A companion piece to the Reference 1491 with small seconds hand was made with a sweep seconds. This watch also has a pink gold case. This collector's piece has a caliber 12''' SC, a design reworked from the caliber 12'''-120 (Fig. 49). This modification did not come from Patek Philippe, but was developed by the Victorin Piguet company. The movement number is 864,993 and the case number is 645,221. The dial is black lacquer and has gold index markers and an imprinted minute circle. The case shape corresponds to the previously described watch. The snap back is 0.5mm thick. The Victorin Piguet movement design, which takes some getting used to, can be seen very clearly in Fig. 49. The hallmarks of the inside back correspond to the case numbers of the previously considered Reference 1491. The watch

shown here was offered on November 14, 2009, at Auktionen Dr. Crott in Frankfurt/Main, but did not sell. The reserve price of €15,000 to €20,000 was likely set too high and the lower offer of €13.500 was not accepted. A yellow gold version was auctioned at Antiquorum in Geneva on November 16, 2002, for CHF 12,500.

To Wear: + To Collect: ++ For Investment: ++

Reference 1516 (Fig. 50)

The Reference 1516 timepieces are among the hardest Patek Philippe watches to find. The author has only seen one of this model, just once. This piece of jewelry is easy to identify, with a caliber 12'''-120, movement number 965,722, and case number 332,339. As with the previous item, this Patek Philippe is more suitable for a woman than a man. The blue color of the dial and the crocodile strap are perfectly matched.

The case, with a 32.5mm diameter, reflects the style of the 1940s. The housing of the two-part design was turned and the striking band lugs soldered on. The solid snap back gives the case increased stability. Perhaps the repercussions of the post-war period played a role in this low-cost solution. In terms of production time, this case certainly represents a cost-cutting solution.

Fig. 48 - It is always a question of personal taste whether a small or sweep seconds hand looks better in the case of identical watches. This model Ref. 1491 with a sweep seconds hand is particularly striking, perhaps due to the black dial (movement no. 864,993, case no. 645,221). *Image Auktionen Dr. Crott.*

Fig. 49 - Manual wound caliber 12''' SC, an adapted version of the caliber 12'''-120 from small to a sweep seconds hand. This modification was done by the Victorin Piguet company. Via the altered train wheel bridge and small attached bridge, the three additional gears (with the same number of cogs) take the seconds strokes from the position of the small seconds hand to the center. This is what we call an indirect seconds drive. Whether this additional construction was especially successful can be queried. With the successor caliber 27 SC, Patek Philippe demonstrated a better solution for this task (see also page 34). *Image Auktionen Dr. Crott.*

Fig. 50 - The elegant Reference 1516, with yellow gold case and blue dial. Only an expert watchmaker can recognize that this is definitely a lower cost watch. The case housing was made with very thin sides, to save a lot of material (gold). The caliber 12'''-120 is not, as was previously usual, screwed to the case, but clipped into the snap back with a dial set on top. When the watch is dismantled, the snap back with movement and dial, are taken out of the case middle. The Reference 1516 was put on the market in 1941 and is among the least costly gold watches on the price list. The watch shown here was made in 1950 and has a Reference number on the inside back (movement no. 965,722, case no. 332,339).

As to the hand-wound caliber 12'''-120, there is no need to speak of compromises. It appears to be in almost new condition, and after a successful servicings it again achieved chronometer ratings. The small Helvetia is found twice on the case, on the case housing by the "4" and on the underside of the left upper band lug. The hallmarks are deeply stamped and the turned snap back deviates somewhat from its predecessor. Marked from top to bottom, first comes the large Helvetia, purity notation, case number, and the casemaker's mark (collective trademark no. 5, key no. 4, Antoine Gerlach SA, Genève, closed in 1977). After a larger gap, comes in four rows "PATEK PHILIPPE & C°", "–GENEVE–", "SWISS.", and the Reference number 1516. There is no grave accent on the GENEVE but the SWISS has

a period. There are only four digits in the Reference number. According to the archive extract, the Reference 1516 was produced in spring 1950 and sold on May 12 the same year. The watch was purchased by a collector from Antwerp, Belgium, on December 31, 2000, for $3750 and then checked by an expert.

Reference 1516 watches are rare. Another Reference 1516 piece has rather dubious fame. In 1957, the Mafia leader Charlie "Lucky" Luciano in Palermo gave his top boss Joseph "The Godfather" Bonanno a Patek Philippe Reference 1516 in yellow gold. He had the original leather strap exchanged for a non-brand bracelet of 14-karat yellow gold at the Patek Philippe concessionaire in Palermo, the jeweler S. Barraja, Via Ruggero Settimo. It could be that, for these Sicilian "men

Fig 51 - This detail of a Reference 1566 watch case shows us the extensive manual work necessary to make the earlier models. The upper area of the band lugs is diamondized; the sides satin finished. The 45° beveled edge is not accurately executed. The same goes for the watch crystal, where the diamond-filed, beveled edges are not totally homogeneous.

of honor", name, look, and a cheaper price came first. He could have chosen a original Patek Philippe gold bracelet, but for three times the price. Furthermore, the Reference 1516 at that time was among the least costly Patek Philippe watches.

This watch was auctioned at Antiquorum in New York on March 4, 2009, and despite its dilapidated condition sold for $36,000 (movement number 966,280, case number 302,352). This watch was accompanied with a notarized letter from the daughter of the previous owner, Catherine Bonanno Genovese, describing the history of the family and the watch.

At Antiquorum in New York, a pink gold Reference 1516 was auctioned on December 1, 2004, for $4080. This watch also was in a really moderate condition. The refurbished dial had the incorrect notation, "SWISS MADE", printed by the "6".

To Wear: + To Collect: + For Investment: +

Between the References

Before we move on, we should mention some rarities in the Reference 1500 group. These include the famous chronograph with perpetual calendar, the Reference 1518 (see Figs. 174 & 175), the Reference 1526 with perpetual calendar, the double chronograph Reference 1563, and the perpetual calendar Reference 1591. The last two models are also worthy of mention because both have a dust cover and screw back. The author has encountered these two time pieces just twice.

Fig. 52 - Reference 1566 after an extensive refurbishing in Geneva. The company inscription corresponds exactly to the production year 1946, but not the "0 SWISS 0" by the "6". This identification for gold index markers was first included in 1968. The caliber 10'''-200 is screwed to the elaborate movement holding plate. It has neither the caliber designation nor the Geneva hallmarks. The two-part snap back has no Reference number; these were given first from 1948 (movement no. 950,371, case no. 642,317).

Reference 1566 (Figs. 51 & 52)

For the numerous men's wristwatches manufactured by Patek Philippe with either square or rectangular cases, we show a pink gold cased Reference 1566. A caliber 10'''-200 was installed with movement number 950,371; the case has the number is 642,317. According to the archive extract, this watch was manufactured in 1946 and sold on March 18, 1947.

The especially harmonious dial is silver-plated. Up to the "6", Roman numerals of pink gold stand for the even hour numbers, with periods for the odd. The lettering "PATEK PHILIPPE & Co, GENÈVE" is typical for the period; only the imprint "0 SWISS 0" under the "6" reveals that this dial was restored by Patek Philippe. The imaginative and multi-faceted case design represents a small work of art (dimensions 25.6 x 35.6mm). The detail of the lower left band lug shows us the diversity of the shape, the surface finishes, and the hand work involved (Fig. 51). The relatively small caliber 10'''-200 was set in a special movement retainer. This consisted of a thin manufactured segment, soldered to a square plate. The elaborate snap back was designed with double sides and circular cut out; when mounted it fixes the above mentioned movement retainer.

The "small Helvetia" is stamped on the left side of the case. In the inside back are listed from top to bottom, "PATEK-PHILIPPE& Cº", "–GENÈVE–", and "SWISS" without a period. After the "large Helvetia" come the gold purity notation "18K/0.750", the case number and the casemaker's mark (collective trademark no. 5, key no. 15, Uli Rotach, Carouge, closed in 1977). This Patek Philippe was bought by an American watch enthusiast for $4800. He had to pay a further €2153,90 to refurbish the movement and renovate the case. The work on the movement, at €1030, and dial restoration (invoice notation: without imprint "SWISS"), at €535.50, were the largest items in the bill (invoice of August 6, 2007). This gem would also be unbeatable as a lady's watch.

Fig. 53 - A comparison of the wristwatches Reference 2449 (right) and 2451 (left) shows the large differences between the two. The case diameter of the right watch is 35.1mm, for the left, 30.5mm. Both dials meet the regulations initiated from 1952. The dial of the Ref. 2451 is still original, the second "E" of the imprint "GENÈVE" has a grave accent. The concessionaire imprint, "TIFFANY & CO", makes this watch even more valuable. This accent was forgotten on the dial of the Ref. 2449, which was refurbished at the end of 2001 in Geneva. The responsible employee should have known better.

Reference 1566 watches were popular at the time and often appear at auctions today. The three following examples have pink gold cases and all come from Antiquorum in Geneva. On April 13, 2003, a version with the company signature "Cartier" was offered and sold for CHF 14,400. On April 24, 2004, a watch was sold for CHF 11,400 and, on November 15, 2007, one was sold for CHF 9600.

To Wear: + To Collect: + For Investment: -

Reference 2449 (Figs. 53 & 54)

Among the attractive men's wristwatches of the Reference 2400 series, is the very rarely found Reference 2449. Powered by the caliber 12'''-400 with movement number 726,775, the case bears the number 670,660. According to the archive

extract, this was made in 1955 of pink gold and sold on December 8, 1957 (Fig. 54). The 18-karat pink gold dial is also noted there. The case, with a diameter of 35.1mm and 20mm wide band lugs, is both aesthetically pleasing and masculine. Band lugs with a 20mm inside measurement are rare and atypical for Patek Philippe for this size case. Could it be that the casemaker did not get exact specifications? The die-stamped snap back is only splash-proof. The movement is edged by a solid bearing ring. The balance staff is not shock proof. As to why there is no Geneva Seal on either the base plate or the barrel bridge, even Patek Philippe specialists could not answer.

The hallmarks on the case housing meet the period standard. The small Helvetia is stamped on the side by the "4" and on the underside of the left upper band lug. On the almost untouched inside back, the large Helvetia and the gold purity notation

Fig 54 - In the opened Reference 2449 (left) and 2451 (right) we can see the different case designs. The pink gold watch has a two-part case with snap back and is only splash-proof. The yellow gold model has an elaborate screw back and a dust cover. The inside back of the Reference 2449 is finely bead polished; that of the Reference 2451 has circular graining. The measure between the band lugs is 20mm for the left watch, only 17 for the one on the right. The Reference 2449 was in produced in 1955, the 2451 in 1952. The left watch has a caliber 12'''-400, the right a caliber 10'''-200 (Ref. 2449: movement no. 726,775, case no. 670,660; Ref. 2451: movement no. 958,667, case no. 668,790).

"0.750" are stamped beneath each other. Then, on the back center, come the company inscription "PATEK- PHILIPPE & C°", "–GENÈVE–", "SWISS", and "RÉF.". Here, the "É" has an acute accent and an abbreviation point. After the case number, the casemaker stamped his mark (collective trademark no. 5, key no. 9, Emile Vichet SA, Geneva, closed in 1960).

This watch was put up for auction on April 12, 2000, by Christies's New York, and bought by a watch enthusiast for $6462.50. The complete refurbishment at Patek Philippe was expensive, coming to DM 2453.40 (about €1254.40) In this general refurbishing, the restoration of the dial at DM 1120 and refurbishing of the movement at DM 365 were the most expensive items (invoice of January 25, 2002). However, considering the newly printed dial and the large number of the replaced components, including the hands, you can almost speak of an as-new condition for this watch.

Watches of Reference 2449 are hard to find. Antiquorum in Geneva sold a yellow gold version on April 20, 2001,

despite the refurbished dial, for CHF 6480. At Antiquorum in New York, a pink gold model was offered on March 23, 2005, and sold for $8040. On the internet auction house "Life Auctioneers", a pink gold version of the Reference 2449 was offered as lot 121, for CHF 13,000. Whether it was also sold at this price was not known by the editorial deadline.

To Wear: ++ To Collect: ++ For Investment: +

Reference 2451 (Figs. 53 & 54)

An interesting counterpart to the Reference 2449 is our yellow gold version of the Reference 2451, with a much more modest diameter. With a case diameter of just 30.5mm, it is the same size as the Reference 96 (see Fig. 39), but also has an elaborate case design. Our Reference 2451 has the hand-wound caliber 10'''-200, with movement number 958,667 and the case number 668,790 (Fig. 54). According to the archive extract, this watch was manufactured in 1952 and bought on December 5 the same year. The dial is silver-plated and fine brushed lengthwise. The signature corresponds to the standards set in 1952, and there is also the name of the American merchandiser and concessionaire "TIFFANY & CO". While the manufacturer's name is in enameled letters, the lettering for the dealer is only imprinted. This difference lets us conclude that this dial was not originally specified for TIFFANY and the company name was added later.

Despite its small size the case has some special features. The bezel and case housing belong together and, along with the band lugs, they were stamped from one piece, turned, milled, and polished. A dust cover protects the movement. The stable screw back is die-stamped and was made as a turned part, and holes were made for the spring bars. Especially noteworthy is the ten-sided closure for the screw back. This closure is recessed, i.e., there is a groove between it and the case back, and the wrench can be easily and securely inserted. The author knows of no other Patek Philippe with such an elaborate watch back design.

Inside the opened watch, we can see all the characteristics of the caliber 10'''-200. This beautifully decorated movement is of chronometer quality. The balance staff still has no shock absorber. The Geneva Seal, rather small, is on the base plate and the barrel bridge. The stable movement retainer ring has a small flange for the dust cover. The hallmarks on the case match the Patek Philippe standard. On the case side by the "4" and on the underside of the left upper band lug, we find the "small Helvetia". The case back inside shows a surface with circular graining and a lot of information.

From the top, these begin with the patent notation and Swiss Cross. Then follow "PATEK, PHILIPPE & Cᵒ", –GENEVE–", and "SWISS", the second without a grave accent and the last without a period. At the diameter center are, from left, the gold purity notation "18K/0750", the "large Helvetia" at center, and at right the casemaker's mark (collective trademark no. 5, key no. 7, Fabior, Oliver Indas, Gimel). Below that are the identification "REF. 2451" and the case number. Comparison with the previously discussed Patek Philippe watches shows just how diverse the hallmarks of the inside back turn out to be, and also often difficult to date, .

This Reference 2451 was acquired by a German collector for about €6.600, and he had to invest approximately another €1600 to refurbish the movement and case. Because of the dealer's notation, TIFFANY & CO., this excellently preserved piece can be assessed for more than is normal for this version. If it does not have to spend all its time in the safe, it would certainly make a very elegant lady's watch. Reference 2451 models are more frequently to be found at auctions or the watch exchanges, and are in high demand, despite their modest diameter of 31mm. First, three examples from Antiquorum in Geneva: a pink gold model was offered on October 14, 1990, and despite the incorrectly refurbished dial, was sold for CHF 8400; on October 14, 2007, a yellow gold model was sold for CHF 9600; and on May 10, 2009, a steel version for CHF 6600. A yellow gold watch was in the auction at Christie's in Hong Kong on December 3, 2008, and knocked for $9721.

To Wear: + To Collect: + For Investment: +

Reference 2469 in yellow and pink gold (Figs. 55 & 56)

Reference 2469 watches are among the especially stylish models that appeared in the 1950s. With their barrel-shaped cases, curved case backs, and attractive dials, they are particular eye-catchers on a lady's wrist. Not to be forgotten is the beautiful, wonderfully shaped caliber 9'''-90, of which we present two different versions (Fig. 56). According to the archive extract, the yellow gold version was made with movement number 974,777 and case number 668,045 in 1952 and sold on February 17 the following year. The dial has alternating point and line shaped index markers and a square seconds hand display.

The red gold version has movement number 976,035 and case number 682,468 and, according to the archive extract, was made in the production year 1954 and sold on November 16, 1955. The hands, index markers, and the three Arabic numerals are also pink gold. In contrast to its yellow gold counterpart, it has no imprinted minute display, and thus a more pleasing effect. The case of the Reference 2469 represents a very elaborate design. It consists of the outer edge, a really complicated chase, and the movement retainer. The first two components were both stamped from sheet gold, curved, and soldered together. The sheet brass movement retainer exactly fits the caliber 9'''-90; the surface is rhodium-plated.

Comparing the movements is interesting. These calibers, the production year 1952 number 974,777 and the 1954 number 976,035, are 1259 pieces apart. Up to the screw balance of the first, and Gyromax balance of the latter, the movements are almost identical. That the 1954 model had no shock absorber, seems at first remarkable. However, the height, taken over from Jaeger-LeCoultre, was too great, and it would not have fitted in the case.

The extensive regulation notations and other inscriptions on the barrel bridge of the second model are striking compared to the yellow gold version. We read "ADJUSTED TO HEAT, COLD, ISOCHRONISM. AND FIVE (5) POSITIONS, EIGHTEEN (18) JEWELS, PATEK, PHILIPPE & CO.", etc. as well as the Geneva Seal (see Fig. 56, watch at right). The gold mark (small Helvetia) is on the outside of the case by the "4". The inside back and the sometimes different inscriptions reveal more. On the older, yellow gold, versions, a symbolized comma separates the letters in "Patek Philippe & Cᵒ"; on the pink gold version a dash. Otherwise, up to the case housing parts, the remaining inscriptions are identical. The five watchmaker's notations on the older watch point to good usage. The pink gold piece could almost be considered like new; there we find no signatures.

The yellow gold Reference 2469 was purchased by a watch enthusiast from an antique watch dealer in Phoenix, Arizona, USA, and cost $7600. Shipping and import sales tax were additional. The pink gold watch was bought in Germany for €6144. The yellow gold model was refurbished at Patek Philippe in Geneva, which cost DM 2738.76 (invoice of February 19, 2002). The largest amounts were for the movement refurbishing for DM 750, the dial restoration for DM 1120, and the crocodile strap for DM 267.

Fig. 55 - Comparison of two different versions of the Reference 2469. The yellow gold watch was made in 1952, the pink gold in 1954. The different company inscriptions on the dials show the new 1952 regulations: the old version is at left, the new at right.

Reference 2469 pieces are hard to find on the market. On May 14, 2006, at Antiquorum in Geneva, a watch comparable to our pink gold model was auctioned for CHF 6200 (movement number 976,845, case number 682,655). The catalog notation of the production year "Made in the 1980's" was rather off the mark. At Sotheby's in New York a pink gold watch was sold on April 19, 2010, for $11,250 (movement number 974,071, case number 668,058).

To Wear: + To Collect: ++ For Investment: +

Reference 2481 in two versions, one with modified case
(Figs. 57, 58, & 59)

The Reference 2481 is another cult status watch, no doubt due to its large-dimensioned case diameter of almost 37mm. The Patek Philippe catalog gives the watch's diameter as 36.6mm. This model was launched in 1950 and made in many different versions. We present two different models. The first comes from the United States, has the caliber 27 SC with movement number 707,885 and case number 2,607,824. The second, not completely faultless watch, comes from a Stuttgart antique watch dealer. With movement number 707,656 and case number 2,607,790, it was, according to the archive extract, manufactured in 1958 and sold on May, 12, 1959. The numbers of both calibers 27 SC are just 229 pieces apart. Both watches came with leather straps. With a stereoscopic microscope, you

can see that the first watch has a dial in original condition, the second a properly refurbished one.

A few words on case design. The impressive and, for the time, over-large bezel diameter of almost 37mm (movement specification 36.6mm) actually represents some deceptive packaging. If you turn the case around, the underlying case cylinder has just a 35.5mm diameter.

The caliber 27SC has been mentioned many times. In both pieces, the movement is very well preserved. The Geneva Seal is stamped on the plate near the caliber designation and on the train wheel bridge. The movement retainer ring has an attractive size and holds the movement securely in place. The hallmarks on both watches are similar, even though the case numbers are far apart. The hallmarks begin at the top of the case back, stamped in three rows: "PATEK, PHILIPPE & Co", "≡GENÈVE≡", and "SWISS". Then comes the "large Helvetia", the gold purity notation "18 K/0.750", the Reference number "2481", case number, and casemaker's mark. The hammer head with the number 171 is collective trademark no. 1, which stands for the company Bernard Dubois, La Chaux-de-Fonds, which was closed down in 1987. The material thickness notation was omitted, but we have determined this as 0.4mm.

The first-noted Reference 2481 comes from an American collector. He bought it for $7563 (about €5957.47) and exchanged it with an interested European party. Another

Fig. 56 - This opened case allows a view of both shaped movements of the caliber 9'''-90 and their elaborate movement mounting. The watch at left still has a screw balance; the right one is fitted with a Gyromax balance. The extensive inscription on the movement at right is also notable (Ref. 2469 left: movement no. 974,777, case no. 668,045, Ref. 2469 right: movement no. 976,035, case no. 682,468).

€854 was invested for the import sales tax. A professional refurbishment of case and movement was under discussion at editorial deadline.

The second example was offered repeatedly by a Stuttgart antique watch dealer, but found no buyers even at a reduced price. A Munich watch enthusiast eventually found one of the reasons for the limited interest. The present band lugs do not match the original design. Only when the dealer was told of this problem, did further details emerge. According to the archive extract, this Reference 2481 was delivered with a crocodile strap. A subsequent owner had the band lugs removed and a solid gold bracelet soldered on. The next owner was not pleased with this soldered bracelet; he had it removed and four band lugs again attached to the case. Unfortunately, the casemaker entrusted with this task did not have any Reference 2481 pattern at hand and attached fancy lugs, which did not match either the Patek Philippe Reference 2482 or the chronograph Reference 1579. The Munich watch enthusiast finally bought this watch for €4500. After a brief first inspection and authentication, this Reference 2481, together with an original version, was sent to a Pforzheim casemaker, who was asked for a proposal for a correct restoration. How this story continued, we learn in the captions for Figs. 58 & 59.

The Patek Philippe Reference 2481 was very popular with princely and royal houses in its time. Saudi Arabian King Saud (ruler from 1953 to 1958), successor to the famous King Ibn Saud (born November 24, 1880, in Riyadh; died November 9, 1953 in Ta'if) was happy to make gifts of the Reference 2481, in a special edition. With the likeness of his predecessor and ruby index markers on the dial, this watch was given to foreign state guests, worthy subjects, or leaders of the many nomadic Bedouin tribes in the country. In 1958, the heavily indebted King Saud abdicated and relinquished power to his half-brother Faisal, resulting in a decline in the good business between Patek Philippe and the royal Saudi house.

The 1961 Patek Philippe catalog still lists the Reference 2481. It gives the case diameter as 36.6mm and the price as DM 1295.

Besides the special editions for princely and royal houses, the Reference 2481 was also marketed with special enameled dials. Watches with cloisonné-enameled dials were considered valuable, unique pieces and were made only in limited numbers. These cloisonné dials displayed palm-tree landscapes, continental maps, and other such motifs. For the dials, first the outlines and shapes of the motifs were made using thin gold wire and soldered on. Then, the outlined areas and shapes were filled with various colored enamel powders and fired.

The lettering "PATEK PHILIPPE" was set in the upper arc under the 12, "GENÈVE" in the lower arc above the 6 and etched in with enamel. Even the grave accent on the second E in GENÈVE was included.

A Patek Philippe Reference 2481 with cloisonné enameled dial was put up for auction on December 16, 1990, at Antiquorum in Tokyo. With its palm tree motif dial, this watch

Fig 57 - The Reference 2481 is one of the sought-after models of the 1950s. With a case diameter of almost 37mm (exactly 36.6mm), it was, at the time, among the "largest Patek Philippe watches." This model was especially in demand by the Saudi Arabian royal family. This watch was also coveted by other princely families and often was made with dials bearing the likeness of particular rulers. This composition shows the Reference 2481 in full detail. This watch was made in 1958. The hand-wound caliber 27 SC has the first shock absorber, which was introduced at Patek Philippe from 1953. The escape wheel cock and train wheel bridge are elegantly raised, to allow housing for the gears for the sweep seconds hand drive (movement no. 707,885, case no. 2,607,824).

Fig. 58 - Making three from two, could be the motto of this picture; we can make such photos thanks to modern image processing. The hand-wound Ref. 2481 at left was already shown in Fig. 57. The middle watch of the same Reference does have band lugs, but the wrong ones. These were later removed by a casemaker and re-made according to the present pattern and soldered on. We see the result of this work on the watch on the right. This example shows us that even a watch with the wrong band lugs does not have to be a hopeless case (at left Ref. 2481: movement no. 707,885, case no. 2,607,824; at right Ref. 2481: movement no. 707,656, case no. 2,607,790).

Fig. 59 - This montage shows the three watches shown above, now one behind the other. At upper right is the original, with longer vertical band lugs. A professional eye recognizes this even without a direct comparison arranged in a row. At the upper right is the original with the movable bezel, satin finished case housing and diamondized snap back. Beneath is the second watch, before and after restoration of the band lugs. An expert eye sees the small differences between original and renovation. The reworked band lugs are set a bit too high and not as cleanly soldered as on the original.

Fig. 60 - This pictures shows all the details of the pink gold hand-wound watch Ref. 2483. The solid pink gold dial has the inscription "FRECCERO." This is the name of the firm FRECCERO SA, of Montevideo, Uruguay, which is still today a concessionaire of Patek Philippe. Only selected dealers were allowed such a signature. On the left we see the opened screw back case with the caliber 12'''-120. On the right lower band lug, the digits 631 were inscribed. They represent the last three digits of the case number 661,631 and make a sure attribution of case and screw back possible. This watch was made in 1952 and the dial conforms to the new regulations introduced that year (movement no. 968,697, case no. 661,631).

achieved CHF 10,160,000 (movement number 702,041, case number 668,415). At Christie's in New York on June 23, 1998, another Reference 2481 with cloisonné enameled dial was auctioned for $178,500 (about DM 319,515). The dial of this watch also had the famous palm-tree motif (movement number 703,043, case number 678,621). A Reference 2481 with the likeness of King Ibn Saud in yellow gold and a yellow gold bracelet (*"Klötzli"* bracelet) was auctioned at Antiquorum on November 6, 2002, for CHF 54,000 (movement number 704,978, case number 689,414). From 2007 to 2009, some dozen normal versions of the Reference 2481 came on the market and were sold for between $9600 and $12,000. With its substantial value, a Reference 2481 should also be considered a mid- to long-term good investment.

To Wear: ++ To Collect: ++ For Investment: ++

Reference 2483 (Fig. 60)

Among the oldest concessionaires in South America is Freccero S.A., Montevideo, Uruguay, where this Patek Philippe Reference 2483 was delivered. The caliber 12'''-120 has the number 968,697, the case the number 661,631. Feccero is also one of the selected dealers who were allowed to put their names on the dial. Pink gold was apparently in high favor with wealthy South Americans at that time. On our Reference 2483, the dial, index markers, and dauphine hands are all made of 18-karat red gold. With its colored case of the same color, this watch has a very elegant and stylish appearance. The dial inscriptions follow the 1952 regulation, with "PATEK PHILIPPE" and "GENÈVE". Of course the "SWISS" is under the "6", though covered by the bezel.

The solid, two-part case has a screw back and is very elaborate. The case housing with integrated bezel was stamped in one operation from one piece, die-stamped, turned, and milled. The diameter is 32.5mm. The upper bezel and band lugs are diamondized and the remaining surfaces satin finished and polished.

The caliber 12'''-120 is in almost mint condition, although the Geneva Seal is not to be found. The watch has no shock absorber.

The hallmarks are interesting and sometimes different. This can be due to the casemaker, who belonged to collective trademark no. 1 (hammer head with number 10, Cédex, Charles Dubois SA, Le Locle, closed down in 1982). On the underside of the band lug by "2" is the "small Helvetia", and by the band lug by the "8" is the number 631. These are the last three numbers of the six-digit case number. This particular identification prevented any potential mix-up and always ensured that each case was screwed to the right back. In terms of production technique, there was also another ground for using this identification. Case and screw back were manufactured separately, including turning the fine threads, the inside thread on the case and the outside thread on the screw back. Afterwards, the various cases were tried out with the different screw backs, and those fitting together best were selected for each other. To prevent mix-ups later, the case always was stamped with the last three case numbers.

The heavy case back is turned and includes six punched slots. It is exactly 0.5mm thick and the inside surfaces have circular graining. On the upper third of the back, the inscription begins with "PATEK, PHILIPPE & Co", "–GENEVE–", and "SWISS". Beneath in a row are the marks of the casemaker, the purity notation "18K/0.750" and the "large Helvetia". Below this are the numbers for Reference 2483 and case 661,631.

The watch shown here comes from the US and was sold on August 12, 2002, for $5750. Including shipping and import sales tax, the watch cost around €6757, and the thorough servicing at Patek Philippe another €693.45.

The new owner did not know that the Reference 2483 was always made with a dust cover. This watch did not get that extra protection. Reference 2483 watches were also made with the caliber 27 SC with sweep seconds. The small seconds hand model is very rare and hard to find. A pink gold version with caliber 12'''-120 was auctioned at Antiquorum in Tokyo on December 16, 1990, for CHF 10,800. Between 2006 to 2009, only a few yellow gold versions of this model were offered, selling for between CHF 7800 and CHF 15000. This waterproof model would also make a beautiful lady's watch.

To Wear: ++ To Collect: ++ For Investment: ++

Fig. 61 - Even the fine watchmaker Patek Philippe made some men's wristwatches which look like a lot but cost little. The Reference 2501/1 shown here is among them. It is a good thing that only the experts, and not the collectors, recognize this fact. All the details of this watch can be seen in this montage. It was produced at the end of 1952 and the dial is original. The graduated, two-step case has a snap back. To take the watch apart, the crystal has first to be snapped open. After both screws holding the movement are turned, the dial and movement are taken out upwards as a unit. The snap back allows inspection and aligning the rather small caliber 10'''-200. Despite all constrictions, this bargain model seems to be popular with collectors. In summer 2010, a watch from the U.S. dealer "Second Time Around Watch Company" was sold for $6800 and another, on the internet portal "Buy & Sell Watches", sold for a full $8000 (movement no. 958,784, case no. 672,412).

Fig. 62 - The manually wound Ref. 2508 with stainless steel case is among the most sought-after collector's pieces. The version with gold case is listed in the 1961 German sales catalog for DM 1355. The steel version, launched as a "budget watch," could be had for DM 900. These five separate pictures show this watch, including with screw back and dust cover, in full detail. Also interesting, is the lead seal around the movement retaining ring, later replaced by a plastic seal. The manual caliber 27 SC can be seen in full detail. This also goes for the movement no. 708,505 on the barrel bridge above right and the case no. 2,614,125 on the lower right inside back. This watch was sold in spring 2009 for €28.500. At Antiquorum auction house in Geneva, a stainless steel Reference 2508 was auctioned on May 13, 2007, for CHF 44,840 (movement no. 710,519, case no. 2,614,135, manufactured in 1963).

5.2 The 1950s boom – Now automatically wound (Reference range 2500 – 3585)

Reference 2501 (Fig. 61)

We selected a Reference 2501/1 timepiece as a good example of a rather casual "budget" men's wristwatch. Here, the minimal solution was used for case design, gold content, and the movement. The caliber 10'''-200, with movement number 958,784, was also made as a lady's watch. The case housing has a two-tiered bezel and a snap back, with number 672,412.

The dial is silver-plated and the surface was brushed, bottom to top. Lettering and the seconds hand display are enameled and in very good condition. The same goes for the baton hands, although that for the small seconds is no longer original

The two-tiered gold case has an outer diameter of 33.6mm; the snap back is 23.4mm in diameter. The crown is recessed, fitting exactly within the outer dimensions. The band lugs are soldered on, with just 17mm between them. The case was milled under each of the band lugs, to allow space for the half-turned band ends. The small caliber 12'''-200, with the dial, is mounted in the case from above and the Plexiglas crystal snapped on. After both screws holding the movement are turned, the case can be shut with the snap back. The movement has a detachable winding stem, which is inserted after the movement is mounted.

The condition of the caliber 10'''-200 can only be given a grade D and a refurbishing is urgently recommended. The partially missing rhodium plating, damaged screw slots, and the numerous watchmakers' marks indicate that this watch has had a lot of wear.

The hallmarks in the 0.4mm thick snap back correspond broadly to the then-standard. From the top are the "large Helvetia", the purity notation and company name "PATEK PHILIPPE & C⁰", "–GENEVE", with the right dash missing, "SWISS", and "RÉF. 2501/1". The casemaker belonged to collective trademark 5, with key no. 1. He was registered as "Ed. Wenger SA, Genève" and closed down in 1992.

Our Reference 2501/1 comes from the USA and was acquired by a watch enthusiast for $4850 or €3870.49. On September 20, 2006, a comparable watch was offered at Antiquorum in New York and sold for $4320. In Geneva, at the same auction

house, a white gold version of this Reference was put up for auction on April 13, 2002, and sold for CHF 8640.

To Wear: To Collect: + For Investment: -

Reference 2508 in stainless steel (Figs. 62 & 63)

The Reference 2508 is another watch very much in demand today. This manually wound watch, launched in 1950, was still listed in the 1961 German Patek Philippe catalog, which stated that with yellow gold case it cost DM 1335. This model was waterproof and had a dust cover and ten-sided screw back. The case could be ordered in yellow or red gold (case diameter 34.8mm). The "budget version" at the time came with a steel case.

First, we shall consider the steel version (see Fig. 62). The watch, which has a caliber 27 SC, has movement number 708,505 and case number 2,614,125. The screw back makes the watch waterproof and there is also a dust cover.

The dial is lacquered and has 12 index markers. At the 12, 3, 6 and 9 o'clock they are wedge-shaped; at the remaining hours are tiny pyramids (Fig. 63). The company inscription "PATEK PHILIPPE, GENÈVE" is written in capital letters. The dauphine hands harmonize with the dial and case. The case housing has an integrated bezel. It is stamped from one piece, turned, milled, and the surface finished.

On the gold version, the inside back has circular graining. The screw back is ten-sided. The older watches have a lead seal; in the newer ones it is made of plastic.

Upon visual examination, the installed caliber 27 SC appears to be in excellent condition, but a Patek Philippe servicing would still be beneficial.

The Geneva Seal is stamped on the base plate by the caliber designation and on the train wheel bridge. The inscription on the machined inside back appears somewhat different from that of previously described watches. Listed one below the other are the patent notation, then the inscriptions "VACUUM", "PATEK, PHILIPPE & C⁰", "–GENEVE–", "SWISS", "ACIER INOXYDABLE", "REF. 2508", and case number 2,614,125.

The watch first belonged to a German watch lover who bought it in spring 2007 from a Swedish collector for €8000.

Fig. 63 - This picture shows the dial of the Reference 2508 with steel case, and in comparison to Fig. 64, the various ways of manufacturing a dial. This dial was first lacquered and then the minute interval marks and company name were printed on it. Finally, the steel index markers were applied and riveted. This dial is still in original condition. Since steel watches were almost a third less expensive than the same Reference in a precious metal (gold), savings were also made on manufacturing the dial.

Fig. 64 - The dial of the 1954 yellow gold Reference 2508 is more elaborately designed than its counterpart above. The company name and minute marks were fired in enamel and then lacquered. When the dial is held flat, the colors drain away from the raised letters and minute interval marks, due to gravity. Finally the index markers were applied and riveted. To refurbish this dial, the index markers have to be taken off and the paint removed. Then the dial is newly lacquered and the index markers reset. Only an expert would know that the dial shown here had been refurbished. This almost seven-times enlargement makes it possible for a layman to see small alterations, such as in the letters of the company logo and the minute marks. Had this dial been refurbished by an expert firm in Switzerland rather than in the USA, the renovation would be barely noticeable (movement no.703,890, case no. 680,970).

Fig. 65 - Reference 2509 watches are among the most popular models. With a small seconds hand, they are even more elegant than the previous model 2508. This picture shows two different watches, one with a yellow and one with a pink gold case. The various angles let us see this model in all relevant details. These include the movement caliber 12'''-120, the case from the back, the inside back with inscriptions and hallmarks, and the dust cover. Two Geneva Seals are stamped on the caliber 12'''-120, one on the base plate near the balance, and one on the barrel bridge, here, however, highlighted with gold. The balance has no shock absorber. The inside back is fine circular graining; all inscriptions and hallmarks are easy to recognize. The pink gold watch is a prominent piece, once belonging to the American entertainer Chuck Barris.

Two years later, the German sold the piece to an American. Although no refurbishing had been done, the American paid €28,500 for this steel watch.

To Wear: ++ To Collect: ++ For Investment: ++

Reference 2508 in yellow gold (Fig. 64)

The second Patek Philippe Reference 2508, the 750 yellow gold counterpart to the first watch we presented, is also powered by a caliber 27 SC. It has the movement number 703,890; the case number is 680,970. The dial has been refurbished and newly lacquered. Since the signature and minute markings are enamel, these were preserved as in the original. This renovation would be barely noticeable had the dial maker not forgotten the "SWISS" under the 6 and set two of the 12 index markers inexactly.

The design of the gold case matches that of its steel counterpart, including the boring of the spring bar holes, the dust cover, and the ten-sided screw back. The screw back is exactly 0.5mm thick. The caliber 27 SC is also identical; however, the movement number is, compared to the steel watch, 4,615 pieces lower and, therefore, about eight years older. The lettering on the barrel bridge is consistent with that on the previously discussed watch. The only difference is with the Geneva Seal, which is stamped on the barrel bridge, not the train wheel bridge.

The "small Helvetia" is stamped on the case housing, on the underside of the left upper band lug, and by "4". The lettering on the circularly grained inside back also matches the previous watch in detail. It includes, in successive rows, the patent notation with Swiss cross, "PATEK, PHILIPPE & Cº", with symbolized comma, "–GENEVE–" and "SWISS". In the middle are purity notation "72/18K/0.750", "large Helvetia", and the casemaker mark (collective trademark no. 5, key no. 11, Manufacture Taubert, Geneva, closed down in 1974). After this comes "REF. 2508" and case number "689,970".

A US collector bought this watch for $8065.78 (about €6077.06); import sales tax came to about €1155. There has been no refurbishment at Patek Philippe, but, considering this reasonable purchase price, it would not stretch the budget. Reference 2508 watches are very much in demand. Two yellow gold models were auctioned at Antiquorum in Geneva on March 16, 2008; a yellow gold model with black dial and attached Milanese gold bracelet sold for CHF 38,400 (movement number 706,435, case number 696,830). A pink gold version with silvered dial and leather strap brought CHF 23,400 (movement number 702,866, case number 677,478).

To Wear: ++ To Collect: ++ For Investment: ++

Reference 2509 in pink and yellow gold (Fig. 65)

Reference 2509 watches are among Patek Philippe's most sought-after and popular models. This Reference was launched in 1950 and remained in production for over 15 years. With its small seconds hand, it is even more elegant than the previously described model Reference 2508. In the 1961 German catalog, the case diameter is given as 34.8mm and the price as DM 1245. Due to the popularity of this model,

we selected both yellow and pink gold watches for this book. The first, with a yellow gold case, is powered by the caliber 12'''-120 with number 938,783; the case number is 673,731.

This watch was made some three years earlier than the pink gold counterpart described below. The case shows that the watch was worn. However, the hallmarks on the case middle by the 4 and under the upper left band lug are still deeply struck, so we can conclude that this case has hardly been refurbished, something also shown by the red coloration of the gold, called gold oxide, on the underside.

Only a trained eye would be able to tell that the dial had been refurbished. The enameled lettering "PATEK PHILIPPE, GENÈVE" and the enameled cross hairs for the small seconds were retained. After the gold index markers were taken off, the dial lacquer was removed and the silver layer below brushed lengthwise. This is how the "SWISS" printed under the "6" was lost. Why the cross hair pointing to the 6 was kept a bit shorter, can't be determined. Another Reference 2509 model delivered to FRECCERO, Montevideo, has similarly shaped cross hairs for the small seconds (movement number 720,057, case number 672,126, pink gold case). After the dial renovation, the gold index markers could have been reset more cleanly and evenly.

The Reference 2509 case has two parts and still has a dust cover. The band lugs have holes. The case housing was die-cut, die-stamped, turned, milled, and given the desired surface features. The ten-sided screw back, which used a 29mm wide wrench, is turned and die-stamped. The back is 0.5mm thick.

The Reference 2509 was made with two different calibers. First, the well known caliber 12'''-120 was used, but from 1950 the successor caliber 12'''-400 also. The caliber here is a 12'''-120 number 938,783, manufactured in 1953, still without a shock absorber for the balance staff. The Geneva Seal is stamped both on the base plate near the balance and on the barrel bridge. Despite being 57 years old, this hand-wound watch looks almost like new and the lack of any watchmaker's notations on the inside back reinforces this conclusion. The inscriptions on the circularly grained inside of the back resemble those of the previously described yellow gold Reference 2508. The manufacturer Taubert in Geneva provided the case. Unlike the pink gold version we have yet to describe, the word "VACUUM" is missing.

This beautiful collector's piece was bought at auction by a German watch lover for $7000 or €5000 in the USA; the import sales tax came to about €800. At editorial deadline, no decision had yet been made to invest in a renovation at Patek Philippe.

The pink gold counterpart was previously owned by well-known American entertainer Chuck Barris, who appeared on radio and television, including the TV series "The Gong Show", one of the most popular programs in the 1970s. This watch was bought at auction at Christie's, New York, on June 22, 1998, for $6037 (about DM 10,806.23). This gem is powered by a caliber 12'''-400 with number 726,820, the case has number 693,707. From the archive extract we learn that this pink gold watch was made in 1955 and sold on November 18, 1957.

Pink gold Reference 2509s with luminescent hands and index markers are rare finds. As a Patek Philippe insider told the author, only 50 of these pieces were made. Our special interest begins with the dial. The archive extract tells us that

Fig. 66 - This detail shows us just how sensitive enameled dials are to pressure and bending. The dial of this valuable Reference 2526 is fractured in several places.

Fig. 67 - Overview of the damaged watch. It could be that it fell on a tile floor and the dial absorbed the full impact from the movement. Since the hand display and the index markers kept their shape, we assume that the destructive force came from behind the dial and in a ring shape. The dial was screwed to the movement by two cylinder pins and set in the case from behind. Inside the case, it is held by the bezel in a ring form. If the impact came via the movement on to the dial, it would be bent in a ring shape and the dial would be fractured. Since Patek Philippe has had no replacement dials with enamel inscriptions in stock for years, only a lacquered dial could be offered in exchange.

this watch was delivered with a black dial. The dial mounted today has the earlier luminescent hands and index markers in pink gold, but a silver-plated surface. The imprint "0 SWISS 0" also shows it was finished after 1968. Since the watch's screw back is really tightly fastened after a Patek Philippe refurbishing, the staff at the Ulm concessionaire could not open it for the photo studio, so we cannot describe or show the inner workings. An article in the magazine *Chronos,* 3-2003 described and showed pictures of this watch. The circularly grained inside back has the inscription "VACUUM"; the collective trademark 5 with key no. 11 tells us the casemaker is the manufacturer Taubert, Geneva.

Reference 2509 watches were always popular. At Antiquorum in Geneva a yellow gold version was auctioned on February 25, 1990, for CHF 8400. On November 14, 1999, a Reference 2509 with steel case was put up for auction at the same house and sold for CHF 14,400. A pink gold model was also offered at Antiquorum in Geneva on March 16, 2008, and sold for CHF 24,000 (movement number 725,448, case number 689,652). A steel Reference 2509 was auctioned at Christie's in New York on October 26, 1998, for $8970, or about DM 14,710.80 (movement number 962,121, case number 2,605,631). At Antiquorum in Geneva, a steel Reference 2509 was sold on March 31, 2001, for CHF 13,800 (movement number 920,350, case number 621,075). The name "WALSER WALD" was imprinted on the dial. This special imprint was for Walser, Wald y Cia, Florida 486, Buenos Aires, Argentina, a Patek Philippe concessionaire until the 1980s; the jewelry business no longer exists.

More important to our discussion is the wrong Reference number. The movement caliber 12'''-120 with number 920,350 was already made in 1940 and the case number 621,075 is from that same time. The watch was, however, not a Reference 2509, but a Reference 565 (see Fig. 40). The Reference 2509 was first launched in 1950, after the Reference 565 which appeared in 1938. The question is if the buyer, who paid CHF 14,400 for this piece, also noted this. If so,

he made a good piece of business. At Antiquorum in Geneva correctly named steel models of the Reference 565 were also sold. One such model was knocked down on March 16, 2008, for CHF 38,400 (movement number 924,674, case number 629,538, production year 1943) and another on November 11, 2007, for CHF 55,200 (movement number 923,330, case number 629,472, manufactured in 1943). Watches did not have stamped Reference numbers then.

To Wear: ++ To Collect: ++ For Investment: ++

Reference 2526 "Calatrava" with cream and black enameled dials (Figs. 66-74)

The automatic caliber 12'''-600 AT gives this watch a fine quality seldom achieved by other brands. In Fig. 70 we see an especially beautiful piece in 750 yellow gold, purchased from the heir of the first owner from Portland, Oregon, USA. The Reference 2526 was manufactured with cases in 750 yellow, pink, and white gold. There were also platinum pieces. The 1961 Patek Philippe catalog shows that these watches were not considered prohibitively expensive at the time. Here, the Reference 3428, successor model to the Reference 2526, is listed with a purchase price of DM 3880.

This book shows three different versions of the Reference 2526 because of its special importance. The first model has a cream dial and yellow gold case; this is the watch from Portland, Oregon, USA. According to the archive excerpt, this automatic with caliber 12'''-600 AT, movement number 763,637 and case number 696,013, was finished in 1956 and sold on June 28, 1957. This statement corresponds to the information and documentation of the first owner, who bought this watch personally on the given date at Patek Philippe headquarters on Quai du Rhône. Ten years later, he returned to Geneva and had his watch checked for the first time. The dial, the real focus of this watch, gleams in unblemished enamel and has survived the last 63 years well. The dauphine hands

Fig. 68 - An automatic Reference 2526 with intact dial. Enameled dials are easy to recognize by the etched in company names and the enamel layers cut into to make the hole for the seconds hand staff. Even the national information "SWISS" under the "6" is done with enamel lettering. All the secrets of enameled dials are revealed on page 28.

Fig. 69 - This automatic Reference 2526 received a replacement dial at Patek Philippe. It was given a high-gloss lacquering to reproduce the appearance of an enameled dial as much as possible. The company logo, minute interval points and second bars are imprinted. The bore for the seconds hand staff is unconstricted and works smoothly; the national notation "0 SWISS 0" is imprinted and meets the new regulations introduced in 1968. We can reckon a 30%-40% markdown for watches which only have lacquered replacement dials. Examples are shown in Figs. 13-16

and the index markers have also not lost any luster. The case diameter is 35.6mm according to manufacturer's catalog. The case consists of housing section with integrated bezel and a screw back. The case housing was stamped from one piece, die-stamped, turned, milled, and the surfaces finished.

The screw back was initially manufactured as a turned part and then die-stamped. The screw back still has a pressed-in steel ring, which holds a spring ring washer. When the back is screwed on, the washer in turn presses on the movement retainer ring. It is important that the two spring ends of the washer are always aligned with the steel ring, or the sharp ends would damage the movement retainer ring when the back is screwed on. Further processing steps are identical to those for the case housing.

The automatic movement is in pristine condition and was given a refurbishing at Patek Philippe. This watch movement is, both technically and aesthetically, one of the best and most beautiful ever made there. The case hallmark, the "small Helvetia" stamp, was done differently on the Reference 2526 watches. On the first of the three versions we are describing, it was struck underneath between the two band lugs below, at the "6". In another watch of this model, the "small Helvetia" was struck twice, as usual between the band lugs and on the underside of the upper left band lug. On a third watch, the hallmark is only on the latter place.

Now we shall examine the inside back. At first, we note the bead-blasted surface. The inscriptions are laid out, beneath each other "PATEK, PHILIPPE & Cº", "GENEVE", and "SWISS". Then follow in a row, from left to right, the mark of the casemaker, the purity notation, and the "large Helvetia"; the case and reference numbers are stamped below. The case supplier, F. Baumgartner, SA., Geneva, was registered with the collective trademark no. 5 and key No. 2. The brand was shut down in 1973.

This watch was sold on the internet on January 24, 2001, for $12,100 and total costs, including shipping and import sales tax, came to some €14,870. This watch was in such good condition that the servicing at Patek Philippe in Munich cost only €568.40 (invoice of February 21, 2003).

Another Reference 2526, with a lacquered dial replacing the enameled dial, was purchased by a watch enthusiast on April 21, 2005, for $12,001 (approximately €9298.78). The movement number of the caliber 12'''-600 AT is 761,484; the case number is 684,544. Including shipping and import VAT, this collector's item cost exactly €10,854. Another €680 had to be paid for a refurbishing by the exceptional watchmaker Martin Becker of Straubenhardt, near Pforzheim. This watch can be seen in Fig. 69.

One of the most beautiful Reference 2526 styles is the model with black enamel, rather than cream-colored enameled dials. The two designs are compared in Figs. 70 & 71.

The international auction catalogs of Antiquorum, Sotheby's, and Christie's have cited production figures for the Reference 2526 in the past two years. A total of 580 pieces were manufactured, 480 in yellow gold, 50 in pink gold, 30 in white gold, and 20 in platinum. Of this total, 10 each of the watches with the yellow and pink gold cases were to be given black enameled dials. Only the then-Production Director François Cart, the manager of the Patek Philippe archives, would be able to tell us if this information is true. But François Cart has not been among the living for a long time, and the guardians of the Patek Philippe archives maintain absolute silence.

The figures noted above were entrusted to the author many years ago by a Patek Philippe employee, who is now long deceased. This information was cited only with reservations, since the author cannot verify it from his personal research.

Enameled dials can retain their appearance over centuries. The only pressures they cannot sustain without damage are shock-like temperature fluctuations and mechanical strain. Replacement dials are a very important issue for this Reference, but Patek Philippe Service has always had a negative response. In the early 1960s, a small series of replacement dials was again introduced, 100 pieces, although this number was not used. These dials can be identified by their color: they do not match their cream-colored predecessors, but turned out more of a clinical white.

Fig. 70 - Every watch collector's dreams include the first Patek Philippe automatic from 1953. It was given the Reference number 2526. The cream-colored enameled dial gives this watch an especially refined appearance. We see the "constriction" of the enamel layer by the bore for the small seconds hand. The case was made with a diameter of exactly 35.6mm. To the right, the cast crown with Patek Philippe signet, used for all automatic watches up to 1964 (movement no. 763,637, case no. 696,013).

Fig. 71 - A black enameled dial suits the Reference 2526 better. According to a Patek Philippe employee, just 580 Reference 2526 pieces were produced, 480 in yellow, 50 in pink, and 30 in white gold, as well as 20 in platinum. Ten each of the yellow and pink gold pieces had a black enameled dial; the model shown here is one of them.

Fig. 72 - This picture shows us how a Reference 2526 case looks without dial and movement. The case is two-part, the case housing with an integrated bezel and a screw back. The first is stamped out from one piece, turned, milled, and given the appropriate surface.

PATEK PHILIPPE
THE WORLD'S FOREMOST WATCH

proudly presents this unique, new selfwinding watch made by its master watchmakers of Geneva, Switzerland.

The price is $800. F.T.I. With hand-wrought 18 Kt. gold bracelet, $1200. F.T.I. At Selected Jewelers.

The story of this timepiece with its thirty jewels and its 18 Kt. gold double-action rotor weight, is so fascinating that we would welcome the opportunity of sending you a descriptive booklet.

Fig. 73 - Advertisement for the automatic Ref. 2526 in *Life* magazine in 1956. This piece, with crocodile strap and gold pin buckle, cost $800; the gold bracelet model cost $1200. At that time, the exchange rate for a dollar was exactly DM 4.2161, so the watch with crocodile strap would cost DM 3372.88, and with gold bracelet DM 5059.32.

PATEK PHILIPPE
präsentieren Ihnen

IHRE BERÜHMTE

AUTOMATISCHE UHR

Fig. 74 - The first automatic Patek Philippe watch, Reference 2526, was launched in 1953. It was presented at the Swiss Watch Fair, an exhibition which is part of the Swiss Industries Fair, from April 11-21, 1953, in Basel, where the brochure shown here was distributed.

Die Gründe

einer unbestrittenen Ueberlegenheit

Das Werk, das von aussergewöhnlicher Güte ist, hat nicht weniger als 30 Steine. Uhrmacher und Regleure, welche die weltberühmte Tradition der Genfer Uhrmacherkunst weiter pflegen, vollenden es in Handarbeit.

Die Aufzugmasse, oder der Rotor, ist aus massivem 18-karätigem Gold. Es ist dies eine äusserst selten anzutreffende Ausrüstung von Uhren höchster Qualität. Die patentierte "Gyromax"—Unruh, eine Patek Philippe - Ausschliesslichkeit, stellt eine aufsehenerregende Neuerung dar. Ihre sehr hohe Regulierfähigkeit zusammen mit den unerreichten aerodynamischen Eigenschaften erlaubt eine absolut wissenschaftliche Gang-korrektur.

Die Zeiger und die lapidierten Ziffern sind aus 18 ct Gold, desgleichen die Schale, welche Dauer-haftigkeit mit Eleganz von sicherem Geschmack verbindet. Es gibt verschiedene Modelle mit Selbstaufzug, namentlich die Ref. 2526, deren Email-Zifferblatt keinen Veränderungen durch äussere Einflüsse unterworfen ist, wie z.B. Trübung durch Sonnenbestrahlung.

Gesamt-Abbildung des automatischen Werkes. Kaliber 12''' 600. — Durchmesser: 27 mm.

Die Patek Philippe-Automatic ist wert-voll zugleich wegen ihrer Pracht, wegen der Schönheit ihrer Linie, wegen der hohen Genauigkeit und der dauerhaften Aufrechterhaltung dieser Präzision. Bei angemessenen, guten Unterhalts-Bedingun-gen und nach individueller Anpassung der Reglage bewegt sich ihre äusserste Abweichung in der Grössenordnung einer Sekunde in 24 Stunden.

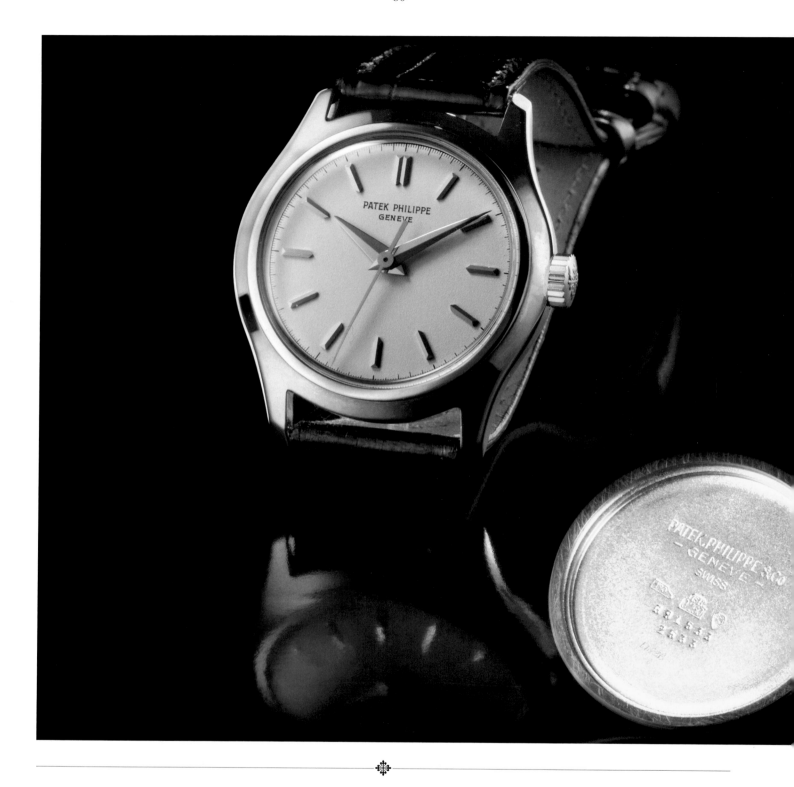

When purchasing a Reference 2526 watch, the dial is of utmost importance. Is it a well-preserved original dial, an original replacement dial, or a lacquer dial fitted as a replacement? The latter can be recognized not only by its lower luster, but also by the lack of constriction at the bore for the small seconds display. It is just this feature that is typical for the enamel coating (see Fig. 68). If there are doubts, when a particularly large investment is in question, the watch can be examined by a concessionaire or at Patek Philippe. Even if opening the watch, dismantling the movement and demontage of the dial would mean paying €500 or CHF 750, one should

not shy away from making this investment, assuming, of course, that the potential seller agrees with this procedure.

One can estimate paying some €12,000-€22,000 for the yellow gold version and €25,000 to 38,000 for the pink gold Reference 2526 watches in good condition. A rare pink gold piece with black enameled dial even attained CHF 157,500 (approximately €102,000) at an auction in Geneva on October 11, 2003 (movement number 761,735, case number 687,422). At Antiquorum in New York on June 18, 2008, a yellow gold Reference 2526 with black enameled dial reached $61,200 (movement number 762,329, case number 689,066). On

September 22, 2004, at the same place, a pink gold Reference 2526, including gold bracelet (*Klötzli* bracelet) was sold for $60,000 (movement number 762,624, case number 691,288). A record price was set by a white gold model with attached *Klötzli* bracelet. It was put up for auction on November 13, 2006, at Christie's in Geneva and sold for CHF 156.000 (movement number 762,700, case number 688,740).

Watches with platinum cases are sold for even more. At Antiquorum in New York on March 24, 2004, such a watch was sold for $78,000 (movement number 761,518, case number 687,558). At the same auction house, on June 14, 2007, another

Reference 2526 with a platinum case was auctioned for $138,000 (movement number 761,412, case number 687,561).

An eBay vendor from Texas, USA, tried to sell a Reference 2526 enameled dial. He offered an intact, cream-colored dial first for $20,000 and later for $15,750 (eBay Item 290 412 971 446, Providence Golf 1157). His offer ended on April 11, 2010, without any buyer response.

An expert can determine production data from the numbers 93 452 listed or stamped on the back. The number "93" stands for the Patek Philippe customer number, the 452 for the running production number. On the replacement dials later

Fig. 76 - Watches with pink gold cases were very much in demand in the 1950s. The Reference 2537 has a case diameter of 34.4mm and curved band lugs. Another unusual feature is the width between the lugs, which is exactly 19.5mm instead of the usual 18mm. The dial is silver-plated and brushed vertically; the company's signature in enamel.

made for the Reference 2526, which were only lacquered, the ID 93 was imprinted for Patek Philippe and 2526 for the Reference, meaning that no more running production numbers were listed. Between the two numbers, we find a five-pointed star, as proof of origin from the company Cadrans Stern.

To Wear: +++ To Collect: +++ For Investment: +++

Reference 2533 (Fig. 75)

There are many outstanding watches in the Reference group 2500. This includes References 2532 and 2533, which have identical cases. The case housing, with integrated bezel and screw back, make this watch waterproof. The Reference 2532 has the caliber 12'''-120 and small seconds hand; the Reference 2533 has the caliber 27 SC with sweep seconds hand. We present the latter here.

There is an archive extract for our yellow gold Patek Philippe, which registers the caliber 27 SC with movement number 705,194 and case number 691,533. The watch was made in 1956 and sold on August 28 that year. It was delivered with a white dial, gold index markers, and leather strap. The cream-white dial corresponds to the typical Patek Philippe design. The bars for the minute intervals are divided

by four strokes for every 12 seconds (see Fig. 75). Dauphine hands show the hours and minutes, which are, like the index markers, 750 yellow gold. The company logo meets the 1952 regulations, reading: "PATEK PHILIPPE, GENEVE", the latter without the grave accent. The case housing is one piece with the bezel. It was stamped from one piece, die-stamped, turned, milled, and given the desired surface finishes. The ten-sided screw back was also stamped from one piece, die-stamped, turned, milled, and the surface finished. The back thickness is, again, exactly 0.5mm. The inside back is bead-blasted. The 34.5mm diameter case has not been polished for decades and, due to the gold oxide, the surface color is getting a reddish tone.

The manually wound caliber 27 SC, protected by a dust cover, deserves good marks for being as good as new. The shock absorber is by Jaeger-LeCoultre. The Geneva Seal is on the base plate and barrel bridge. Surprisingly, it was also at first designed as gold-colored and painted gold bronze. The "small Helvetia" is at the bottom of the right upper band lug; the last three digits of the case number (533) can be found on the underside of the left lower band lug.

The inscription of the inside back is very discretely designed and runs as follows: stamped under each other "PATEK, PHILIPPE & Co", "-GENEVE-", and "SWISS".

Fig. 77 - The Reference 2537 opened and from the back. The caliber 12‴-400 has a balance with shock absorber. The snap back bears an engraving. The engraver must have forgotten a period by the right letter. If a new owner did not like such a monogram, they could have it professionally removed. An example of this can be found in Fig. 102.

In a row then come the casemaker's mark, purity notation "18K/0.750" and the "large Helvetia". Lower we find case and Reference numbers. Two watchmakers' repair notations, as well as the good condition of the case, let us conclude that this watch was rarely worn.

The casemaker's mark, collective trademark no. 1, a hammer head with the number 170, reveals the casemaker. This was the company Cédex, Charles Dubois SA, Le Locle. It went out of business in 1982 and was the same casemaker as for the Reference 2483 in Fig. 60.

This Patek Philippe was sold on April 12, 2000, at Christie's in New York for $5875; the refurbishing done in Geneva cost another DM 4424.24, or €2262.07. The two largest single items in this general repair work were the refurbishing of the movement for DM 2535 and restoration of the dial, for DM 1125 (invoice dated January 25, 2002).

Reference 2533 watches have not come up for sale very often in recent years. A yellow gold version was sold for CHF 13,800 at Antiquorum in Geneva on October 16, 2005.

To Wear: ++ To Collect: ++ For Investment: ++

Reference 2537 (Figs. 76 & 77)

Patek Philippe rarities include the Reference 2537, a hand-wound watch with a 34.5mm case diameter. The pink gold version, presented here, has the movement number 728,086 and the case number 424,446. This watch, according to the archive extract, was manufactured in 1957 and sold on August 12, 1959. The author has seen this Reference only twice. The dial is silver-plated and brushed vertically; the company logo and crosshairs for the small seconds are enameled. The index markers are striking; the two for the 12 are wedge-shaped and the others are single and straight.

The case is in two parts, the case housing and a snap back, the former designed as a turned part with 34.4mm diameter. The band lugs are soldered. Another unusual feature is the 19.5mm width between the lugs. The snap back is die-stamped and exactly 0.5mm thick. A milled slot gives the winding stem free passage. The caliber 12‴-400 is in a sturdy movement retainer ring marked "metal". The balance wheel is protected by a Jaeger-LeCoultre shock absorber. The Geneva Seal is on the base plate near the balance and on the barrel bridge. The movement is in good condition and was refurbished in Geneva.

Fig. 78 - If you want to be inspired by watches, you must have a Patek Philippe. The Reference 2540 is the second automatic winding model by the Geneva manufacturer The really beautiful crown was set on the automatic watch cases until 1964.

Fig. 79 - The opened Reference 2540 offers a clear view of the caliber 12'''-600 AT as well as the inside back. The movement is set in an intricate movement retainer ring, which, in turn, is screwed to the case with four cylinder head screws (movement no. 764,811, case no. 699,844).

The "small Helvetia" can be found on the outside of the right lower band lug. The inside back surface was bead-blasted. The inscription and identification are somewhat different from the previous watch. In the upper third of the inside back, are stamped "PATEK, PHILIPPE & Co", "-GENEVE-", and "SWISS". Below, in the lower third, are the purity notation, "18K/0.750", the "Helvetia", and the mark of the casemaker. Below come numbers for case and Reference, with header "REF". The mark shows that the case-maker was in the collective trademark no. 5 with no. 23 key: this company, Eggly & Cie., Geneva, closed in 1990. Four watchmaker's notations, the last from 1977, testify to the regular wear of the watch.

Worth mentioning is the owner's engraving "P.H.H."; the engraver forgot the period by the last "H". This watch was bought by a collector for $4850 (approximately €3861.93) in the U.S. and its credentials properly established. The collector paid a further €1619.36 for the complete refurbishing in Geneva (invoice dated July 9, 2004).

Reference 2537 watches rarely come up for auction. A pink gold version was auctioned on June 15, 2005, at Antiquorum in New York and attained $10,800. On October 16, 2005, a yellow gold piece was sold for CHF 13,800 at Antiquorum in Geneva.

To Wear: ++ To Collect: ++ For Investment: +

Reference 2540 (Figs. 78 & 79)

Patek Philippe's second automatic wristwatch was given Reference number 2540 and was launched in 1954. It got the nickname "TV Patek Philippe". The piece presented here has a pink gold case and a caliber 12'''-600 AT movement; it is in absolutely mint condition. The movement number is 764,811, the case number reads 699,844. According to the archive excerpt, this watch was made in 1957 and sold on May 28, 1958. The dial is silver colored and has baton hands and bar index markers of pink gold. The square case has base dimensions of 31.5 x 31.5mm and soldered lugs.

Fig. 80 - With a 36mm case diameter, the Reference 2551 was among Patek Philippe's largest watches in the 1950s. The intricately molded case was turned; the band lugs are soldered on. The model at right is still in the mint, original condition and has probably never received a refurbishing. The watch at left has a refurbished dial. Comparing it with the version at right we can see clearly that the company name was printed too large and thick on the watch on the left. The dial surface is silver-plated and brushed vertically (watch at right: movement no. 766,071, case no. 2,608,560; watch at left: movement no. 766,216, case no. 2,608,524).

The square back is die-stamped, and is just 0.4mm thick at the thinnest point. The case surface is polished overall; only the back is satin finished. The caliber 12'''-600 AT is set in a very intricate three-tiered movement retainer ring which is square outside (Fig. 79). It is screwed to the case housing with four cylinder-head screws. The movement itself is secured in the movement retainer ring with three screws.

The "small Helvetia" is on the underside of the top left band lug. The company identification on the inside back, consists of "PATEK-PHILIPPE & Cⁱᵉ", "-GENEVE-" and "SWISS". On the lower third of the back, we find in a row, the casemaker's mark, the purity notation "18K/0.750" and the "large Helvetia". Below are the case and Reference numbers, with heading "RÉF.". The mark corresponds to the collective trademark no. 5, the key has the number 26. This belonged to the company Ponti, Gennari & Cie., Geneva, which was closed in 1969.

A yellow gold piece was sold for CHF 16,800 at Antiquorum in Geneva on November 13, 2005; a pink gold one sold for CHF 22,800.

The model discussed here is from the U.S., where it was purchased for $12,500. A refurbishing at Patek Philippe in Geneva cost another €1877.46. All in all, a good business deal, which shows that such exceptional watches will always be in demand into the future.

Fig. 81 - Here we see the opened still-like-new Reference 2551. One particular feature of the automatic movement 12'''-600 AT is the guilloche gold rotor; another is the Gyromax balance with Masselotte weights on the outer hoop. The refurbished watch can be seen from the back above left. The flat surface of the screw back was re-turned to 0.05mm, and the material thickness reduced from 0.5 to 0.45mm. Was this perhaps to fix some damage or remove existing initials?

To make sure attentive readers and dedicated collectors do not get irritated, we shall deal with the References 2540/1 and 2540/2. Both models had a manual movement. The Reference 2540/1 is equipped with the caliber 12'''-400 with small seconds hand, while the hand-wound movement 27 SC with sweep seconds hand ticks in the Reference 2540/2.

Both versions very rarely come up for sale. A yellow gold Reference 2540/1 was offered for auction at Christie's in Geneva on November 17, 2008, and sold for CHF 20,000 about $16,770 (movement number 727,470, case number 694,485). At Antiquorum in Hong Kong on May 27, 1991, a yellow gold version of the Reference 2540 2 was sold for CHF 38,400 (movement number 706,642, case number 694,540). Its value can also be gauged by an auction at Sotheby's New York, where a yellow gold Reference 2540 2 was sold on April 14, 2005, for $12,000 (caliber 27 SC no. 705,799).

To Wear: ++ To Collect: +++ For Investment: ++

Reference 2551 in two different conditions (Figs. 80 & 81)

There can be no question that Reference 2551 watches, launched in 1954, are among the most beautiful creations by Patek Philippe. For this reason, we present two watches.

One can be considered in untouched condition; the other has already some refurbishings behind it. Below we will present both watches in parallel and discuss possible differences. For clarity, we will call the almost mint condition watch the first, and the other the second piece.

Both watches are equipped with the caliber 12'''-600 AT. The first one has the movement number 766,071 and case number 2,608,560. According to the archive extract, it was produced in 1958 and sold on October 9, 1959. The second watch has the movement number 766,216 and case number 2,608,524. This movement is 145 pieces later than the first; the case 36 pieces earlier. We cannot reconstruct now what ordering principle was used at that time for making Patek Philippe movements, dials and cases. Both watches were made in 1958.

The differences between the dials are interesting. For the first watch, it was decided to make the index markers and hands in rod shape. This dial is still original, as can be seen by the company logo "PATEK PHILIPPE, GENÈVE" as well as "SWISS" under the "6". The second watch has wedge-shaped index markers and dauphine hands. The dial was refurbished. The silver-plated surface is vertically fine brushed and the company name, crosshairs for the small seconds hand, and national origin were partially printed too large or too thick. Because this work, in terms of pure craftsmanship, is cleanly executed, the differences are likely to only attract the attention of a specialist or in direct comparison.

The two-part case of the Reference 2551 is very complex. The case housing with integrated bezel was created as a turned part, and the band lugs, which were die-cast, are soldered on in profile, thus, exactly matching the outside shape of the case. The screw back was turned from one piece, die-stamped, once again turned and diamondized. The case diameter of the first watch is 36.0mm; 35.8mm for the second. The screw back material thickness measures 0.5mm for the first; 0.45mm for the second. The original diamondized back surface of the second watch was re-turned, which caused the difference in material thickness.

From the still well defined edges of the first watch, we can see, in general, that the case has kept its original shape. The movements of both watches have been renovated in Geneva and brought to an almost-new condition.

Only the first watch has hallmarks on the case. The "small Helvetia" is stamped on the outside of the right lower band lug. The hallmark has been polished off the second watch. The inner surface of the back was bead-blasted when it was manufactured. Why both backs were refinished with emery paper, could only be explained for the first watch. Did someone wish to remove possible repair notations on the second watch?

The inside back inscriptions are identical for both watches, since the cases come from the same maker. Listed top to bottom are "large Helvetia", purity notation "0.750", "PATEK-PHILIPPE & Cᵍ", "-GENEVE-" and "SWISS". Below follow the Reference number "RÉF 2551", case number and the casemaker's mark, which belonged to collective trademark no. 5 with key no. 1, Ed. Wenger SA, Geneva, which was closed in 1992. The first watch also has a watchmaker's repair notations scratched in, "W 8215439". According to the owner, this watch's movement was given a refurbishing in March 1994, at the Munich company, Antike Uhren Eder. Some 10 years later it was again refurbished at Patek Philippe in Geneva.

The second Reference 2551 comes from another collector, who bought his watch in the 1990s for DM 12,500. The watch was refurbished 10 years later at Patek Philippe in Geneva for €1024.40.

Reference 2551 watches are in high demand at auctions. A platinum-cased watch was sold at Antiquorum in New York on December 7, 2006, a for $66,000. A month earlier, on November 12, 2006, a model with a pink gold case sold at Antiquorum in Geneva for CHF 36,000. At other times, buyers have paid between CHF 12,000-CHF 14,000 for yellow gold watches.

To Wear: ++ To Collect: +++ For Investment: ++

Reference 2552 in two different versions (Fig. 82)

In 1955, Patek Philippe launched its fourth automatic watch, the Reference 2552. Due to the wide, two-tiered bezel, this watch seems very large, although it has the same 36mm diameter case as the previously described Reference 2551. Because these automatic watches are so important, we are presenting another two models. The first watch has the movement number 762,058, case number 688,312 and was manufactured in 1955. The second watch has movement number 762,428 and case number 689,767. According to the archive excerpt, it was manufactured in 1955 and sold on May 14, 1956. Thus, the movements are around 370 numbers apart, the cases 1,455 numbers apart. The Reference 2552 was made with yellow, red, and white gold, and platinum cases.

The dial is made of gold, was galvanically silver-plated and lacquered. The company name, the interval marks and crosshairs for the small seconds hand are enameled. The national origin mark "SWISS" under the "6" is printed. The first watch we show has a dial still in its original condition. The index markers are made of 18K gold and riveted. The Dauphine hands complete the watch's elegant appearance.

The dial of the second watch had been refurbished, but the result is not authentic. Instead of a seconds display with crosshairs and eight interval marks, the watch was given an irregular crosshairs and a seconds hand that is too short. The Patek Philippe Service Department in Geneva was only satisfied with the proper appearance of this dial after a second effort.

The case with integrated bezel was manufactured as a turned part. The band lugs are soldered on. The bezel is two-tiered, the cast crown half inset. The two-tiered bezel represents the most distinguishing feature of this model. The screw back was turned from one piece and die-stamped. The six notches ensure secure closure. The entire case is diamondized and only the smooth back surface was turned. For the first watch, the back piece's material thickness is only 0.40mm, instead of the designed 0.50mm. Either a dedication engraving was removed or the back was refinished for some reason.

The movement caliber 12'''-600 AT is in very good condition. The watch received a complete refurbishing at Patek Philippe in Munich. The "small Helvetia" was stamped on the outside of the right lower and left upper band lugs. Unfortunately, only remnants of both hallmarks can be seen. The case was polished too often and, perhaps, unprofessionally. The inside back inscriptions of both watches are identical up to the case number, since both were supplied by the same

Fig. 82 - The Reference 2552 was, in its time, one of the largest Patek Philippe watches, with a case diameter of exactly 36mm. The case was made as a turned part and the lugs are soldered on. The crown is mounted half recessed for protection. The watch at left has its original dial, the right hand one was refurbished. The interval marks for the small seconds display were inadvertently made in an atypical style. The Reference 2551 dial shown in Fig. 80 has cross hairs like these (left watch: movement no. 762,058, case no. 688,312, watch on the right: movement no. 762,428, case no. 689,767).

Fig. 83 - The 2554 is one of the extravagant watches, also known as the "Manta-Ray" among aficionados The special design was also used for the anniversary model Reference 5100 *"10 Jours"* made for the beginning of the third millennium. This watch not only has a special design, but also a very intricate case construction. The 9'''-90 shaped movement, which has been made since 1934, is impressive and is set in a special holder. The Gyromax balance with adjustable Masselotte weights can be easily seen. The snap back is closed in a way that the lip, visible from the front, serves to half hold the winding stem (movement no. 976,999, case no. 696,927).

casemaker. Stamped on the inside back, from the top beneath each other, are the "large Helvetia" and the purity notation "0.750". Then follow the company name "PATEK-PHILIPPE & C℗", "-GENEVE-" and "SWISS". In the lower third come Reference number "RÉF. 2552" and the case number .

The casemaker's mark is at the bottom. For both pieces, this is the collective trademark mark no. 5 with key no. 1, belonging to the firm Ed. Wenger SA, Geneva, which closed in 1992. The inside back of the first watch was probably bead-blasted again, presumably after the previously described repair of the back. Three watchmakers' repair notations are engraved. The inside back of the second watch was sanded down, so that neither the bead-blasted surface nor any watchmakers' repair signs are visible. The back material thickness measures 0.50mm.

A German watch lover bought the first listed Reference 2552 for DM 15,000. The second version is from the U.S. and cost $5569.99 (€4655.24). It was turned over to Patek Philippe in Munich and a complete refurbishing, including the dial, was commissioned. This cost €2291.94, with the biggest costs being a refurbishing of the movement for €1140 and the dial restoration for €530.

Reference 2552 watches are all very popular with watch enthusiasts and are also often offered at international auctions. This watch was also popularly called the "Disco Volante".

A white gold case model was put up for sale at Antiquorum in Geneva on October 15, 2006, and changed hands for CHF 50,400 (movement number 762,442, case number 690,970). On November 11, 2007, at the same auction house, a watch with yellow gold case and dial imprint "TIFFANY & CO." was auctioned for CHF 22,200 (movement number 762,586, case number 689,840). At Antiquorum in New York, a rare platinum version was offered on October 16, 2008, for $60,000, but found no buyer (movement number 761,840, case number 688,392). Perhaps the ongoing financial crisis at the time caused potential buyers to hold back.

To Wear: ++ To Collect: ++ For Investment: ++

Reference 2554 (Fig. 83)

Reference 2554 is one of Patek Philippe's most extravagant men's watches.

The rectangular dial and the curved case sides give it its special design. It is no coincidence that this design was rediscovered and used for the anniversary model to celebrate the third millennium of our era. Under Reference 5100 "*10 Jours*", this hand-wound watch has a power reserve of around 10 days.

The men's wristwatch Reference 2554 with caliber 9'''-90 was launched in 1955. The model shown here has the movement number 976,999 and case number 696,927. According to the archive extract, it was produced in 1956 and sold on September 16, 1957. This watch was available with yellow, red, and white gold or platinum case. In the 1961 German Patek Philippe catalog, it was listed in yellow gold with a price of DM 1285. The white gold model cost DM 1475, the platinum DM 2740.

The dial is painted silver and has rod-shaped index markers and matching baton hands. The case is made in two parts and very elaborately finished. The back is also really complicated and was soldered together from many parts. The half-shell

bearing on the snap back guides and stabilizes the winding stem. The movement is in mint condition. It was incorporated and set precisely in a special movement retainer (see Fig. 83). There are no hallmarks on the outer surface of the case. Inside the case housing, the number 27 is stamped by the "8", which are the last two digits of the case number .

The notations on the inside back are slightly different from the previous versions. Crosswise we find, from top to bottom in a row, first the purity notation "0.750", the "large Helvetia", and the casemaker's mark. Then follow "PATEK, PHILIPPE & C℗", "-GENEVE-", and "SWISS". Below come the case number 696,927 and "REF 2554". The back surface is bead-blasted. The casemaker's mark belongs to collective trademark mark no. 5 and key no. 7, which was Fabior, Olivier Jude, Gimel, which is still in business today.

The watch shown here was purchased by a collector for €8800 at a Hamburg art auction house. Refurbishment cost another €1396.64. All in all, a good deal and a decent investment. Reference 2554 watches often come up for auction. At Antiquorum in Geneva on April 2, 2000, a pink gold watch sold for CHF 40,800. The same auction house in New York auctioned a yellow gold design on July 12, 2007 for $25,200.

To Wear: + To Collect: ++ For Investment: +++

Reference 2573 (Fig. 84)

Though the model is considered less spectacular today, the Reference 2573/2 was once considered an elegant men's watch. The 1961 German catalog listed this watch in yellow gold for a price of DM 1475. The Reference 2573/1 has no small seconds display, but is otherwise identical, and then cost only DM 1460. The watch shown here works the manual caliber 10'''-200 with movement number 748,484 and case number 424,900. The dial is brightly lacquered and the inscription "PATEK PHILIPPE, GENÈVE" and the crosshairs for the small seconds hand are enameled. There are two bar-shaped 18-karat yellow gold index markers at the "12" and one each at the other hour intervals. This gives a pleasing appearance together with the bar hands.

The case is designed in two parts, measuring 33mm in diameter and has a snap back. The case housing was turned and the four lugs soldered on. The snap back is die-stamped, turned, and diamondized. The material thickness is 0.4mm. In addition to the crocodile strap with pin buckle, this watch also has an original type O, gold bracelet. In 1961, the Reference 2573/2 cost DM 2620 with this bracelet.

The movement is held in the movement retainer ring with two screws. The caliber is in good condition and this watch was given a complete refurbishing at Patek Philippe in Geneva. The Geneva Seal is stamped both in the base plate near the balance and the train wheel bridge, the latter highlighted with gold paint. The "small Helvetia" hallmark is stamped twice, at the underside of the left upper and right lower band lugs. The inside back inscription reads, top to bottom "PATEK-PHILIPPE & C℗", "-GENEVE-", and "SWISS". The next line has the purity notation "18K/0.750", the "large Helvetia", and the mark of casemaker. Below are case and Reference numbers, the latter with "REF: 2573".

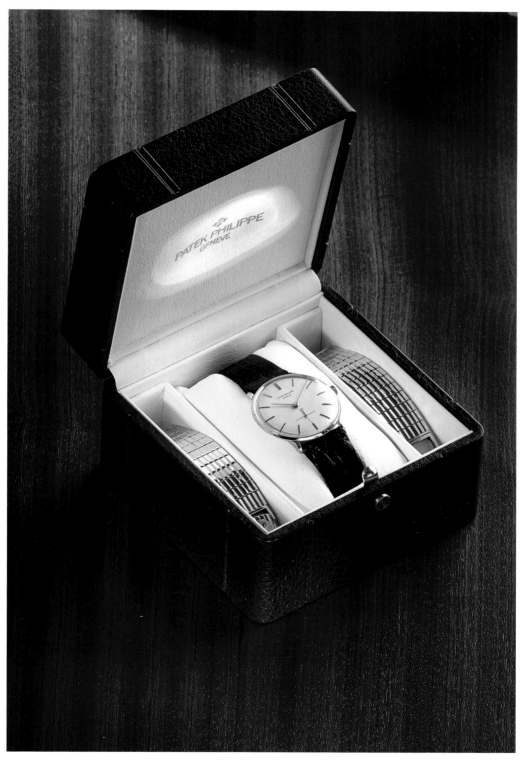

93

Fig. 84 - The Reference 2573 was certainly an interesting watch, at least when introduced in the 1950s. The 2573 was available with crocodile and suspended-style gold bracelet. This special box allowed you to keep the watch and its changeable bands. With a 33mm case diameter and only 7mm height, it was considered an elegant men's watch and had many fans. Shown here with the gold bracelet, this watch cost DM 2620 in 1961 (movement no. 748,484, case no. 424,900).

Fig. 85 - The Reference 2583 (left) and 2584 (right) are among the automatic watches with a 36mm case diameter. Above right is the Reference 2583 from the rear; the snap back has a small lip. The clever design and a special rubber seal makes both watches waterproof (Reference 2583 left: movement no. 763, 399, case no. 697,241. Reference 2584 at right: movement no. 765,654, case no. 2,606,355). On the dial of the watch at right, "KOCH" is imprinted below the center; this was the name of the concessionaire in Frankfurt am Main.

Under the large Helvetia we can just see an English import hallmark for 18-karat gold, probably by the Assay Office at Chester. The casemaker mark is for collective trademark no. 5 with key no. 23, which belonged to the company Eggly. & Cie., Geneva, which closed down in 1990.

This watch belonged to an Englishman living in Paris, who sold it for €4800 to a German collector. The buyer had to invest another €785 for refurbishing at Patek Philippe in Geneva.

The model Reference 2573/2 was made with cases of yellow, white, and pink gold, and often appears at auctions. A watch with pink gold case came up for auction at Antiquorum in New York on June 14, 2006, selling for $5280. On October 14, 2007, a white gold version was sold at Antiquorum in Geneva, for CHF 11,400.

To Wear: + To Collect: + For Investment: -

Reference 2583 (Fig. 85)

After the References 2551 and 2552, there are only three more automatic models in the Reference group 2500. The References 2583 and 2584 have case diameters of 36mm and snap backs. Models of the Reference 2585 only come with a 35mm diameter steel case and screw back. Reference 2583 watches are hard to find. The watch shown here has the caliber 12'''-600 AT, with movement number 763,399; case number 697,241.

Fig. 86 - Caliber 12'''-600 AT with automatic winding mechanism. This first automatic movement by Patek Philippe is one of the most beautiful movements that was ever made. The movement works in the Reference 2584, which is shown in Fig. 85, right. The guilloche gold rotor, the Gyromax balance, and fine adjustment are clearly visible. The latter is actually set too high. On the one hand, the watch's rate is regulated by the eight Masselotte weights of the balance. When the slots in these Masselotte weights are set outwards, the lower moment of inertia (GD2) makes the balance vibrate more rapidly. There is also a regulator with fine adjustment, via micrometer screw and swan neck spring, on the balance cock. The regulator is also set on "faster" at the middle. This caliber has 30 jewels and is adjusted in five positions.

The appropriately sized 32mm diameter dial is silver-plated and vertically fine-brushed, with applied golden line index markers; only the "12" is an Arabic numeral. The watch has matching baton hands. The company logo "PATEK PHILIPPE, GENEVE" and the interval marks for the small seconds are enamel. Only the accent grave on the second "E" of "GENEVE" did not survive the dial renovation undamaged.

A lot of effort went into making the cases for Reference 2583 watches. The bezel was made as a turned part and snapped onto the case housing. The latter is also manufactured as a turned part. The solid band lugs are soldered on in profile with the case. The snap back is die-stamped, the material thickness is 0.5mm. Its small lip makes it easier to open this waterproof case. This last advantage was accomplished through a clever design and a rubber gasket. The distance between the lugs is 20.2mm, itself something unusual for Patek.

The "small Helvetia" is stamped on the outer side of the right lower band lug. The information on the inside back tells us more. The notations start at the top with "PATEK, PHILIPPE & Cᵒ", "GENEVE-", and "SWISS". Then follow in a row the casemaker mark, the purity notation "18 K/0.750", and the "large Helvetia". After a wide space come the case and Reference numbers.

The surface of the inside back is bead-blasted. There are a total of seven watchmaker's notations cut into the case, which indicates the extensive wear this watch has had. The signature "W.E. WARDMAN, 1958" on outside back tells us who was probably the first owner of the watch.

This collector's piece was completely refurbished at Patek Philippe, and the caliber 12'''-600 AT is in a corresponding mint condition.

In recent years the author has seen just two pieces of this Reference. On October 15, 2006, such a watch was auctioned at Antiquorum in Geneva for CHF 18,000. The watch shown here was bought by a collector for $5609 (€4739.53) in the USA. The servicing by Patek Philippe cost a further €758.32. These are rare and sought-after watches, which can be expected to increase in value in the future.

To Wear: ++ To Collect: ++ For Investment: ++

Reference 2584 (Fig. 85 & 86)

The model Reference 2584 was one of the watches Patek Philippe manufactured in larger numbers. The watch shown here reveals the former concessionaire who sold it, by the small mark "KOCH" below the center of the dial. This was the jeweler R. Koch, Kaiserstrasse 25, Frankfurt am Main. In Frankfurt today, only the wholesale dealers Wempe and Bucherer remain. The Institute for the History of Frankfurt am Main's company archive W1 tells us more about the history of the jeweler who later became a concessionaire for Patek Philippe: "In 1879, Robert Koch opened a jewelry store, in which his brother Louis became a partner. They soon gained international fame. They opened a branch in Baden-Baden. Since their clients included numerous dynasties, including the House of Hohenzollern, the Koch brothers were given the title of court jewelers at the turn of the century. Even after the death of the Koch brothers, the business kept its exclusive focus. The business continued to operate until 1986".

The caliber 12'''-600AT has the number 765,654, the case the number 2,606,355. According to the archive excerpt, the watch was manufactured in 1958 and sold on March 12, 1959. The lacquered dial is original and still gleams in its old glory, despite its 52 years. The company logo and the seconds interval marks are enamel, and the grave accent on the second "È" of the city of origin, looks like new.

Even the case with its cast crown looks almost flawless. The bezel and case housing are a single piece. The snap back is die-stamped, turned, and diamondized; its design can be considered very intricate. A screw back would not have been much more expensive. The distance between the lugs is 19.5mm.

The movement is in as-new condition; there can be no question of any other assessment after the complete servicing at Patek Philippe in Munich.

The "small Helvetia" hallmark is on the outside of the left upper band lug and also stamped on the case housing section by the "6". In the inside back we read, from top to bottom "PATEK, PHILIPPE & Cᵒ", "GENEVE-", and "SWISS". In a row in the middle are the casemaker's mark, the purity notation "18K/0.750", and the "large Helvetia". Beneath come case and Reference numbers. The inside back surface has not been refinished. The casemaker's mark, collective trademark no. 5 with key no. 2 represents F. Baumgartner SA, Geneva, which closed in 1973.

The watch shown here belongs to a German collector. He purchased it on the internet for $7200 and paid another €2999.76 for the complete servicing. This amount included refurbishing the movement for €1140 and renovating the dial for €530 as the largest items (invoice dated December 10, 2008).

Reference 2584 watches are not often found at international auctions. A yellow gold version of the Reference 2584 was sold for CHF 20,400 at Antiquorum in Geneva on May 13, 2007. Whether this watch was in a condition similar to the sample piece presented here, we cannot say.

To Wear: ++ To Collect: ++ For Investment: ++

Reference 2585 in stainless steel (Fig. 87)

Another rare Patek Philippe piece is the Reference 2585, which we show in stainless steel. For some time the author knew only of the specimen shown here, though he encountered it twice at auctions. According to archive excerpt, this rare piece was manufactured in 1958 and sold on November 4, 1960. The caliber 12'''-600 AT has the number 765,932, the steel screw-back case the number 694,413. The dial is silver-plated, has steel index markers and Dauphine hands of the same material. The case is in two parts, consisting of the middle part with integrated bezel and a screw back. The case housing was stamped from one piece, die-stamped, milled, turned, and given the appropriate surface finish. The case diameter is exactly 35.0mm, the case design almost identical to that of the Reference 2577 R-SCI, one of the few watches with an enameled dial. We also see similarities in the little grooves inserted between the band lug tops and the cylindrical part of the case. The caliber 12'''-600 AT is screwed in three places. The inscription on the inside back matches those of the Reference 3417, up to Reference and case numbers (Fig. 95).

Fig. 87 - The Reference 2585 in stainless steel is one of the really rare watches shown in this book. No one except Patek Philippe itself, can say how many pieces of this rarity were ever manufactured; the author estimates that it could not have been more than three or four pieces (movement no. 765,932, case no. 694,413). Patek Philippe made only a few watches with automatic winding and waterproof steel cases. Besides the Reference 2582, these include the Reference 3466, Fig. 117, and the Nautilus Reference 3700/1, Fig. 168. *Image Christie's*

This rare watch has a story that is interesting both for the reader and the author The author himself once collected wristwatches in the 1980s and early 1990s. His goal was to collect watches with automatic winding mechanisms and screw backs, which meant that only the fine quality products of Patek Philippe and Vacheron & Constantin came into question.

The author was at a Sotheby's auction, on Monday, October 28, 1996, in New York. The pictured Reference 2585 was being auctioned as lot number 256. The author bid up to $9000, the price rose, and the watch was finally sold for $10,000 or $11,500 including a 15% premium. This was unfortunate for the author, as we shall see later, because, except for the Patek Philippe Reference 3454 (Fig. 113), this model was then the only one still missing from his collection.

Almost nine years later, the same watch resurfaced at Christie's in Geneva and was offered at the auction on May 16, 2005 for CHF 40,000. After a fierce bidding match, the watch was eventually sold to its new owner for exactly CHF 104,400 (approximately $85,194).

In almost nine years, the value of this watch had risen by $73,695 or 740%. This certainly is a remarkable example of value appreciation. However, less spectacular instances can also generate substantial returns, as we shall learn in this book.

Finally, a few words as to how many Reference 2585 pieces there are. The author now knows of two and watch expert Dr. Helmut Crott knows four of these rare timepieces. It will be interesting when one of these rare specimens comes up for auction.

To Wear: ++ To Collect: ++ For Investment: +++

Reference 3403 (Figs. 88-90)

The Reference group 3400 includes many interesting wristwatches, with the first notable one being the Reference 3403, a waterproof gold watch with automatic winding mechanism. The archive records that this watch was made in 1956 and sold on August 30, 1958. The caliber 12'''-600 AT has the number 764,061 and the case number is 309,891.

It seems astonishing that the archive says the watch was manufactured in 1956, since Patek Philippe reports that the Reference 3403 was first launched in 1958.

The watch dial is painted cream and is still in its original condition. The lightly applied patina is not unpleasing here. The company imprint "PATEK PHILIPPE, GENÈVE", the concessionaire logo "TIFFANY & CO.", and the interval marks for the small

Fig. 88 - Comparison of the References 3403 in yellow gold (right) and 3415 in pink gold (left). Both watches are powered with the automatic caliber 12'''-600 AT and have a waterproof case with screw back. The two watches differ only in case diameter. The right is 32.5mm, the left 35mm. Both watches have the original dials. The right shows the dealer's logo, "TIFFANY & CO." The dial of the Reference 3415 contains many special features. The hour interval marks for the "12", "3", "6", and "9" are applied index markers. The remaining hour marks done by faceting, in which a wedge-shaped depression is cut into the dial with a diamond stylus. This reveals the gold of the dial from under the coating.

Fig. 89 - Here we see both watches with open screw back, right, the Reference 3403 in yellow gold, at top left the Reference 3415 in pink gold. The identical calibers 12'''-600 AT are set in different movement retaining rings. The case of the Reference 3404 was stamped; the Reference 3515 is turned. Both inside backs are finely bead brushed and still in original condition (Reference 3403, movement no. 764,061, case no. 309, 891, Reference 3415: movement no. 766,091, case no. 2,608,806).

seconds hand are enameled. The enamel concessionaire's logo is a novelty since, as a rule, the names of preferred concessionaires are imprinted after the dials are finished.

Bold, profiled index markers and Dauphine hands tell the wearer the exact time. The harmonious case diameter measures exactly 32.5mm. This figure measured with a caliper conflicts with some data in the literature, which often refers to 32 or 33mm. The case consists of a solid housing with integrated bezel. It is stamped from a single piece, turned, die-stamped, milled, and the surface finished. The sturdy, ten-sided and stepped screw back is also die-stamped and turned.

Also worth noting is the lavish dedication engraved on the screw back. The company FOREST OIL gave its manager RALPH. E. WARNER this watch in 1958. FOREST OIL CORPORATION was founded in 1916 in the USA and is now one of the largest, still-independent companies engaged in exploration, production, and marketing of oil and gas.

After a complete refurbishing at Patek Philippe in Geneva, the movement shines like new. The Geneva Seal is both on the base plate and on the reverser bridge, both gold paint-filled. Many watch enthusiasts consider the caliber 12'''-600 AT the finest automatic movement ever made.

The "small Helvetia" is stamped on the case by the "4". Looking through the stereo-microscope, we can recognize the letter "G" for the Geneva Assay Office under the Helvetia head. We also get the impression that this case has not been refinished. The markings on the inside back are a bit different from the usual style. Above are the "large Helvetia", the purity notation "0.750", and the casemaker's mark. "PATEK, PHILIPPE & Cᵒ", "-GENEVE", and "SWISS." are stamped below. The grave accent and right hyphen are missing on the "GENEVE" and the "SWISS." has again been given a period. Below comes the Reference number 3403 without pre-notation. The inside back surface appears to have been very

Fig. 90 - Regulator of the caliber 12′′′-600 AT enlarged some 20 times. Not only a watchmaker can recognize all the important components. First, a note about the Gyromax balance. In the first design, the Masselotte weights were positioned in recesses of the balance wheel. Also clearly visible are the Breguet spring, the stud support, the regulator and the micrometer screw. You can also see other details, such as the fact that the swan neck spring is doubly screwed underneath.

Fig. 91 - References 3415 and 3429 look exactly alike at first glance. The case housings with integrated bezel are identical; only the case backs differ in small details. The dial is a reliable distinguishing feature. That of Reference 3429 has only applied index markers, the Reference 3415 is faceted, as illustrated in Fig. 88. In the two watches below, you can see the faceting clearly on the right hand one. This Reference 3415 in yellow gold bears the concessionaire's imprint "WILH. SCHAAFF, HEIDELBERG". This business closed in the early 1980s. In the top row, the pink gold Reference 3415 is at left, the Reference 3429 on the right side. You can only tell that different calibers tick in these two References by opening the back: the Reference 3415 has the 12′′′-600 AT and the 3429, the successor caliber 27 460.

Fig. 92 - The lower right band lug of the yellow gold Reference 3415 has the "large Helvetia" stamped on it. Looking more closely, you see on the left the "G" for the Assay Office in Geneva. The various scratches and warping of the material by the screw back groove show the heavy wear this watch received. The depth of the hallmark, however, indicates that this case was probably never refinished.

Fig. 93 - This band lug is part of a Reference 3415, this time a pink gold piece. In a watch from 1958, it is no longer possible to ascertain who turned out such shabby workmanship. The fact is, that here 2-3 tenths of a millimeter of valuable gold was pointlessly removed, but no attention was paid to the original surface finish, since, in the factory, the entire case for a Reference 3415 was only diamondized. The refurbishing of a watch case should always be well thought out.

slightly bead-blasted, since the loops made while the turning the piece are still to be seen. The collective trademark no. 5 with key no. 4 tells us the casemaker, Antoine Gerlach SA, Geneva. This company closed in 1977.

The watch shown here comes from Christie's in New York and was purchased on October 24, 2001, for $14,100. A servicing at Patek Philippe in Munich, including archive extract, cost another €1052.17. The movement refurbishing for €445 and the exchange of the gold rotor for €260, were the largest items (invoice dated November 11, 2002).

Reference 3404 watches are rarely up for sale. At Antiquorum in Geneva on October 12, 2003, a yellow gold version was auctioned for CHF 16,800. Another yellow gold model was auctioned at Antiquorum in New York on December 1, 2004, for $16,800.

At the same auction, another Reference 3403 with dial imprint "TIFFANY & CO" and the gift engraving of the company "FOREST OIL CORPORATION" sold for $14,400 (movement number 764,444, case number 309,897). Our Reference 3403 pictured here, with case number 309,891, is only six pieces earlier. The watch auctioned at Antiquorum had been sold on the internet three years previously. The antique e-dealer, Hess Fine Art in Tampa-St. Petersburg, Florida, USA, had offered this item on eBay and sold it on April 28, 2001 for $13,555. With the later auction result of $14,400, taking commission and buyer's premium into account, the seller lost about $2500.

To Wear: + To Collect: +++ For Investment: ++

Reference 3415 in yellow and pink gold (Figs. 88-91)

We are including two examples of the Reference 3415 here. These watches differ in other details besides the different pink and yellow gold cases. These details are both exciting and

instructive for the collector and are worth cash when buying these collectibles. Such facts and details are really valuable to know, even for experienced professionals and distributors, when buying and selling watches of this brand.

Both watches are powered by the automatic caliber 12'''-600 AT. The movement number is 766,091 in the pink gold watch, 766,095 in the other. The numbers are just four digits apart, meaning that the movements were probably produced on the same day. The case numbers are 2,608,806 for the pink gold piece and 2,608,696 for the yellow gold one. The case numbers differ by just 110, and both cases were made by the same maker. We have the archive extract for the yellow gold Reference 3415, which says that the watch was made in 1958 and sold on September 29, 1959.

Let us begin with the comparative description of the dials, which are still in original condition. As usual with Patek Philippe, both dials were made of 750 gold sheet, the first pink gold, the second yellow gold. We will see how important this distinction is, in the design of the two dials. The company name "PATEK PHILIPPE, GENÈVE" and the interval marks for the small seconds hand are enameled, the surface painted a lightly pink or yellow gold toned cream color. The hour indicators for "3", "6", and "9" each have one index marker, the "12" has two. The remaining hours are faceted. For faceting, a wedge-shaped depression is cut into the dial using a diamond stylus (at an acute angle of 60° or 90°). This rarely used technique happens after painting the dial. The dial is set on an indexing head and faceted at the right angle and to the desired length. The dial must be 18-karat gold, so that the surface of the wedge-shaped cuts will not oxidize, as mentioned earlier.

The word "SWISS" under the "6" is not visible; whether it is there at all can only be determined the next time the watch is refurbished. "WILH. SCHAAFF, HEIDELBERG", the name of the concessionaire, was printed on the yellow gold watch. The jeweler WILH. SCHAAFF, Hauptstrasse 34, Heidelberg, is listed in the 1961 German Patek Philippe catalog, one of the 15 concessionaires in Germany. According to a relative of this long-deceased jeweler, the business continued up to the 1980s. Today there is no longer a concessionaire for Patek in Heidelberg.

The case of the Reference 3415 is made of two parts: the case housing with integrated bezel and the screw back. The housing is manufactured as a turned part and the lugs soldered on. The solid screw back was stamped, die-stamped, and turned; the round parts are diamondized. In the flat area, the screw back material is 0.5mm thick. The diameter of the case measures 35.0mm. The middle is slightly tapered twice in the bezel part. The outer surface is cylindrical, with a small indent and tapered closure. Such a case contour can only be made by turning.

Discussion of the original surfaces are very valuable here. The case of the yellow gold piece had significant wear, but still has the factory-made surfaces. All the case housing surfaces were diamondized without exception. The "small Helvetia", which is stamped on the outside of the right lower and left upper band lugs, is still deep, and the "G" for the Assay Office in Geneva is still recognizable. The rounded parts of the screw back, which has six notches, were diamondized; the flat part of the back is turned.

The polisher responsible for the pink gold case did not follow exact specifications and worked at his own discretion. As a result, the cylindrical part is satin-finished lengthwise, the graduated bezel and the lower tapered part of the case correctly diamondized. The outer surfaces of the lugs were satin finished vertically, which took a lot away from the small Helvetia set there. It is hardly recognizable (Fig. 93). The screw back, however, still has the right surface.

The pink gold Reference 3415 was refurbished at Patek Philippe in Munich, as required by the movement's condition. Apart from the lack of lubrication the second watch's movement was in good condition. A comparative view of the two inside backs is also exciting. That of the pink gold piece still has its original surface. After all the information was imprinted, this inside back was very finely bead-blasted. The only addition is that a watchmaker noted the initials "L.F." with a fine felt-tip pen.

The inside back of the yellow gold case looks a little different. Here the back was clamped in the chuck of a lathe and the interior surface refinished with sandpaper. The marks suffered under this inappropriate treatment. As a rule, we must conclude from such reworking, that someone wanted to remove previous watchmaker's markings. A watchmaker's signature was engraved as "9674 RPU+" only after the sandpapering.

Except for the case number s, the information is the same in both inside backs. We can see in some detail that the same casemaker made both. From top to bottom, the "Helvetia" the purity notation "0.750", "PATEK, PHILIPPE & Cᵒ", "-GENEVE-", and "SWISS" appear. A bit below is "REF 3415", the case number and the casemaker's mark. The casemaker belonged to collective trademark no. 5, with key no. 1, for Ed. Wenger SA, Geneva, which closed in 1992.

The pink gold Reference 3415 comes from the Munich watch dealer Bachmann & Scher and cost €10,400. The author has known Thomas Bachmann for over 20 years and appreciates him as a serious and competent professional. The refurbishment at Patek Philippe in Munich came to €497.90.

The yellow gold version was auctioned at Henry's auction house in Mutterstadt for €7198.18. No refurbishing was done as of our editorial deadline.

At Antiquorum in Geneva on April 23, 1995, such a model was sold for CHF 6840. Ten years later, a pink gold version was sold there on October 16, 2005, for CHF 15,000 (movement number 766,165, case number 2,608,800). The production year 1960 listed in the auction catalog, was probably not quite right, since this watch comes from the same year as our two examples presented here.

Finally, we emphasize that watch cases which are still in their original condition, should be left that way. Even small traces of wear on the original case are far less of a problem than an improperly refinished watch as the two Reference 3415 watches proved here (see Figs. 92 & 93).

To Wear: ++ To Collect: ++ For Investment: ++

Reference Amagnetic 3417 (Figs. 94-96)

Among today's most sought-after watches from the Geneva manufacturer is the Reference 3417 "Amagnetic", which only came with a steel case. It was listed on page 11 of the 1961 Patek Philippe German catalog with the price of DM 900. Today, watches of this Reference sell for 30 to 40 times as much.

The collector's piece we show here is powered by the caliber 27-AM 400, with movement number 732,829. The case has the number 2,633,182. The watch dates from 1963. The dial is painted silver, manufacturer's name and the minute interval marks are printed. Not all the original dials still have the "SWISS" imprint by the "6". Except for the Arabic numeral "12" and no number at the "6", the hours have bar index markers that match perfectly with the baton hands.

The case is very elaborately designed, ensuring no magnetic fields could disturb its exact rate. This is done with a special dial, a movement retainer ring and a special inside back, all made of permallium-type soft iron. The outer case consists of case housing with an integrated bezel and very sturdy screw back, both made of stainless steel. The case middle is stamped from a solid piece, turned, milled, and the surface finished. The diameter is 35.0mm.

The back was made as a turned piece and has six die-stamped notches. The material thickness is 0.5mm. The inside back is also turned from one piece and is set like a cartouche in the soft iron ring of the movement. Two small, milled notches allow free passage for the winding stem and the fixing pin for the exact position of the movement.

The caliber 27-AM 400 differs from the caliber 12'''-400 in many details. The components of the train are manufactured from non-magnetic material (the lever of gilded beryllium bronze, the roller of brass, escape wheel of duro-chrome). For the caliber 27-AM 400, the shaft for the seconds hand and the minute pinion are also longer than in the caliber 12'''-400, to compensate for the increased thickness of the soft iron dial.

The Reference 3417 was issued in two series. In the second series, the mark "Amagnetic" was omitted and the seconds hand display made more simply. Why some dials were marked "SWISS" and others not, could not be clarified at Patek Philippe in Geneva.

Fig. 94 - The Reference 3417 "Amagnetic" is one of today's most sought-after watches from our Geneva manufacturer; it comes only with a steel case. In 1961, this watch, which was protected against electromagnetic fields, was available for DM 900. Today, you have to pay 30 to 40 times that amount. The Reference 3417 was manufactured in two series. Only the watches of the first series bear the inscription "Amagnetic", and they often attain higher prices at auctions. Only a few professions require watches protected against electromagnetic fields; investment bankers are certainly not among them. Rather, it is electric locomotive engineers or high-voltage-current electricians in power plants who really require such watches (movement no.732,829, case no.2,633,182).

Fig. 95 - The open Reference 3417 "Amagnetic" with dust cover and screw back. Unlike other watches, such as the Reference is 2508 or 2509, the dust cover is not die-stamped of soft iron, but made as a more complex turned part. This cup-shaped cover is set on the movement, and the two visible notches allow passage for the winding stem and fixing pin. The caliber 27-AM 400 differs from the caliber 12‴-400 in many details. The components of the vibration system are made of non-magnetic material (the lever of gilt beryllium bronze, the roller of brass, escape wheel of duro-chrome). For the caliber 27-AM 400, the seconds hand and cannon pinion staffs are also longer than in the caliber 12‴-400, to compensate for the increased thickness of the soft iron dial.

Differing from cases of precious metals, the inside back inscriptions here are much simpler. From top to bottom are stamped the company logo "PATEK, PHILIPPE & Co", "≡GENEVE≡", and "SWISS". Then come, without additional designation, case and Reference numbers. The surface has circular graining, and there are three watchmaker's notations. This watch was purchased by a collector for $10,700 in Los Angeles, California, United States. The professional refurbishing at Patek Philippe in Geneva cost another €1090.40. All in all, a good investment.

A Reference 3417 was sold at Antiquorum in New York on March 24, 2004, for $18,400. At Sotheby's in Geneva on May 16, 2006, a Reference 3417 made in the second production run (without imprint "Amagnetic") changed hands for CHF 32,400. At Christie's in Geneva on November 16, 2009, a Reference 3417 with hinged Milanese steel bracelet was sold for CHF 42,500 (movement number 728,934, case number 2,610,407, manufactured in 1960).

To Wear: ++ To Collect: ++ For Investment: +++

Reference 3419 (Figs. 97 & 98)

The development engineers at Patek Philippe in Geneva came up with another ingenious design for the hand-wound watch Reference 3419, also only made in steel. An expansion on the previous model Reference 3418, which was also available with a steel case, the Reference 3419 had an integrated system to exchange the leather strap for a flexible steel bracelet.

At first glance, watches of these two References cannot be distinguished. Only the expert will recognize the small differences. The Reference 3419 case has an indent for the crown; that is, the crown is slightly recessed in the case.

We have an archive extract for the Reference 3419 presented here. The caliber 27-AM 400 has the movement number 730,715 and the case number 2,619,877. The watch was produced in 1962 and sold on April 13 that year. As the pictures show, they came with leather straps. The dial is silver-plated. The company name, minute interval marks, the small seconds display, and the national origin "SWISS" are printed. Except for the "6", all the hour marks are faceted, twice for the "12". The baton hands match. The case is of stainless steel and the prospectus gives its diameter as 34.4mm. This case has an intricate design: the case housing with integrated bezel consists of two interlocking turned parts. The outer ring has special indents beside the "6" to hold the connecting pieces for either leather strap or flexible steel bracelet.

The inner part is cylindrical, with the fine thread for the ring nut turned on its outside. The inner case holds the movement and is closed with a six-notched screw back. When the band attachments described above are inserted in the case outside, the ring nut can be screwed open or closed. A special wrench is required to tighten the ring nut, which meshes the drive pins into two radial millings in the ring nut (Fig. 97).

The caliber 27-AM 400 is set in a soft iron ring, similar in design to that in the Reference 3417. Since this watch was serviced in Geneva, the movement is also in almost new condition. The Geneva Seal is stamped on the barrel bridge and on the base plate near the balance wheel. A gasket ensures the guaranteed waterproofing. The design and lettering of the inner back are the same as that of the Reference 3417. The Reference 3419 described here is from the U.S. and was acquired by a German collector for $4950, who had to pay another DM 1111.28 for the complete renovation (invoice dated June 25, 2001).

Fig. 96 - The caliber 27-AM 400 works in the Reference 3419 as well as in the Reference 3417 "Amagnetic." The screw back has been removed, but the outer ring, more exactly called the ring nut, is still screwed on. Their importance is described in the next picture.

Fig. 97 - The Reference 3419 has an integrated system for changing the watch band. The case housing has special indentations above the two lugs, which can fit a leather strap or a steel bracelet, depending on the style. If the two adapters are used, they are held by a ring nut, screwed with a fine thread to the case. In this picture, the case back is screwed back on.

These models are rarely auctioned. A Reference 3419 sold for CHF 5040 at the auction house Antiquorum in Geneva on April 13, 1997. Seven years later, at the same auction house in New York, another piece was sold on March 24, 2004, for $6960. At the HERITAGE auction house in Dallas, Texas, a refurbished model was offered on May 10, 2010, and attained $15,535 (movement number 729,198, case number 2,606,134).

To Wear: + To Collect: ++ For Investment: +

Reference 3420 (Figs. 99-100)

Reference 3420 is one of those watches equipped with the previously described, magnetic-field-proof protected caliber 27-AM 400. This unassuming model was launched in 1960 and is listed in the 1961 German Patek Philippe catalog with a price of DM 1175, and a diameter of 34.0mm. The archive extract states that the caliber 27-AM 400 had the movement number 734,094 and the case number is 432,458. The yellow gold watch was produced in 1967 and sold on December 9 that year. All the parts of this still almost untouched collector's item, are still in original condition. The dial is silver-plated and has a protective varnish. The hour index markers are designed as gold bars and set double at the "12". The company name, the interval marks for the small seconds hand and the national origin "SWISS" are imprinted. The watch has matching baton hands.

The case has three parts. The bezel is made as a turned part and snapped on, the housing is also turned with the four lugs soldered, and the snap back was made as a die-stamped and turned piece with a wall thickness of exactly 0.50mm. The petite, knurled crown is 4.4mm in diameter. The movement gleams in almost-new condition. The Witschi instrument measurements confirm its chronometer quality. A single watchmaker's mark from 1981 shows the watch was little worn.

The case, still in original condition, has the "small Helvetia" stamped on its side by the "2". This hallmark is so unspoiled that we can still recognize even the "G" for the Geneva Assay Office. On the circularly grained inside back we find the manufacturer's name "PATEK-PHILIPPE & Cⁱᵉ", "-GENEVE-", and "SWISS". On the lower third of the back in a row, from left to right, are the purity notation "18K/0.750", the "large Helvetia", and the casemaker's mark. Below follow the case and Reference numbers, the latter with "REF: 3420" noted. The casemaker's mark is collective trademark no. 5 and key no. 23, which stands for Eggly & Cie, Geneva, which closed in 1990.

The question of why the non-magnetic caliber 27-400 AT came to be installed in a gold case watch without a "soft iron cage", was answered by a retired Patek employee. Since demand for the References 3417, 3418 and 3419 was less that the number of pieces manufactured, there were excess calibers 27-400 AM available, and these were put in the following Reference 3420 instead of the caliber 12'''-400.

Watches of this Reference have often come up for auction. This model was sold on October 14, 2001, in Geneva for CHF 10,800. Two years later in Zurich, more precisely on November 16, 2003, a piece was sold for CHF 16,800. On October 14, 2007 this watch was even worth CHF 21,600 to a buyer in Geneva (movement number 733,869, case number 432,603). The version presented here was acquired by a collector in the U.S. for $4239.99 (approximately €3490.28). A professional servicing at Patek Philippe in Geneva was done, including two gold spring bars, at no charge; the only cost was €90 for the archive extract. Compared to the previously mentioned auction prices, all in all a good investment.

To Wear: ++ To Collect: + For Investment: +

Fig. 98 - The Reference 3419 was only made with steel cases, like the Reference 3417. It is not easy to distinguish from the previous model 3418. Both models have the band-changing system shown in the picture at left. The best way to distinguish these two References is by the crown, which is slightly recessed, only on the Reference 3419. The model shown has all its original parts, including the dial with faceted hour bars. For this piece, the dial was silver-plated only after the faceting, so the indents would not oxidize (movement no. 730,715, case no. 2,619,877).

Fig. 99 - The Reference 3420 we show here is a very popular collector's watch. Why this gold watch also got the anti-magnetic-field caliber 27 AM 400 will be explained in the accompanying text. The case only has a snap back (movement no. 734,094, case no. 432,458).

Fig. 100 - When you look at the back of the Reference 3420, you come to the assumption that the watch was designed to save material. The case middle, with its outer diameter of 34mm, is sharply tapered inwards, so that the rim diameter for the snap back measures to no more than about 29mm. There is no separate movement retainer ring or fixing pin, unlike the References 3417 and 3419. The snap back quality deserves recognition. With a 0.5mm material thickness and good sized fit length, the snap back will close securely.

Reference 3425: Two instructive examples (Figs. 101-102)

Reference 3425 was the third Patek Philippe watch equipped with the new caliber 27-460. With a case diameter of 33.5mm, it appears rather unpretentious from the outside, but shows its real strong points after just a short acquaintance. We again show two examples of this model. First, because the first piece is still almost new and was generally kept maintained in that shape; secondly, the second piece was badly worn and rather disfigured. Besides the comparison, we will show in full detail how the second watch was, despite all handicaps, thoroughly refurbished and restored to almost-new condition.

This comparison is particularly interesting because Patek Philippe in Geneva generally does not offer such comprehensive and costly restorations. The first Reference 3425 contains the caliber 27-460 with movement number 1,114,454 and case number 2,639,270. As the dial imprints tells us, this watch was delivered to the concessionaire Hausmann & Co in Rome. The second piece has movement number 1,114,987 and case number 2,666,201. Thus, the automatic movements are 533, the cases 26,931 figures apart.

Our first automatic has been kept as new. An Italian watch lover bought it on December 8, 2002, from a dealer in New York for $4500, and later invested a net €1470.30 for refurbishing by Patek Philippe (invoice dated August 26, 2003). The watch had been purchased from the jeweler

Hausmann & Co. in Rome in 1966. Hausmann & Co., one of the oldest Italian concessionaires for Patek Philippe, celebrated its 200th anniversary in 1994. The company name tells us that this jewelry business has German roots.

The second watch is from the U.S. and was acquired by a German watch enthusiast over the internet. Our comparative description tells us that this Patek Philippe had to endure a great deal in the last 40 years. We note in advance that the Reference 3425 was listed in the 1961 German Patek Philippe catalog, and sold for DM 1755 in yellow gold.

The dial of the first watch is painted silver. The company name "PATEK PHILIPPE, GENÈVE", the minute interval marks, the small seconds hand, the concessionaire name "HAUSMANN & Co." and the national origin "SWISS" are printed in one passage. The index markers are bar form and riveted. The baton hands match this design exactly.

The second watch dial has been refurbished, but with some shortcomings. The company logo is somewhat too large and the accent grave has been forgotten for the second "È" of "GENÈVE". The arrangement of the interval marks for the seconds hand does not correspond, either in diameter or in line width, to the original. Even the "SWISS" under the "6" was omitted.

This rather out of order dial was sent to the dial maker Bethge & Söhne near Pforzheim and professionally redesigned, according to the original style of the first watch,

Fig. 101 - The following two Reference 3425 wristwatches have a particularly interesting story to tell. This model is an elegant men's wristwatch with automatic winding and 33mm case diameter. Introduced in 1960, some watches of the first production series were equipped with the caliber 12'''-600 AT; all the rest with the successor caliber 27-460. This picture shows a watch in mint condition (bottom) in comparison with a battered version (middle) and how the latter was refurbished to almost new condition (top). This goes for both the dial and the case. Together with the like-new watch, the dial, which had been refurbished in the U.S., was sent to the watch factory Bethge & Söhne in Ispringen for a new renovation. The result was so successful that even experts can barely distinguish the two dials. In the picture at bottom, we see the model watch with original dial, in the middle, the piece which came from the U.S., and above the dial with the new imprint Bethge & Söhne.

Fig. 102 - This picture shows at center an image of the Reference 3425 from the U.S. The extensive inscription was certainly meant well, but makes the watch hard to sell. Modeled after the mint-condition piece, the back was removed and renovated by a specialist from Pforzheim. Using laser and gold wire, the inscriptions were filled in and in a second step, re-turned and diamondized. The upper watch shows the results: a virtually new screw back. In a criminal case, X-rays could make the original engraving visible again (mint condition Reference 3425: movement no. 1,114,454, case no. 2,639,270; renovated Reference 3425: movement no. 1,114,987, case no. 2,666,201).

at a cost of €280. When the dial was re-mounted, both watches became almost indistinguishable to a non-expert. In a direct comparison, a professional would note primarily the somewhat lighter color of the newly made dial (Fig. 101).

The Reference 3425 case is in two parts and closes with a screw back. The case housing with integrated bezel was manufactured as a turned part; the four lugs are soldered on. The bezel is tapered; the case housing cylindrical. The screw back is die-stamped, turned, diamondized, and has six notches. The outside is tapered twice, but flat in the middle. The wall thickness there is 0.50mm.

The case of the second piece is generally identical. Only the screw back has an extensive inscription. The complete engraving reads: "50 YEARS OUTSTANDING SERVICE, PRESENTED TO C.S. WHITE-SPUNNER, DECEMBER 1969 BY TURNER SUPPLY CO.". The Turner Supply Company was based in Mobile, Alabama, USA, and was founded in 1905. Today Turner is a distributor of industrial products of leading manufacturers such as 3M, Norton, Sandvik, and many others.

Since a Patek Philippe with such a "beautified" case could only be sold for a significant price discount, the case was sent to a Pforzheim casemaker for refurbishing, with the first watch used as a pattern. A special picture was taken of its screw back and all the inscriptions filled with gold using a laser. Subsequently, the back was turned, diamondized, and restored to its original condition. The comparison in Fig. 102 confirms the casemaker's successful work, which cost €214.80.

Unlike other watches, there was no gold hallmark on the outside of the Reference 3425 case. The inscription on the inside back showed that both cases were made by same supplier. From top to bottom, run the "large Helvetia", the purity notation "18 K/0.750", the company logo "PATEK-PHILIPPE & Cº", "-GENEVE-", "SWISS", the notation "RÉF. 3425", the case number, and the mark of the casemaker. This last belongs to collective trademark no. 5 with key no. 1, which stands for the company Ed. Wenger SA, Geneva, which closed in 1992.

The surface of the inside back of the first watch is finely bead-blasted and has no watchmaker's repair notations. For the reworked piece, after the renovation of the screw back, the inside was bead-blasted, albeit the result was slightly grainier than the original.

Reference 3425 watches are almost always in demand. Whether for everyday wear or as a collector's item, they always retain their value. At Antiquorum in Geneva on October 20, 1991, one such watch was sold for CHF 7200. At the same auction house in New York, a Reference 3425 in yellow gold was sold on June 20, 1998, for $6348. Finally, a version in white gold came up for auction at Antiquorum in Geneva on March 29, 2009, and brought CHF 9600 (movement number 1,113,274, case number 2,636,947).

To Wear: ++ To Collect: ++ For Investment: +

Reference 3428 (not pictured)

Before we go to the next watch illustrated, a few notes on rare Reference 3428. Some pieces of this model were also made with an enameled dial. The case is identical with that of the Reference 2526, but was only made in yellow and pink gold and platinum. Instead of the automatic caliber 12'''-600 AT, it is powered by the successor caliber 27-460. This watch is listed in the 1961 German catalog. The case diameter is given as 35.6mm. The list price for the yellow gold version is DM 1915; white gold cost DM 2150 and platinum DM 3880. The value of these watches today is shown by three examples from Antiquorum in Geneva. On October 19, 2002, a yellow gold piece sold for CHF 40,800; on October 24, 2004, a watch of the same color went for CHF 34,800, and on April 24, 2004, a version in pink gold sold for CHF 64,800 (movement number 1,111,864, case number 2,614,560).

To Wear: +++ To Collect: +++ For Investment: +++

Reference 3429: Two examples (Fig. 103-104)

Another favorite automatic is the Reference 3429. It was produced with yellow and pink gold cases. The case housing with integrated bezel is just like that of the Reference 3415 case, except that the screw back is neither round or spherically diamondized, but tapered in two tiers. At first glance, it could easily be confused with the Reference 3415, if the latter did not have faceted index markers on the dial.

The first of automatic watches, again shown in comparison, has the caliber 27-460 with movement number 1,113,443 and case number 2,644,656. The second is powered by a movement with number 1,113,233; the case has number 2,631,702. The comparison is made because of the differences between the cases, while barely visible, are worth noting. The two watches are pictured in Fig. 91 together with two Reference 3415 pieces.

The Reference 3429 dial is yellow gold and the company logo and the interval marks for minute and small seconds hand are enameled. Following this preliminary work, the dial was silver-plated and given a sunburst finish. The gold bar index markers are riveted, with two side-by-side markers at the "12". Then the matching baton hands were mounted. The national origin "SWISS" is printed under the "6". Both dials are original.

According to the 1961 sale catalog, the Reference 3429 case diameter is exactly 35mm. The case of the first watch has a "small Helvetia" stamped on its side by the "4". In contrast to the original finish, which is untouched on our second copy, the four lugs were incorrectly vertically satin-finished. However, at the factory, all the case surfaces, except for the turned back, were diamondized. Anyone who does not know that, would barely notice the difference .

The two watches and calibers 27-460 were refurbished by Patek Philippe in Munich and restored to a visually new condition. The model with movement number 1,113,443 was in such good condition that the servicing fees were limited, and Patek Philippe in Munich charged only €750.52 (invoice dated December 13, 2002). In comparison to the one just described, the watch with movement number 1,113,233 was almost worn out and needed a number of replacement parts during the refurbishing. The total cost was €2544.22 (invoice dated November 17, 2009), with the movement refurbishing for €585, the spare parts for €273, and the new gold rotor for €1127 being the largest items. This comparison not only shows the price increase over seven years, but also the VAT increase in from 16% to 19%. After this work, both watches were again at chronometer performance levels.

Fig. 103 - The Reference 3429 is one of the most pleasing wristwatches made by the Geneva manufacturer. Except for the partially faceted index markers, it looks very similar to the Reference 3415. The screw back of Reference 3429 is tapered twice; that of the 3415 round or spherically diamondized. Instead of the caliber 12'''-600 AT, here the successor caliber 27-460 is at work. Fig. 91 shows a direct comparison of the two models (movement no. 1,113,443, case no. 2,644,656).

The second piece has no external hallmarks on the case. The inscription on the inside back, however, appears identical in both watches. The casemaker's mark shows that this was the same supplier as for the previously described Reference 3425. Comparing the two References shows two interesting differences. One is that the Reference 3429 inside back surface was more strongly bead-blasted. The other lacks the previously described "RÉF." before the Reference number. The material thickness is just 0.5mm for both examined Reference 3429 pieces.

The first described Reference 3429 was bought on August 22, 2002, from an antique watch dealer in New York for $4785 (€4800). The watch still had its original gold pin buckle, golden spring bars, and original crocodile strap (Fig. 104).

The second Reference 3429 comes from Paul Duggan Co., a famous antique watch dealer at 333 Washington Street, Boston, Massachusetts. The watch bought on September 10, 2009, had a small handicap that probably could only be corrected at Patek Philippe itself. The bearing for the gold rotor was damaged so badly that the rotor lay loose in the case. This lowered the price to $4984.50 or €3512.94. Here, besides the initial low price, the currency parity (€ 1= $1.42) at the time, also played a role.

The 1961 Patek Philippe German catalog lists the prices for a yellow gold Reference 3429 at DM 1755, and for a white gold piece at DM 1930. The auction house Antiquorum in New York sold a yellow gold version on June 14, 2006 for $9000, and on May 28, 2007, a white gold piece for $26,400 (movement number 1,115,296, case number 2.644,740).

To Wear: ++ To Collect: ++ For Investment: ++

Reference 3433 (Figs. 105-106)

The Reference group 3400 watches, which have a case diameter of 36mm, include the Reference 3433. This piece is listed in the 1961 German Patek Philippe catalog on page 14, with the case diameter specified as 36mm. The yellow gold version is listed DM 1855. This Reference was also made with a platinum case, but perhaps this was not available in Germany. The automatic model shown here is a successor to the Reference 2551 and looks very similar, but is driven by the caliber 27-460. The movement has the number 1,112,899, the case number is 2,626,193. The dial was exchanged during refurbishing by Patek Philippe in Munich. This dial is lacquered a creamy white; the rounded beam-index markers, with their upper parts painted black, are riveted on. The indicator for the "6" is shorter because of the second-display cross; three index markers are riveted at the "12". The watch has matching baton hands.

The case has two parts. The bezel is integrated in the case housing, both of which were manufactured as a turned part. The four lugs are soldered in profile, that is, exactly matching

Fig. 104 - Patek Philippe pays attention to the smallest detail. The Reference 3429 is shown at left, with crocodile watch strap removed (genuine Louisiana alligator strap). This hand sewn strap is generally known as the "Umbugg". By it are the pin buckle and spring bar, both of 18-karat yellow gold. If you want to remove the strap from the watch case, use the special Patek Philippe tool or a prepared tooth pick, to push the pin in and then remove the strap. The Reference 3429 case is made as a turned piece. The soldered lugs are clearly visible. The bridge width is 18mm.

the case shape. The back is die-stamped and turned, and the surface finished. Like the screw back of the Reference 3429, it tapers twice and the flat area is turned. Why the six die-stamped notches turn out to be much smaller than in the Reference 3425 and 3429, can no longer be explained.

Patek Philippe in Munich gave this watch a complete refurbishing, which cost €3031.20. The largest individual amounts were €1400 for the restoration, €635 for the replacement dial 148TJ, €132.50 for the center wheel and cannon pinion, and €122 for the ball bearing for the gold rotor (invoice dated May 17, 2006). After this work, the movement was restored to an almost new condition and its performance ratings are again as good as new.

The marks on the inside back again reveal the casemaker's signature. Stamped in sequence from top to bottom are the "large Helvetia", the purity notation "0.750", the company name "PATEK-PHILIPPE & C°", "-GENEVE-", and "SWISS". Then comes "REF 3433", the case number, and casemaker's mark. The collective trademark no. 5 and key no. 1 show this was the firm Ed. Wenger SA, Geneva; unfortunately, this mark is no longer in use, as the company closed down in 1992.

The automatic shown here is owned by a German collector. A watch from Italy was purchased at the Uhren-Technik watch fair in Munich for €4800. Reference 3433 watches do not come on the market too often. At an auction by Christie's in Geneva on November 13, 2006, a yellow gold piece was sold for CHF 16,800. A year before that, on July 10, 2005, a platinum case model was auctioned by Antiquorum in Hong Kong, and hit HKD 600,000, about €60,000 (movement number 1,111,112, case number 2,616,375). Another platinum piece was offered on May 12, 2008, by Christie's in Geneva and sold for CHF 85,000, about $81,284 (movement number 1,232,822, case number 2,626,268).

References 3435, 3438, and 3439 (not illustrated)

There are three other models worth mentioning after the automatic Reference 3433. These include the Reference 3435, which has a case diameter of 34mm and a waterproof snap back. This watch in yellow gold cost exactly DM 1855 in 1961 in Germany. Reference 3438 was the next model with caliber 27-460. With only a 31mm case diameter and snap back, it was not as well known. Despite these minor drawbacks, this model seems to be in demand with those collectors who value having a complete collection. Thus, on February 2, 2000, when a Reference 3438 in yellow gold was offered at Antiquorum in Geneva, it sold for CHF 24,000 (movement number 1,111,458, case number 312,683).

The last automatic we should mention is the Reference 3439. With a case diameter of only 32mm, it does not meet current notions, but is still a very sought-after collector's

Fig. 105 - The Model Reference 3433 is rarely available for sale. It is the successor to the Reference 2551, expanding the case diameter to 36mm. From the outside, only the screw back is different. In the Reference 2551, the back is round and diamondized; in the Reference 3433 it is twice tapered. We could not determine why the die-stamped notches are much smaller than usual. Fig. 81 provides a direct comparison.

item. The automatic Reference 3403, shown in Figs. 88 & 89, appears similar to the Reference 3439, but the case diameter, at 33mm, is about one millimeter larger.

The automatic Reference 3439 version with a sapphire crystal display back is especially important. This piece was manufactured as 3439/1. Launched in 1965, the watch was the first that let curious watch freaks see the movement in full detail. The author has seen this model only twice. We will give a full description of the special features of such a transparent display back when we present the successor model Reference 3561 (see Figs. 143 & 144).

Reference 3444 (Fig. 107)

We should deal with the automatic model Reference 3440 before the automatic Reference 3444. This model has a 35.0mm case diameter and screw back. It is powered by the caliber 27-460. The design of this model is something most watch collectors have to get used to, because the case housing has, among other things, a double V-shaped profile.

The model Reference 3444 we present here is one of the automatics which is very rarely for sale. The archive extract states that this watch was produced in 1961 and sold on October 2 that year. The caliber 27-460 has the movement number 1,111,024 and case number 2,619,254.

The dial is still in its original condition and a joy to behold. The company name "PATEK PHILIPPE, GENÈVE", the interval marks for the minutes, and the small seconds chapter are enameled. When this was done, the gold dial was silver-plated and given a sunburst finish. Then the index markers were riveted on. These are wedge-shaped at positions "12", "3", "6", and "9". The remaining eight hours have index markers which taper toward both ends. No watches previously presented at auctions have this style hour index markers.

Under the "6" you can still just see the national origin "SWISS". The Reference 3444 case is very intricate. The case housing with integrated bezel has several tiers is rounded, and manufactured as a turned part from one piece. The remarkably solid band lugs are soldered on in profile. The screw back is die-stamped and tapered, and has six notches for opening.

Fig. 106 - The Reference 3433 has a two-part case with soldered lugs and screw back. Both the case shown here and that of the Reference of 2551 were supplied by the same casemaker. Comparing the screw back to the one pictured in Fig. 81, you can see the hallmark with key no. 1 on both pieces. The supplier was Ed. Wenger SA, Geneva, which closed in 1992 (movement no.1,112,899, case no. 2,626,193).

All surfaces are diamondized. Patek Philippe in Munich gave this watch a complete refurbishing, with the result that the movement gleams in almost new condition. The gold rotor was also replaced.

A small, circular abrasion can be seen on the inside back, the traces of one of the three cylinder screw heads fastening the rotor, which was not screwed tightly enough. It emerged too far and left its marks on the back (machine processed).

Probably because there is no convenient place to inscribe it, the case has no small Helvetia outside. But the inscription on the inside back is interesting. At top are the manufacturer's certificate with "PATEK, PHILIPPE & Co", "≡GENEVE≡", and "SWISS". In the center come the casemaker's mark, purity notation "18K/0.750", and the "large Helvetia". Unlike previous versions, the casemaker's mark runs vertically upwards. The case and Reference numbers are on the lower area, the latter without any additional notes. The inside back is finely bead-blasted and there are two watchmaker's repair signs. The casemaker's mark belongs to the collective trademark no. 5 and key no. 4, the hallmark for Antoine Gerlach SA, Geneva, which closed down in 1977.

A collector bought this watch for $7000 at the jeweler TNS Diamonds Inc. in Philadelphia, Pennsylvania, USA. The store price was marked as $12,950, but, after a lengthy discussion, this was reduced to $7000. Another €778.26 went for the refurbishing (invoice dated December 10, 2008).

Reference 3444 pieces are rarely seen at auctions. One such model was offered at Antiquorum in New York on March 28, 2007, and sold for $12,500 (movement number 1,111,096). At Christie's in Geneva on November 13, 2006 a Reference 3444 went for CHF 22,800 (case in yellow gold, movement number 1,112,096, case number 2,628,014).

To Wear: ++ To Collect: ++ For Investment: +++

Reference 3445 in four versions (Fig. 108-112)

In 1961 Patek Philippe manufactured its first automatic with date display. It received the Reference number 3445 and was initially powered by the caliber 27-460 M; this was changed to the caliber 27-460 M PM for the last production run. "M" stands for "mono-date", "PM" for *piton mobile,* in English

Fig. 107 - The Reference 3444 is very rare. Case and band lugs are very intricately made, and the screw back does not match the previously seen designs. There is also an interesting small detail of the screw back. Because they were not fully screwed in, one of the three cylinder head screws, which attach the rotor, has left its mark at the center. The screw touched the inside back, leaving this mark. Had it been a bit looser, the rotor would have probably been blocked (movement no. 1,111,024, case no. 2,619,254).

"mobile stud carrier". The latter caliber is easy to recognize, since the seven-digit movement number always begins with the three numbers 123.

In the 1960s, the Reference 3445 was the most popular model. It was made with cases of yellow, pink, and white gold and platinum. Because so many were manufactured with many dial styles, we are going to present four different models. Before going into the various styles, we shall describe the design of this automatic wristwatch. Depending on the case, the dial is made of yellow or white gold. If it was to have index markers applied, the required holes were bored and the

dial was then silver-plated. The next step was the sunburst finish and lacquering, if required. Then the company name and interval marks for the small seconds hand were imprinted, and finally the dial received a protective coating.

The case is two-part, with a housing and screw back. The two-tiered bezel is an integral part of the housing. The middle is first cylindrical and then tapers below. It is turned from solid metal, and the plain lugs are soldered on. As was the practice, all surfaces are diamondized. The screw back is also turned from solid metal and milled. The sturdy ten-sided back closes tightly. The area by the lock and the rest of surface, except

Fig. 108 - Patek Philippe made its first watch with date display in 1961, which was given the Reference no. 3445. The watch shown here was bought by someone interested in watches at the Bodenhagen GmbH pawnshop in Mönchengladbach for €3710. The watch then had the dial shown below right. A check of the dial number "93Y3514A" showed that this dial does not belong to this Register, but rather to Register 3514, a later model. The Reference 3514 has the caliber 27-460 M and, thus, the same dimensions for the dial. There was further damage on the incorrect dial; the Roman numerals IV, X and XI were set manually, but not professionally. A new dial was professionally installed during a Patek Philippe refurbishing. This cost €1307.90 (movement no. 1,118,030, case no. 328,637).

Fig. 109 - Detail of the dial of our second version of the Reference 3445. The automatic with a white gold case has an impressive dial. This is of white gold, which was silver-plated and then given a sunburst finish and finally painted gray. Then the Roman numerals and the intervals for the small seconds display, the points for the minutes, and the company logo were imprinted. The special coating makes the Roman numerals look like enamel. The hands are also of white gold and painted.

the fine threading, were bead-blasted. The flat surface of the back is turned, the rounded transition to the ten-sided top is diamondized. The case diameter is 35.0mm, the total length with band lugs is 41.5mm and the height is about 10mm.

We have already noted that by the end of the 1960s these watches used the caliber 27-460 M and later the modified version 27-460 M PM. Besides the inscription on the base plate, we also recognize the differences in the balance cock. A slot radial to the balance staff, has a cylinder head screw to release and adjust the stud. This makes it possible to exactly set the drop, i.e., the symmetry, of the oscillating system.

The inscriptions and surfaces of the inside back are identical in all four watches, since they were made by the same casemaker. This was, as already stated for the Reference 3444, the collective trademark no. 5 with key no. 4. This stood for the firm Antoine Gerlach SA, Geneva, which closed in 1977. Therefore, we shall describe only one of the four inside backs (see picture on Fig. 108). The "large Helvetia" is stamped at the top, followed by the purity notation "18 K/0.750", the company name "PATEK, PHILIPPE & Co", "≡GENEVE≡", and "SWISS.". Then come the case number, Reference number, and casemaker's mark.

The first Reference 3445 presented in this book has the movement number 1,118,030 and case number 328,637. According to the archive extract before us, this yellow gold watch was produced in 1970 and sold on May 5, 1971.

After 31 years of wandering, in places we do not know, it ended up in 2002 at the pawnshop Bodenhagen GmbH in Mönchengladbach. This automatic, offered for sale on the internet, was eventually sold for €3710 on December 6, 2002, to a German watch lover (Fig. 108). All the problems already noted by the seller were checked and confirmed in the buyer's initial examination of the newly acquired watch. On the dial, still in original condition, which had Roman numerals, the damaged "IV", "X", and "XI", had been repaired by hand, if not masterfully. The dial was replaced with a far more beautiful one during a Patek Philippe refurbishing in Munich. The new one is silver-plated and has a sunburst finish. On the silvered dial, the larger Roman numerals create a much more pleasing overall effect. The servicing, including issuing an archive extract, cost €1307.90. This included the movement renovation for €445 and replacement of the dial with an old original version for €290.50, as the largest items (invoice dated July 8, 2002).

The next automatic Reference 3445 watches we present both have white gold cases. The first one has movement number 1,230,663 and case number 318,158 (Figs. 109, 110, & 111). The dial is impressive. It has a sunburst finish and was then painted dark blue. The national origin "0 SWISS 0" under the "6" tells us that this dial had golden, in our case white gold, index markers riveted on. As described in Section 4.3, this regulation only came into effect from 1968.

Fig. 110 - View of the caliber 27-460 M PM with movement no. 1,230,663. PM stands for *piton mobile*, in English "mobile stud support." On the balance cock near the "Incabloc" shock absorber, we see a long hole radial to the arbor with a cylinder head screw. This screw shifts and locks the mobile stud support. The second generation Breguet spring and Gyromax balance are also important. Here, the Masselotte weights are no longer on the balance wheel, but mounted inside on small consoles. Another small detail: the original factory mounting screw (one of three) was replaced by a cylinder head screw with special washer.

This watch is from Japan and was purchased by a German watch enthusiast on August 31, 2001, for $4550 (approximately €5056). Another €1424.48 went to Patek Philippe in Munich for a complete refurbishment. In addition to €400 for the movement refurbishing, the other largest items in this sum were the replacement of the gold rotor for €196 and exchange of the dial for €271 (invoice dated January 22, 2003).

The second white gold Reference 3445 has the movement number 1,230,402 and case number 329,656 (Fig. 111). According to the archive extract before us, this watch was produced in 1972 and sold on June 10 that year. The surface with sunburst finish was painted gray and printed with cream white Roman numerals. At first we thought that the Roman numerals were enameled. Company name and interval marks for the small seconds hand are printed in the same way.

The chased bezel is anomalous; it was most likely finished later. This watch also comes from Japan and was bought by a European watch lover for $7000 (€5000). Refurbishment at Patek Philippe in Munich cost another €1650. Despite everything, a good deal, because this version of the Reference 3445 rarely comes up at auction and cannot be purchased for under €12,000 and up to €15,000.

The inside backs of both white gold watches are still in original condition and have no repair markings.

The fourth version of the Reference 3445 has a yellow gold case and some unusual features (Fig. 112). The archive extract statement gives the exact Reference designation 3445/6, but on the case back, it is 3445 6. The caliber 27-460 M PM is number 1,230,981, the case number is 329,328. The watch was produced in 1971 and sold on April 25, 1972. The archive extract also reveals that this piece was delivered with a silvered dial and rod-shaped index markers. When it was refurbished at Patek Philippe in Geneva, the dial, including the baton hands, was removed and replaced with a blue lacquered dial with Dauphine hands. This change made the watch even more impressive. The second difference is in the case. The case of the 3445 6 version has shorter lugs, and is just 38mm long. The inside back is still in original condition and shows two watchmaker's repair signs.

Reference 3445 watches often come up for auction. A piece with white gold case and silver-plated dial was sold at Antiquorum in New York on June 18, 2008 for $19,200. The Patek Philippe refurbishing notation certainly also influenced this price. On May 10, 2009 at Antiquorum in Geneva, a yellow gold model was auctioned for CHF 15,600.

Watches offered on the internet at www.chrono24.com are of interest to collectors; there are often ten or more copies of the Reference 3445 available. A sampling by the author revealed that none of the watches on offer for €8500-€13,500 still had all the original or factory-made case surface finishes.

To Wear: ++ To Collect: ++ For Investment: ++

Fig. 111 - Two particularly striking examples of the Reference 3445 in white gold. The dials of both watches are made of white sheet gold and given a sunburst finish. Then the right model was enhanced by blue lacquer and white gold index markers. The frame for the date window is in white gold. The piece on the left has a gray finish and imprinted Roman numerals. This special lacquer gives an impression almost like enamel. The white gold hands are painted in the same color. The bezel of this watch is chased, that is, a steel stylus is used to make decorative patterns. Both watches are from Japan and were later refurbished by Patek Philippe. The case diameter is exactly 35.0mm. The semi-recessed crowns are a protective measure (watch left: movement no. 1,230,402, case no. 329,656; watch right: movement no. 1,230,663, case no. 318,158).

Fig. 112 - Here is a clear overall look at our fourth Reference 3445 in all relevant views. This watch was completely refurbished at Patek Philippe in Geneva and by special request a dark blue dial, yellow gold index markers, and Dauphine hands were affixed. The details about the caliber 27-460 M PM are clearly recognizable. The inscriptions and hallmarking on the case inside back are clear. The fine bead-blasted surface is still original. A closer look shows two watchmakers' repair signs (movement no. 1,230,981, case no. 329,328).

Reference 3454, an almost unknown watch (Figs. 113-116)

Now we present one of the sensations of this book: the automatic Reference 3454. This model has not been previously mentioned in the literature and also cannot be found in the Patek Philippe Museum in Geneva. The author himself has recently seen this gem for only the second time.

We have an archive extract for this watch. The caliber 27-460 has the movement number 1,112,614, the case the number 312,558. The watch was manufactured in 1962 and sold on October 16, 1963.

The dial is painted a cream color and restored to its original condition. The company name, the minute interval marks, the crosshairs for the small seconds hand and the national origin "SWISS" are imprinted. Specially shaped beam index markers are at the hours, and those for "12", "3", "6", and "9" are doubly wide. The watch has matching baton hands.

The two-part case measures 34.6mm in diameter. The narrow, partially fluted bezel is integrated, the four lugs soldered in profile. The case housing was turned from solid metal, has only one short cylindrical section and is tapered below. This shape fits well with the two-tiered tapered screw back. This was turned from one piece, die-stamped and finished with diamondized and turned surfaces.

This screw back is shown with the watch, but it is now closed with subsequently made sapphire crystal back. We will go into this later.

The case housing is still in original condition and has no surface hallmarks. This case, like those of the four previously described automatic Reference 3445s, was made by Antoine Gerlach Company SA, Geneva. Except for the Reference number, the inside back inscriptions are identical. The original fine bead-blasted surface of the inside back was improperly sanded afterwards, and one can see two watchmaker's repair marks.

This rare piece was auctioned on February 4, 2006, at Antiquorum in Geneva and the price reached CHF 21,600. When he received his watch, the new owner came to the author and asked him for his comment. We inspected the

Fig. 113 - The Reference 3454 shown here created another sensation. Only four or five pieces of this model were manufactured and it is not in the Patek Philippe Museum in Geneva. Even Oswaldo Patrizzi has not discussed this watch in his various and comprehensive books. What is more, our piece shown here has had a checkered history (movement no. 1,112,614, case no. 312,558).

Fig. 114 - The Reference 3454 with newly attached transparent display back; next to it at the right is the factory-installed back. This back showed clear traces of reworking. A check of the material thickness showed that the originally 0.5mm thick back was just 0.4mm thick. The new transparent display back was supplied by a casemaker in Pforzheim. Instead of die-stamped notches, this has six mill cut notches. The originally fine bead-blasted inside back was later sanded, probably to cover up unwanted traces.

Fig. 115 - The transparent sapphire crystal back shown at right was mounted on this Reference 3454 at an Antiquorum auction, but with two primary errors. First, this additional back was not of yellow, but pink gold; second, when it was correctly tightened, the rotor was blocked. Using an external measurement, the "case specialist" had probably miscalculated the inside height by 0.3mm. Nothing beats good craftsmanship.

Fig. 116 - Our approximately 20-fold magnification shows us important details of the caliber 27-460. The Gyromax balance regulator is in the foreground. This second generation piece is of 18-karat gold and was made by die casting. The cast piece was drilled, turned, and diamondized. Six of the Masselotte weights are set with steel arbors on brackets and two more on the balance arms. The Breguet spring with bent end-curve is just as visible as the "KIF anti-shock" system for the balance pivot. The end of the balance spring is locked in a stud support. We can easily identify the newer and older watches by comparing this image with Fig. 90.

watch itself first, and then both screw backs. On the watch, we first noted the incorrectly refurbished dial; furthermore its timekeeping accuracy left much to be desired. The two screw backs revealed more. The original piece, which was loosely attached, had small dents and traces of refinishing inside. The outer surface had been re-turned. For pieces like this watch, we can conclude that the repair work was done to remove some damage or an inscription. Checking the thickness of back was informative, as this was down to 0.4mm from the original 0.5mm.

The additional sapphire crystal back showed wear and blemishes. The inner height was not sufficient, so that when screwed on, the sapphire back touched the gold rotor and eventually blocked it. We can also consider the material selected as an error, since the back was made of pink gold instead of yellow.

The new owner first entrusted this rare automatic to Patek Philippe in Munich and commissioned a refurbishing, which cost €1658.27 (invoice dated March 2, 2007). The biggest single items were the complete refurbishing for €560 and the replacement dial for €664. Later, he arranged with a casemaker in Pforzheim to create a new sapphire glass display back and paid €1030 for this optically suitable cover. Including import sales tax, a new bracelet and gold clasp, and all associated shipping costs for valuables, the total investment for this watch came to around €17,800. All in all, it was a safe and valuable investment, especially since there is no copy of this watch even in the Patek Philippe Museum in Geneva.

Because the Reference 3454 is very rare, the author has researched this watch extensively and learned of peculiar goings-on. In December 2001, a yellow gold automatic Reference 3454 was offered for $10,000 on eBay, but the seller from West Hollywood, California, USA, did not find a buyer. On November 15, 2004, Christie's in Geneva offered a Reference 3454 and sold it for CHF 14,340 (approximately $12,276). The author concentrated his further research on this watch, because, despite a different appearance, the movement and case numbers were identical to those of a Reference 3454 presented in this book. What happened here?

The first clues came from the description of this watch in the Christie's catalog, which stated that the dial had baton index markers and a concessionaire's imprint, "B.D. HOWES & SON". On the rear side, or the screw back, was a very long engraved dedication, which we reproduce here only in parenthesis (Los Angeles Realty Bord [sic] XX, Service Watch Presented to George H. Shellenberger, February 16, 1967, Los Angeles, Most Useful Citizen in 1966). The Christie's description ended with the note that only four examples of this Reference are known. What happened with this watch, between the time it was auctioned at Christie's for CHF 14,340 in November 2004, and its sale at Antiquorum on April 2, 2006, for CHF 21,260?

First, the dial was refurbished, but very moderately so. Then the inscription was removed from the back, but this still left visible traces. Thus, our previous assumption has been confirmed. Using our Automatic Reference 3425 as an example (Fig. 102), we can see that all these processes could have been done much more professionally and that even a reworked back can be kept at its original dimensions.

What did the seller want to camouflage with all this work? Perhaps the fact that this watch had already been sold two years before at Christie's? What would be the point of this unprofessionally reworked screw back in this operation? Was this another diversion, or an another effort to lead people to believe that the watch had gone up in value? After deducting the premium and 20% commission, only about CHF 14,160 remained for the seller; it is very likely that a collector or speculator was at work here, who had initiated the dial correction and the making of the new sapphire crystal display back. This conjecture has yet to be proven.

This story teaches us one thing: if buyers use the checklist in this book when purchasing their watches, this would certainly prevent such stories as this one (see Chapter 8).

To Wear: ++ To Collect: +++ For Investment: +++

Reference 3466 (Figs. 117-118)

The very hard-to-find Reference 3466 is one of Patek Philippe's treasures. This automatic was launched in 1965; it was only manufactured with a steel case (diameter 35.0mm) and in limited numbers. It has a screw back.

It would be difficult to surpass the simple beauty of this timepiece. The caliber 27-460 has movement number 1,116,171 and case number 2,664,436. The dial is silver-plated. The company name and interval marks for the small seconds hand are imprinted. The index markers are riveted on, with two for the "12". The bezel is integrated in the case housing. However, we cannot absolutely determine how the band lugs were made. The seams are so finely executed that it is impossible to tell if they are soldered or not. The sturdy screw back was pre-turned from one piece, die-stamped, turned, and diamondized. The six large notches close the case securely.

The screw back inner surface as circular graining. The identifying marks include the company name "PATEK, PHILIPPE & Co", "≡GENEVE≡", and "SWISS", the last much larger than in a gold watch. Below are the case and Reference numbers.

The Reference 3466 shown was sold for CHF 12,266.40 on November 19, 2003, at Sotheby's in Geneva. The owner commissioned a Patek Philippe servicing and sent them this watch, which was in very good condition. This work cost €468.64 (invoice dated November 2, 2004). On May 15, 2006, another Patek Philippe Reference 3466 was offered at Christie's in Geneva. This time, however, the buyer had to pay a lot more: the hammer price was CHF 33,600 (movement number 1,116,692, case number 2,664,370).

To Wear: ++ To Collect: ++ For Investment: +++

Reference 3470 (Figs. 119-120)

Even Patek Philippe sometimes produces "ugly ducklings" like the Reference 3470. We can no longer determine just what standards the company directors set for the product planners and designers at the time. It can be assumed that the plan was to manufacture a very small and inexpensive men's wristwatch with a price far below the normal cost

Fig. 117 - After the Reference 2585 (see Fig. 85), the Reference 3466 is the second automatic watch with a steel case. Here we see this rare watch from front and rear. The bezel is integrated into the case middle part. The screw back is die-stamped, turned, and diamondized.

Fig. 118 - This image allows a glimpse at the inner workings of the rare Reference 3466. The caliber 27 460 is fastened to the movement retainer ring by three screws; two can be seen. The inside back has circular graining and, compared to gold cases, is very "generously" inscribed (movement number 1,116,171, case number 2,664,436).

Fig. 119 - Even Patek Philippe has some "ugly ducklings", such as this Reference 3470. Presumably, the product planners had to manufacture a small and very inexpensive men's wristwatch. The white gold case has a diameter of only 29.5mm, there was also cost-cutting by eliminating the small seconds hand. The width of the lugs is only 16mm. The above-left pictured dial had been freshened up in the U.S., but not in a typical way. In the refurbishing at Patek Philippe, the dial was replaced and one matching the 1968 regulations installed. Because of the white gold index markers, "0 SWISS 0" is under the "6".

Fig. 120 - The opened Reference 3470 allows us a glimpse of the inside back and of the movement caliber 175. The Gyromax balance has only four Masselotte weights. There is a second indent in the snap back, next to the counter bearing for the winding stem (movement no. 1,130,984, case no. 316,240).

for a Patek Philippe watch. The manual caliber 175, with movement number 1,130,984, is at work in this white gold man's wristwatch; the white gold case is only 29.5mm in diameter and has the number 316,240.

We have an archive extract for this watch, which states that this model was produced in 1964 and sold on October 16 that year. There is neither a Reference number nor a gold stamp on the back of the dial. The dial is silver-plated and shows fine gold bar index markers, and matching baton hands. When the watch was given a servicing, the dial was replaced with a brand new one. The extremely simple case consists of middle part and snap back. The width between the lugs is only 16mm. There are no hallmarks on the case exterior.

The inscription inside this back is not exactly typical. From top to bottom, are imprinted the "large Helvetia", the purity notation "18K/0.750", the company name "PATEK, PHILIPPE & Co", "≡GENEVE≡", and "SWISS". Below follow the numbers for case and Reference, and casemaker's mark. The collective trademark no. 5 and key no. 4 stands for Antoine Gerlach SA, Geneva, which closed in 1977.

The watch is from the U.S. and was acquired on the internet by a collector for $2500. It was only after the buyer received this timepiece, that he realized what he had let himself in for. Brass extensions had been soldered to the outer sides of the

band lugs to make it possible to attach a wider leather strap, now more likely to be 19mm wide, instead of the original 16mm wide leather strap. The dial turned out to be refurbished, the time keeping values were beyond belief.

The seller, a professional photographer from Los Angeles, was very surprised at all the criticism and at first categorically refused to take the watch back and refund the purchase price. It took a lengthy discussion to convince him that legal measures could only be avoided if he would help pay for the repair costs. The watch was then sent to Patek Philippe in Munich for a complete refurbishing; the disfigured case was entrusted to a competent casemaker. The collector only got his watch back after almost half a year. In addition to the replaced dial and the renovated caliber, the case gleamed in its old form and splendor, without, however, having changed the basic impression of this small men's wristwatch. Such a design would be better fit the wrist of a graceful lady.

The refurbishment cost DM 1624.05 and case renovation a further DM 160. The overall investment for this collector's item was DM 6787.05; the biggest single items in the servicing were the movement refurbishing for DM 672, the replacement balance for DM 469 and barrel bridge for DM 149. We should also note here that refurbishing a manually wound caliber 175 is not easy work and not something that Patek Philippe

Fig. 121 - The author has only seen this extremely rare watch, Reference 3473, twice. This is also the only Patek Philippe piece with a finely fluted bezel. Watch and cufflinks work stylishly together. Simply beautiful. This model is powered by the caliber 27-460 with automatic winding mechanism. The case is constructed in three parts and has a screw back. Everything about this watch is original; it probably was seldom worn. The current owner acquired this watch through a happy coincidence. The purchase price, import fees and the refurbishment at Patek Philippe added up to exactly DM 9449.36. Today this watch could only be bought for twice that if you could ever find one (movement number 1,112,437, case number 2,629,723).

Fig. 122 - The cast crown on a Reference 3473 magnified about 12-fold, where we see the PP logo in its distinguished symmetry. All automatic models received this special cast crown up to 1964.

⊹

watchmakers enjoy very much. Even after the seller agreed to pay half the costs, this was hardly commercially successful business, but certainly instructive.

The Reference 3470 is not among Patek Philippe's bestselling models, and is rarely offered for sale. On September 20, 2006, a yellow gold model was auctioned at Antiquorum in New York for $3360. A version with a pink gold case was offered on the internet and changed hands on April 4, 2010, for €2783.

To Wear: ? To Collect: ? For Investment: -

Reference 3473 (Figs. 121-122)

The automatic Reference 3473 is one of the watches that the author has been able to see only twice. With its fluted bezel and screw back, it is one of the Reference group 3400 waterproof watches, and the second to last automatic of this group, before the Reference 3485 with square or *carée* case. The model presented here is powered by the caliber 27-460, with movement number 1,112,437. The case has number 2,629,723. The dial is painted cream and the riveted index markers are the same as for the Reference 3454 dial on Fig. 113; there are matching baton hands. The company name, the crosshairs for the small seconds hand and the national origin "SWISS" are imprinted.

The case is three-part. The bezel is finely fluted. The case housing was manufactured as a turned part from one piece. The case diameter is 35mm and the lugs soldered on. The sturdy screw back ensures the watch is waterproof.

The watch shown here, in fact, is a very special piece and has quite an interesting story. It was first offered at auction on March 10, 1998, at Christie's in New York as lot number 30, with a reserve price of $4500-$5000, but found no takers. Perhaps the bad photo in the auction catalog contributed to this: the picture showed the watch quite awkwardly, with the crown pulled out. The watch owner sent his unsold piece to the competitor, Sotheby's, New York, where this Patek Philippe was offered as lot number 121 at the auction on June 22, 1998. It sold for $4025. A German watch collector, on the telephone, won the bidding. With the dollar to DM exchange rate of DM 1.79, this watch, including and import VAT, cost exactly DM 8513.42.

Patek Philippe in Munich refurbished the watch and restored the movement to almost-new condition. The buyer had to spend DM 936.12 for a new crocodile strap and gold pin buckle. The total investment for this Reference 3473, therefore, came to exactly DM 9449.36.

The Reference 3473 very rarely comes up for auction. One was offered at Antiquorum in Geneva on April 14, 2002, and sold for CHF 22,800 (movement number 1,112,289, case number 2,629,719). Another was auctioned at Christie's in Geneva on November 13, 2006, for CHF 21,600 (movement number 1,112,496, case number 2,629,734). To date, the author has not seen a third piece.

To Wear: ++ To Collect: ++ For Investment: ++

Reference 3483 (Figs. 123-124)

The next watch is in tune with modern trends, since demand for steel watches from high-quality brands is on the rise again. Reference 3483 is among the very rare models of the Geneva-based brand. This waterproof, hand-wound watch was only

Fig. 123 - Wearing a stainless steel Patek Philippe wristwatch is now considered particularly chic. The Reference 3483 is not only an extreme rarity, but has a modern size with its 35mm case diameter. This model was launched in 1963, but in small numbers. The case has a design comparable to the Reference 3466 (see Fig. 117). Due to the lower height of the caliber 27 SC, the screw back has a different shape.

Fig. 124 - The Reference 3483 from the back, at left with solid screw back with deep notches, in the middle, the manually wound caliber 27 SC, and at right the circularly grained and inscribed inside back. This watch was made in 1963 and sold on Sept. 19 that year. It was delivered with a crocodile strap with steel pin clasp. These watches have rarely come up for auction in the last 10 years (movement no. 710,826, case no. 2,632,453).

Fig. 125 - The Reference 3514 was Patek Philippe's second model with date display after the Reference 3445; it was launched in 1965. This watch was made in many versions and in large numbers. Despite its case diameter of 33.6mm, this model was very popular; it came in yellow gold, pink gold, white gold, and platinum cases. Given the special importance of this watch, we are including four versions. At the far left is a piece with white gold case, silver-plated white gold dial and index markers, and hands of 750 white gold. As in all other watches, the automatic caliber 27-460 M is at work here (movement no. 1,126,585, case no. 322,943). This watch must have had an attached white gold bracelet because we can still see the small rounding to hold

produced with a steel case (diameter 35mm) and in small quantities. We have an archive extract for this watch, which says that it was produced in 1963 and sold on September 19 that year. The watch, as delivered, had a leather strap and steel buckle. The caliber 27 SC has the movement number 710,826 and case number 2,632,453. The dial is silver-plated, the index markers are in bar form, and the baton hands in steel. Company name and national origin "SWISS" were stamped.

The steel case is two-part and provided with a stable screw back. The case housing with integrated bezel was made as a turned part, the four lugs are soldered on. The screw back was die-stamped and turned, and has six notches for secure closing. The case is almost identical to that of the Reference 3466 and differs only in the height of the case housing and the design of the screw back (Figs. 117-118). The caliber 27 SC is held in a sturdy movement retainer ring.

The lug counter-pieces on the band lugs. This counter-bearing is shown in Fig. 136. The second version at the left has a yellow gold case. This watch dial is made of sheet metal, silver-plated and painted silver (movement no. 1,123,956, case no. 320,650). A yellow gold Milanese bracelet was soldered on the third model. In the early 1970s, such combinations were very popular (movement no. 1,124,557, case no. 319,469). The watch on the far right represents the standard version of this Reference, a simple beauty for every day (movement no. 1,123,252, case no. 319,417). This model was produced in 1965 and sold on March 31, 1966.

❖

The Geneva Seal is stamped on the base plate near the screw balance and on the train wheel bridge, the latter highlighted with gold paint. After a servicing at Patek Philippe in Munich, this beautiful movement gleams like new.

The inscriptions on the inside back, which was circularly grained on all surfaces, include the company name "PATEK, PHILIPPE & Co", "≡GENEVE≡", and "SWISS". Under these follow case and Reference numbers.

The watch documented here was put up for auction on March 24, 2004, at Antiquorum in New York and sold for $6480. Including shipping costs and import VAT, the German watch lover had to pay €6525.17 for the watch. The refurbishment cost an additional €880, so that the total investment amounted to precisely €7405.17.

As mentioned earlier, the manually wound watches of the Reference 3483 are very rare. The last example known to the

Fig. 126 - This detail of the automatic caliber 27-460 M is almost like a work of art. The approximately 17-fold magnification reveals all the details of this miraculous little movement. The Gyromax balance with Masselotte weights, Breguet spring, "KIF" shock absorber, and balance cock with its regulator can be identified to the smallest detail. In addition, you can see the different surface finishes, such as the circular graining at bottom right and the Geneva stripe on the bridges, cock, and rotor. In the foreground, the Geneva Seal highlighted with elegant gold color.

author came up for auction in the late 1990s. In June 2010, a Reference 3483 was offered for sale by the Paris antique watch dealer Romain Rea for €15,500 or $18,693. At this point in time, it is not known if this Patek Philippe was eventually sold.

To Wear: ++ To Collect: ++ For Investment: ++

Reference 3514 in four different versions (Figs.125-126)

The second wristwatch with date display marketed by Patek Philippe had the Reference number 3514. This was also the first automatic in the 3500 Reference group. Reference 3514, like the previous model Reference 3445, is among the Geneva brand's most popular and best selling watches. The case with 33.6mm diameter was made in yellow, pink, and white gold, and in platinum. In addition to numerous dial styles, you could buy this model with either suspended or soldered Milanese gold bracelets. We will present the reader with four different versions, because of this watch's special importance.

Our principal description of this model, launched in 1965, is based on a watch from the first production year. According to the archive extract available, this watch was manufactured in 1965 and sold on March 31, 1966. The caliber 27-460 M has the number 1,123,252 and case number 319,417. The dial, made of gold, was first silver-plated and then given a sunburst finish. The company name, the interval marks for the small seconds display, and the national origin "SWISS" are printed in black. Matching baton hands are mounted with the beam-index markers for the hours. The case housing with integrated bezel and lugs was stamped from one piece, turned, and given the desired surface finishes. This bezel and band lugs are diamondized on the upper surface, while the side areas are satin finished. The downward-tapered case housing was also diamondized. The design diameter of the case is 33.6mm, not 33mm or 34mm, as is often stated in the literature or in auction catalogs. The solid screw back is turned from a solid piece, milled, and diamondized. The ten-sided back is milled and the key width is 29mm. The back material thickness is 0.5mm.

After being refurbished at Patek Philippe in Munich, this caliber 27-460 M gleams almost like new again. The servicing, including an archive extract, cost exactly €1743.60; the movement refurbishing for €445, the two automatic bridges for €151, and the exchange of the gold rotor for €260.60 were the biggest items (invoice dated November 11, 2002). For the two versions presented here, with yellow gold case and crocodile strap, the "small Helvetia" was stamped on the underside of the upper right and lower left band lugs.

On watch cases with soldered Milanese gold bracelets, the "small Helvetia" is found on the case housing by the "4". The white gold case has no such hallmark, because it was delivered with a suspended-style white gold bracelet. You can recognize this fact by the slight indentations on the underside of the lugs, to accommodate the band counter-bearing (Fig. 135).

The inscriptions on the inside back are, in principle, identical, since they were all made by the same casemaker. The inner surface is finely bead-blasted. Stamped from top to bottom are the "large Helvetia", the purity notation "18K/0.750", the manufacturer's name "PATEK, PHILIPPE & Co", "≡GENEVE≡" and "SWISS.". Below come the case and Reference numbers and casemaker's mark. This is the collective trademark no. 5 with key no. 4, which stands for Antoine Gerlach SA, Geneva, which was closed in 1977.

The second model has a gold case with silver lacquered dial and black Roman numeral markers. To match, the yellow gold baton hands have been painted black. The dial is made of sheet steel and galvanic silver plating. The identification 93Y3514A was imprinted on the dial back: the number 93 stands for Patek Philippe; 3514 for the Reference. It is identical to the dial shown in Fig. 111. This watch, made by Patek Philippe as Reference 3514 J, has the movement number 1,123,956 and case number 320,650.

This watch was discovered by a Munich watch lover on the internet and bought on November 30, 2003, for $6301 (approximately €5252.80). With shipping costs and import VAT, this investment came to around €6166. A servicing commissioned at Patek Philippe in Munich cost €1090.40 (invoice dated June 4, 2004).

The third version, with soldered Milanese gold bracelet, was made by Patek Philippe as Reference 3514/1 J; inscribed on the inside back were only the numbers 3514. The watch's movement number is 1,124,557 and case number 319,469. This yellow gold model was offered for sale on the internet. A collector contacted the seller, BIJ-Monsa in Geneva, and purchased this beautiful piece for CHF 5500 on January 30, 2003. The subsequent servicing done by Patek Philippe in Munich cost €1197.70.

Although all three of the watches with yellow gold cases were refurbished by Patek Philippe in Munich, the white gold version went to the *Service-après-vente* in Geneva. This piece was put up for auction on October 17, 1993, at Antiquorum in Geneva and sold for CHF 7000, plus premium. However, after Christophe Harsch, the then-service manager at Patek Philippe in Geneva, checked the watch, the new owner was no longer very happy. The cost of the thorough refurbishing came to CHF 1121 (movement number 1,126,585, case number 322,943).

If current auction prices are any measure, automatic Reference 3514 watches seem now to be in great demand. A yellow gold Reference 3514 was offered at Antiquorum in Geneva on April 2, 2006, and sold for CHF 18,000. At Antiquorum in New York on March 28, 2007, a yellow gold Reference 3514 was auctioned for $13,200. At the same auction house, on September 26 the same year, another yellow gold model 3514 was offered and sold for $18,800. Live Auctioneers sold a Reference 3514 with a platinum case that attained $30,000 (movement number 1,124,043, case number 320,385). With the trend towards a more "unassuming" white gold watch, the automatic with white gold case pictured here, bought years ago, represents a good investment.

To Wear: + To Collect: ++ For Investment: ++

Reference 3541 (Figs. 127-130)

Patek Philippe's third men's wristwatch with date display was launched in 1967 and received the Reference number 3541. At first glance, this model can be easily confused with the predecessor model Reference 3445 (Fig. 108). Only the partially recessed crown and the larger diameter make it possible to see the difference. The Reference 3541 was made with yellow and white gold cases. The piece shown has the movement number 1,124,874 and case number 320,933. The dial was galvanically silver-plated and given a sunburst finish. The company logo, Roman numerals, and the interval marks for the small seconds display are imprinted.

Fig. 127 - The Reference 3541 is a successor model to the Reference 3445 and is the third model with date display. A distinguishing feature is the almost completely recessed crown. The case diameter is exactly 35.60mm, or 0.6mm more than the Reference 3445. The watch shown here is very elegant. From behind you can see the screw back with turned surface and the 29mm ten-sided cover with key width 29mm.

Fig. 128 - An opened Reference 3541. The automatic caliber 27-460 M demonstrates the highest level of watch making expertise. The easy-to-read identification notes on inside back reveal the origin of this watch. A small note: The national origin SWISS has a period (movement no. 1,124,874, case no. 320,933).

Figs. 129 and 130 - Direct comparison of the References 3541 (left, Fig. 129) and 3542 (right, Fig. 130) which are quite similar except for the date display, reveals some interesting differences. The dial on the left is silver-plated, has a sunburst finish and minute points. The seconds marks are longer in the main axes. The hands are yellow gold. The right dial is painted silver and matt, and the hands are also yellow gold, but painted black.

Fig. 131 - The Reference 3542 was only manufactured in small numbers. Its case diameter was exactly 36.0mm. The version presented here has a silver lacquered dial and black lacquered hands. The solid case is closed with a screw back. For protection, the crown is almost completely recessed.

The case could have been stamped from one piece, turned and diamondized, since there are no traces of soldering or other attachment on the band lugs, but this case could also have been made as a turned piece and the lugs soldered on. The crown is recessed to 2/3 of its height and thus well protected. The bezel is integrated in the case housing, which is primarily cylindrical, then stepped downward and finally tapered towards the screw back. A most elaborate design. The case diameter is exactly 35.60mm, although the literature and auctions like to give it as 36mm.

The solid screw back is turned from a single piece and has a ten-sided cover with 29mm key width. The surfaces and outer curves of the present watch's back were turned. The caliber 27-460 M was refurbished at Patek Philippe in Munich, but the case, since it was like new, was left as is.

The "small Helvetia" is on the underside of the right upper and left lower lugs. The inscription on the fine bead-blasted and still unspoiled inside back, is, except for case and Reference numbers, exactly like the backs of the four listed Reference 3514 watches. Again the casemaker is the same, with the mark showing key no. 4, for Antoine Gerlach SA, Geneva, the supplier for Patek Philippe.

The model shown here was bought by a European watch enthusiast for $7200, after bidding by telephone at a Sotheby's auction in New York on April 6, 2004. Shipping and import VAT totaled some €936 and the refurbishment at Patek Philippe in Munich was another €770.24. Although the total investment adds up to €8402.24, the new owner can be satisfied. At Christie's in Geneva on May 12, 2008, a yellow gold Reference 3541 was auctioned for CHF 13,125 (approximately $12,531). On April 2, 2006, a yellow gold piece was sold at Antiquorum in Geneva for CHF 17,400, (movement number 1,124,855, case number 320,952). At the same auction house on October 15, 2006, a watch with a white gold case was sold to the new owner for CHF 25,200 (movement number 1,128,794, case number 321,093).

To Wear: +++ To Collect: ++ For Investment: ++

Fig. 132 - The Reference 3542 from the rear with open screw back. After a servicing at Patek Philippe, the caliber 27-460 is almost like new. The inside back is finely bead-blasted and reveals no repair notations (movement no. 1,115,027, case no. 321,169).

Reference 3542 (Figs. 131-132)

The next automatic has Reference number 3542, although it has some differences to the just-discussed Reference 3541. Since so few pieces were manufactured, this model is considered rare. The case diameter is a verified 36.0mm, exactly 0.4mm more than the Reference 3541. The caliber 27-460 movement number is 1,115,027 and case is number 321,169. The dial is painted silver, and the Roman numerals, the company name, the interval marks for the small seconds display, and national origin "SWISS" under the "6" are printed.

The direct comparison in Figs. 129 & 130 is more meaningful than this description. The Reference 3542 case construction was designed slightly differently from that of the Reference 3541 case. The case housing with integrated bezel was apparently made as a turned part. Then the four lugs were soldered on. That they were so recessed during turning, might reinforce the author's conjecture. The sturdy screw back has a ten-sided cover with 29mm key width; the outside diameter is completely re-turned. Excepting the Reference and case number s, the inscriptions on this finely bead-blasted inside back are identical to those on the previously described Reference 3541. Patek Philippe used the same casemaker as a supplier here (Figs. 131-132).

Reference 3542 watches are hard to find. A watch of this model in yellow gold was auctioned for CHF 15,000 on April 2, 2006, at Antiquorum in Geneva (movement number 1,116,234, case number 321,245). A collector bought the watch shown here on September 13, 2004, for $6000 (approximately €4894.14). This watch was fitted with a suspended-style Milanese gold bracelet. A Patek Philippe, Munich, servicing cost another €984.26. Considering how rare this watch is, and the noted auction price, the collector has made a safe investment, since it was not known if the watch that made CHF 15,000 at Antiquorum had been previously refurbished at Patek Philippe.

Fig. 133 - Time and again people try to copy valuable objects, in order to get as much money for doing very little. Since Patek Philippe can only replicate older movements with enormous effort, someone here tried a "marriage". A "marriage" means a watch assembled from parts that did not originally belong together. Patek Philippe made neither the case nor the dial of the watch shown here. The latter may be readily detected when the movement is taken out and the dial lifted. The expert would also see, from certain characteristics of the case, that this watch did not come from the factory in Geneva. Patek Philippe never made band lugs in this shape.

Fig. 134 - The opened "marriage" watch from the rear. The movement caliber 10'''-200 with movement no. 959,100 is original and was probably produced in 1952. The case no. 675,442 has been tampered with; Patek Philippe gave this to a watch with a gold case. A small but crucial feature unequivocally demonstrates that this steel case is not by Patek Philippe. Under the company logo on the inside back, the place of origin is printed as "=GENEVE=". However, Patek Philippe never used this form with two dashes. Watches from our manufacturer only get either three dashes or just one, that is, "≡GENEVE≡" or "-GENEVE-". The mandatory notice "ACIER INOXYDABLE", the mostly circularly grained surfaces and the patent protection notice are all missing. The author would have liked to receive such comprehensive information from Patek Philippe.

A yellow-gold Reference 3542 was offered on eBay in Germany, where it was sold on May 14, 2003, for €8250. The seller had stated in his tender that this watch had been given a Patek Philippe refurbishing for €1450.

To Wear: +++ To Collect: ++ For Investment: ++

An instance of tampering (Figs. 133-134)

The manually wound watch in stainless steel shown in Figs. 133 & 134, is one of our most interesting pieces. This watch, also previously unknown to the author, was purchased by a collector on July 28, 2002, on eBay in the USA, for a substantial $6600. Shipping and import VAT were additional. Thus, the entire investment amounted to around €7743. The new owner sent it to the German branch of Patek Philippe in Munich and asked for a refurbishment. After more than three months, the watch was returned, but unrepaired. In a letter dated March 27, 2003, Patek Philippe Genève wrote as follows: "Movement number 959,100, case number 675,442. The case and the dial were not manufactured by Patek Philippe. The movement is original. The watch is returned without repair".

A few years later, the owner asked the author for his comment and later made his collector's piece available for this book. The caliber 10'''-200 powers the watch, with movement number 959,100. The case number is 675,442. The dial is painted silver. The index markers for the hours are made of steel and riveted, two at the "12". The Dauphine hands are made of stainless steel. The company name, the marks for the small seconds display and the national origin "SWISS" are printed in black. After closer inspection under a stereo-microscope, one could almost assume that this is an original Patek Philippe dial. More exact information could be found on the back of this dial, but at this time, the collector did not want to disassemble the watch.

The case is structured in three parts and has an outer diameter of 32.5mm. The bezel consists of a cylindrical ring, which is tapered upwards. It was produced as a turned part. The case housing was stamped from one piece, turned and milled, and given the existing surface finishes. Punch marks can be seen between the lugs, which is something Patek Philippe would never allow. The lugs have holes for the spring bars. The back is snapped on and has a material thickness of 0.4mm. Altogether, the shape of the lugs and their surface finish do not match the Patek Philippe standards we have seen previously.

The same applies to the outer surface of the snap back. The caliber 10'''-200 with movement number 959,100 was probably produced in 1952. The Geneva Seal is stamped on the base plate near the caliber designation and on the barrel bridge, the latter highlighted with gold paint. There are three locking screws in the movement retainer ring which holds the movement. The movement itself may be considered well-maintained, even if a refurbishing might be appropriate.

The inscription on the inside back is very close to an original from Patek Philippe. In the middle is the company name "PATEK, PHILIPPE & Co", followed by "=GENEVE=" and "SWISS." and the case number. That the "=GENEVE=" is framed by only two dashes is however, incorrect. Steel and gold cases usually have either one or three dashes (≡GENEVE≡), see Reference 3417 (Fig. 95), Reference 3466 (Fig. 118), and Reference 3483 (Fig. 124). Cases made of precious metals were stamped with "–GENEVE–", up to Reference no. 3433 (see Fig. 106) and subsequently with "≡GENEVE≡". That change was made in 1960. The Reference numbers 3444 and 3445 already have these new inscriptions (Figs. 107-108). But even here there were aberrations from these regulations.

All in all, one can make the following assertions about this watch: the movement is genuine; but there are doubts about the dial and case housing, especially because of the unusual band lugs. The case back is another anomaly. As can be seen from other watches in this book, the case number here, 675,442 is between the case number 667,674 of the Reference 565, made in 1952, and case number 688,312 of the Reference 2552, manufactured in 1955. Despite this, no Reference number was stamped on the back of our steel watch, as was common in 1948 at Patek Philippe.

The author considers this watch to be a hard-to-recognize "*marriage*", in which only the movement comes from Patek Philippe. To be certain, we searched for the case number 675,442 in the Patek Philippe archives in Geneva. There it emerged that this case number belongs, not to a steel watch, but to one of precious metal. Armed with this information, the watch collector contacted the seller in the U.S., but with negative results. After such a long time, he would not consider a reverse transaction of this business. Then the irritated buyer sought out an international law firm and described his mishap. There he learned that for such a civil case, the American contract lawyer would first require an advance of about $3000, to be able to take any action at all. Given the demand for such a high fee, our watch enthusiast decided against any further legal action and retained this "*marriage*". However, two years later, a collector was willing to pay nearly twice the original purchase price for the watch, restoring our collector's pleasure in this unique piece.

Reference 3558 in two different versions (Figs. 135-141)

The Reference 3558 has a special place among all the previously presented watches with caliber 27-460 or 27-460 M. Its gold case has the largest material volume and thus the highest weight in gold. This model was very popular in the U.S. and came with yellow or white gold case. To show some varying types of this watch, we present two different models. The first has the caliber 27-460 M PM with movement number 1,230,449 and case number 2,695,315. This watch was produced in 1971 and provided with a leather strap at the factory, which later was replaced with a hinged Milanese gold bracelet from Patek Philippe. This pleasing bracelet also suits References 3428, 3429, 3433, 3435, and 3444 very well, and cost just DM 970 extra in 1961.

The second version of the Reference 3558, with a blue dial, has the previous caliber 27-460 M still ticking, with movement number 1,118,342. The case number is 2,689,535. This watch was produced in 1970 and delivered to the U.S. Both models had the same case supplier, the company Ed. Wenger SA, Geneva, which closed in 1992.

The dial of the Reference 3558 is made of 18K yellow gold and has a sunburst finish. For the second piece, the dial was given another blue lacquering. The index markers are made of 18-karat yellow gold, but for the first piece, these were painted black, including the hands. The company name, the interval marks for the small seconds display, and the national origin "SWISS" are printed.

The case has a very complex design. The snap-on bezel is turned cylindrically, tapered, and diamondized. The case middle was stamped from one piece, turned, milled, and given various surface finishes. The case diameter is just 33.8mm, even if the watch looks much larger. The solid screw back is turned from one piece, die-stamped, and tapered in two steps. Six notches provide for a secure seal. The bezel, the 45° refraction of the lugs, and the two tapered surfaces of the screw back are diamondized; the rest are satin-finished or turned.

Both watches and their movements received a complete servicing at Patek Philippe in Munich, so the movements are in almost new condition and have excellent performance results. The "small Helvetia" is stamped on the bottom of the right upper band lug. Although the cases of both watches come from the same casemaker, a small difference can be detected in the inscriptions on the inside back. In the older watch, in the upper area the "large Helvetia" and the purity notation "18K/0.750" are stamped next to each other; in the newer watch, they are beneath each other. Then follow the company name "PATEK-PHILIPPE & Cᵍ", "-GENEVE-", and "SWISS". Beneath in three rows are the Reference designation "REF. 3558", case number, and casemaker's mark. This last is for the collective trademark no. 5 with key no. 1, the company Ed. Wenger SA, Geneva.

Both watches are from the United States. Including shipping and import VAT, the first one cost €5850 and the second around €5600. The cost of the complete refurbishings was, for the first watch, €1241.20 and €1600.55 for the second. The Reference 3558 is not available for sale very often. At Antiquorum in Geneva on November 19, 2000, a yellow gold

Fig. 135 - The Reference 3558 is one of Patek Philippe's more attractive models. It came on the market in 1967 and was especially popular in the United States. The case was made with the largest material volume and, thus, the highest weight in gold of all the watches made in that period. Since this model is so important, we are showing two different versions. The first watch has a gold dial and index markers; the hands are gold, but painted black. The case is composed of three parts: bezel, case housing, and screw back. Even if the watch appears much larger, the case diameter is exactly 33.8mm. The archive extract says that this watch was delivered with crocodile strap and buckle, but later a Patek Philippe Milanese gold bracelet was attached.

Fig. 136 - The Reference 3558 from the back, with opened case; the caliber 27-460 M PM can be seen in the long slot on the balance cock. The cylinder head screw there is used to adjust and lock the stud support. The attached Milanese gold bracelet is also interesting. You can see the counterpiece or bearings on the lugs, between the spring bar pinion and the watchcase, which keep the end of the bracelet smoothly in place (movement no. 1,230,449, case no. 2,695,315).

Fig. 137 - A second version of the Reference 3558. The blue dial and a crocodile strap give this timepiece an even more elegant appearance. An ideal finishing touch for a dark-blue business suit.

Fig. 138 - At left, Reference 3558 with open screw back. The caliber 27-460 M represents masterful watch-making, probably unmatched by any other Swiss watch manufacturer. The inside back still has its finely bead-blasted surface and all markings are clearly legible. This is not entirely the case for the two watchmaker's repair notations to the right of the national origin "SWISS" (movement no. 1,118,342, case no. 2,689,535).

Fig. 140 - This image shows us just how different watches of the same Reference can appear. Perhaps the Reference 3558 with Milanese bracelet is right for a birthday celebration; the one with a blue dial and matching cuff links, for the opera. The old idea that one should only wear white gold watches on such occasions is outdated. A Patek Philippe wristwatch as beautiful as this one is always stylish with matching cufflinks. This was something Erica Pappritz, also known as "the Countess" of post-war West Germany, always enjoyed.

Fig. 141 - The clasp of a Milanese gold bracelet, already seen in Fig. 135. The approximately four-fold magnification shows us the beautiful detail work one expects from Patek Philippe products.

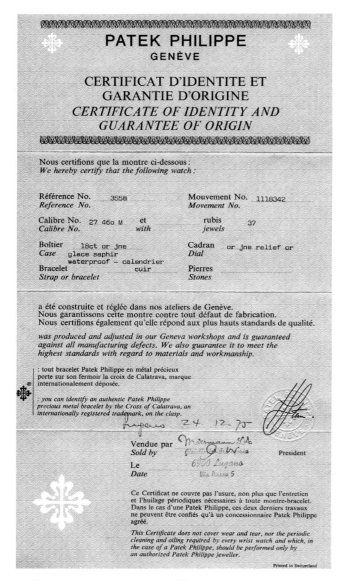

version was auctioned for CHF 12,000. On May 13, 2007, at the same auction house, a white-gold model with a blue dial was auctioned for CHF 30,000 (movement number 1,230,245, case number 2.695,410).

To Wear: ++ To Collect: ++ For Investment: ++

Reference 3561, a real rarity (Figs. 142-144)

The automatic Reference 3561 is one of the rarest of Patek Philippe collectors' pieces, and the second one the firm gave a screw back with sapphire crystal, after the Reference 3439/1. This meant that the inside back was not available to record all relevant information. However, we have an archive extract for our watch.

The caliber 27-460 has the movement number 1,116,766; case number is 2,681,327. This watch was produced in 1970 and sold on October 6, 1971. We also know the life story of this timepiece. We can see from the warranty certificate, which the author has before him in the original, that this rare piece was purchased from the concessionaire "SWISS STORES LTD." in Jamaica on March 15, 1975 (Fig. 203).

The dial is made of 18-karat yellow gold, which was then galvanically silver-plated and satin finished lengthwise. The company name, the interval marks for the minutes and small seconds hand, and the national origin "SWISS" are printed, and the watch has matching baton hands. The case is made in two parts and has a screw back. The diameter is 33.5mm. The case housing with integrated bezel was manufactured as a turned part and the four lugs are soldered. In addition to the cylindrical housing, the bezel is fluted and the screw back attachment tapered. All surfaces are diamondized.

The screw back was made as a turned part, die-stamped and diamondized. The sapphire crystal display back is glued. The movement has been serviced by Patek Philippe in Munich and looks like new again, as a look through the crystal back shows. Since this watch had probably spent most of its time in a safe, the case did not need any new work.

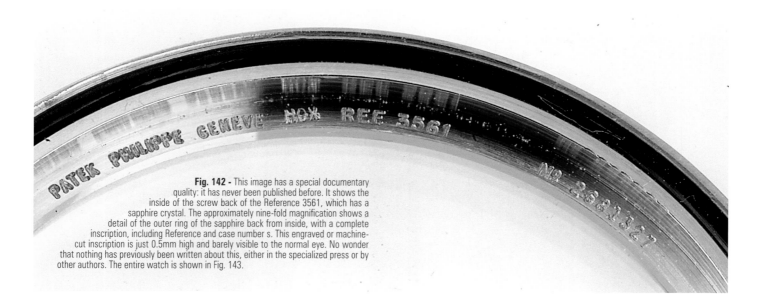

Fig. 142 - This image has a special documentary quality: it has never been published before. It shows the inside of the screw back of the Reference 3561, which has a sapphire crystal. The approximately nine-fold magnification shows a detail of the outer ring of the sapphire back from inside, with a complete inscription, including Reference and case number s. This engraved or machine-cut inscription is just 0.5mm high and barely visible to the normal eye. No wonder that nothing has previously been written about this, either in the specialized press or by other authors. The entire watch is shown in Fig. 143.

Fig. 143 - The Reference 3561 was launched in 1968 and is a successor model to the Reference 3439/1 from 1965. Both watches have screw backs with sapphire crystal inserts; this was the world's first watch with a transparent back. Even if other watch manufacturers might today make that claim for themselves, such assertions should not be taken seriously. Here again, Patek Philippe was the pioneer, as it has been in other areas. Since there is no screw back inside available for the usual markings, the following was inscribed between the band lugs by the "6" from left to right: the purity notation "0.750", the "small Helvetia", and the mark of the casemaker.

Fig. 144 - Our Reference 3561 from the back, with sapphire screw back and opened. The screw back ring is made of a turned part, in which six slots were made by die-stamping. In the 1960s, sapphire crystals of this size could only be manufactured with considerable effort and were very expensive. Only 20 years later, when it was possible to produce synthetic crystals more simply and cheaply using new technologies, did watches with transparent backs become more widely available.

We want to highlight the fundamental differences to the previously presented watches. The purity notation "0.750", the "small Helvetia", and the casemaker's mark are all stamped between the lower lugs, from left to right. This arrangement represents an innovation. The "18K" is still stamped on the bottom of the right lower band lug, presumably by the customs authorities of the island state of Jamaica (a Commonwealth member with the same customs regulations as Great Britain).

When the screw back is open, the differences are even more obvious. On the back outer ring, "PATEK PHILIPPE GENEVE REF. 3561 no. 2,681,327" is engraved inside (Fig. 142). If you take out the movement, you can determine that Reference and case numbers are also hand engraved by the "12" and the "6" with a steel stylus (cut).

This finding has important implications. Patek Philippe watches with display backs often come up for auction. Most of these were automatic models of the Reference 3445, which had subsequently been fitted with an extra sapphire crystal screw back. If the original back is also available to be delivered with such pieces, one can calmly undertake this business. If not, hands off.

The watch presented here comes from an Indian engineer who had emigrated from India to Canada and bought the watch, as its first owner, on March 15, 1975, in Jamaica. After he retired, he sold the watch for $6195 to a German watch lover. Including shipping and import sales tax, the purchase price was exactly DM 14,522.40. The servicing at Patek Philippe in Munich cost a further DM 880.44 (invoice dated November

7, 2001). Because this watch was in mint condition, the only things replaced in Munich were the crown, winding stem, mainspring, and various small parts.

Reference 3561 watches are hard to find. An example of this rare Patek Philippe was auctioned at Antiquorum in Geneva on February 4, 2006, and sold for CHF 21,500 (movement number 1,116,781, case number 2,681,339). Seven months later, the same watch was re-auctioned at Antiquorum in Geneva and this time attained only CHF 18,000. A bitter loss for the seller. The watch auctioned twice in Geneva had a movement number that was 15 figures different from the one presented here and a case number that was12 figures different, so they both should have been manufactured during the same week.

To Wear: + To Collect: ++ For Investment: +++

Reference 3563 in white and yellow gold, the "Backwinder" (Figs. 145-148)

No other watch from Patek Philippe created so little joy, as the models of the "Backwinder" series. This was due to the new caliber 350, whose design went in totally new directions. Details have already been discussed in the presentation of automatic calibers in Chapter 4.5. The unstable regulator, the low power reserve, and the vulnerability of the outer rotor led to so many complaints that the Patek Philippe office in New York had to take back the watches en masse. The multiple problems with the ball bearings for the rotor and the reverser for the two-way winding mechanism could never be satisfactorily resolved, making it necessary to develop this caliber further.

In 1979, the new version appeared, with the designation 1-350. An 18-karat gold segment replaced the heavy metal weight, a new ball bearing, eliminating the reverser, and the improvement of the manual winding and setting mechanism not only benefitted the watch wearer, but also made it much easier to service. Patek Philippe was, however, never quite satisfied with this caliber and production ended in 1985.

The Reference 3563/2 shown here, in 18-karat white gold with integrated bracelet of the same material, was made available to us by a Japanese collector. He had previously purchased it on the internet for $2300. It was expertly renovated by Patek Philippe in Geneva and afterwards showed acceptable performance rates. The renovation cost €1157.10 (invoice dated August 10, 2002). In this amount, the movement servicing for €443.50 and the replacement of the dial at €484 were the largest items. When this watch was accidentally dropped from a height of about 30 cm onto a wooden table while it was being photographed, the just-renovated watch was again totally out of adjustment. Patek Philippe in Geneva did another renovation, however, free of cost as a gesture of goodwill.

So that we can describe the two calibers 350 and 1-350, and also compare the models with and without the gold bracelet, we have selected two of these watches. The first has already been described. It has a white gold case with soldered bracelet and the caliber 350. The second piece has a yellow gold case with leather strap and the successor caliber 1-350. We have an archive extract for the first model, which states that the Reference 3563/2 was produced in 1974 and sold on March 14 that year.

The caliber 350 has the number 1,185,655; the case number is 2,727,909. The yellow gold counterpart was produced in 1984. The caliber 1-350 has the number 1,449,198 and the case the number 2,698,334. The Reference 3563 was made with many different dials. In models with soldered gold bracelets, blue-painted dials created a pleasing effect. The hour index markers and matching baton hands are made of gold. As with the second "Backwinder" with crocodile strap shown here, 18K gold guilloche dials were very popular. These came with golden, graduated index markers and with their upper surfaces painted black. Baton hands were added to match.

The Reference 3563 case is 34.4mm in diameter and intricately made. The case housing with integrated bezel is manufactured as a turned part and the thin lugs soldered on. The width between the lugs is 20mm, not a standard measure for normal Patek Philippe watches. A cup-shaped, die-stamped and turned back, which has a fitting notch by the "6" and the "12", is screwed on with a ring nut with six notches. The back has to be precisely positioned to fix the setting crown, which is screwed on after the back is closed. The gold back is 0.50mm thick. You get an overall impression from the case design that product planning for this Reference took an economical approach to the use of the precious gold. Otherwise the material thickness of the case and band lugs would not be so sparingly thin.

The caliber 350 and 1-350 have already been introduced and their major differences described (see page 38). In addition to the difference between the caliber 350 rotor with its heavy metal segment and the golden rotor weight of the caliber 1-350, the barrel bridge reveals an interesting detail (Fig. 148). When the caliber 350 was reworked, no changes could be made in the area of the barrel bridge, which allowed continued use of this component without problems. Since large numbers of this movement part were available in stock and, originally, nobody had considered modifying this movement, the existing pieces were milled with an end mill and the gold colored caliber designation 350 was simply removed and the new caliber designation 1-350 was engraved into this open space. This was done even on the movement of the yellow gold case watch shown here, although it was item 9198 of 10,000 produced. This means that the movement shown was manufactured in the last production year of this caliber type.

The "small Helvetia" is printed on the outer side of the back. The bead-blasted inside back reveals more. From the top are inscribed the purity notation "18K/0.750" and, below side by side, the casemaker mark and the "large Helvetia". Following come the company name "PATEK-PHILIPPE & C°", "-GENEVE-", and "SWISS". Below are the Reference number 3563 3 and the case number. The commissioned casemaker belongs to the collective trademark no. 5 with key no. 1, standing for Ed. Wenger SA, Geneva, which was closed down in 1992.

The yellow-gold Reference 3563/3 was bought by a German watch lover on the internet in the U.S. for $4000 (approximately €3150.85). With shipping and import sales tax, the total for this sale came to €3809. What is notable about this purchase was the fact that neither the PPC pin clasp nor original PPC crocodile watch strap were provided, but the two golden spring bars were.

Fig. 145 - Reference 3563/2 with soldered watch bracelet in 750 white gold. This model was launched in 1969 and was available both with crocodile strap and gold bracelet. This watch was considered especially chic in the U.S.A. and the Far East because of its new design, without a crown, and initially found many admirers. Only when the problems with the new automatic movement 350 became clearer, did the interest in this watch wane. The version shown here was produced in 1974 and sold on March 14 that year in Japan (movement no. 1,185,655, case no. 2,727,909).

Fig. 147 - The bezel and dial in the hobnail pattern decoration (*Clous de Paris*) give this Reference 3563 "Backwinder" a chic appearance. Although the case diameter is just 34.4mm, the lug width for the crocodile strap is 20mm. For this reason, the lugs are somewhat narrow.

Fig. 146 - The yellow gold version of the Reference 3563/3 already has the improved caliber 1-350. This watch has a very pleasing design, even if the revised automatic movement did not meet the high expectations. In the U.S., this watch was called the "Backwinder," because the crown was set on the back. You wound the movement with the crown in position 1; when pulled out to position 2, you set the time (movement no. 1,449,198, case no. 2,698,344).

Fig. 148 - This image shows us how an open "Backwinder" looks. The outer revolving rotor has a golden swing weight. We can also see part of the ball bearing under the note "NO OIL". On the case back, there is a small notch in both the top and bottom rims. If the back is set on the case, the two notches must exactly meet the corresponding notches in the case. This precisely centered the winding stem projecting from the barrel bridge in the through hole. Only when everything fits together, can the ring nut be set on and turned. A small detail on the barrel bridge: A slot-shaped depression has been milled there with an end mill. There we find the caliber designation 1 350.

Fig. 149 - The Reference 3565, also known as the IOS watch. While it is not to every one's taste, we must not leave it out of this book because of its significance and the large number of pieces. This model was made according to the wishes of the major customer at the time, the investment company "INVESTORS OVERSEAS SERVICES (IOS) LTD." If one of the company's traders exceeded the turnover level of $1 million, they were presented with one of these watches as an award. We describe on page 176, why this model is definitely an inexpensive watch. Savings were made even on the fine caliber 27-460 M and the small seconds display was omitted (movement no. 1,127,995, case no. 2,673,809). It is not fully comprehensible why this watch is sought-after by collectors and commands high prices.

Reference 3563 watches, especially the version with soldered gold bracelet, are not much in demand among collectors, although they are still sought-after today in the Far East. On December 3, 2008, a white-gold Reference 3563 3 with white gold bracelet was offered at the auction house Christie's in Hong Kong, and sold for $9721. As of the deadline on June 20, 2010, internet auctions in the U.S. were offering a white gold 3563 3 for $11,900 and a yellow gold 3563 2 for $10,950. Whether they have been sold for those prices is not known.

To Wear: + To Collect: + For Investment: -

Reference 3565, the IOS watch (Figs. 149-153)

Reference 3565 1 is certainly not to everyone's taste as a wristwatch, but still, we cannot ignore it. The Patek Philippe archive extracts refers to this Reference as 3565/1, at auctions it is often listed as 3565-1. However, 3565 1 is what is printed on the back.

This watch has an interesting background and history. It is a model that looks like a lot, but should cost little. This watch was made according to the wishes of the firm's biggest purchaser, the investment fund Investors Overseas Services (IOS) Limited, which operated as a corporation from its headquarters in Panama. Bernard (Bernie) Cornfeld, founder of this initially quite successful company (born August 17, 1927, in Istanbul, Turkey, died February 27, 1995, in London), was the son of a Jewish family originally from Romania. In its prime, IOS employed more than 20,000 people and was managing assets worth approximately $2.5 billion. If a trader surpassed the turnover threshold of $1 million, he received one of the watches described here as special recognition. Although Patek Philippe has never published production figures, the estimated number of pieces of this model is over 1500. IOS was the only buyer and was a direct customer, not receiving it via a concessionaire, thus saving the seller's discount.

The representative watch shown here, is powered by the caliber 27460 M with movement number 1,127,995 and case number 2,673,809. The production year was 1968. The dial is gold-plated and has a sunburst finish. The company name, the Roman numerals, and national origin "SWISS" are printed. The notation "0 SWISS 0" under the "6" may be considered a small faux pas. This designation is appropriate only for golden index markers. The baton hands are not made of gold, but of steel and painted black. As already described, black-painted gold hands are a standard Patek Philippe feature.

Fig. 150 - The dial of the Reference 3565 looks really costly at first glance. However, it is made of sheet steel and galvanically gilded. The two hands are also made of steel and, like the matching Roman numerals, painted black.

Fig. 151 - The case was made as a simple turned part. It is closed by an IOS-signed snap back. The Milanese gold bracelet is soldered on.

Fig. 152 - Inside of the snap back. Reference 3565 is stamped at the bottom. The various watchmakers repair signs point to the good wear this watch got. Such markings are not allowed legally and prohibited by Patek Philippe.

Fig. 153 - The Milanese gold bracelet of the Reference 3565 has a special clasp, which makes it possible to securely fasten the band, at whatever length. However, with a hard steel ridge that touches soft gold each time you put the watch on, it is certainly not a technically perfect solution. But this has not disturbed anyone so far; quite the contrary, this watch is in great demand with collectors.

Austerity measures were also applied to the cases. The bezel is turned and snapped on. The case middle was made as a compact turned part with a matching flange for the snap back. The case diameter is exactly 35.0mm. The crown setting is half recessed. After loosening the winding stem, the bezel, dial, and movement are taken out upwards. For wearing, the watch has a soldered Milanese gold bracelet with a special clamp clasp. The bracelet was 17.5mm wide at the watch-attachment and 15.4mm at the clasp. The special clasp allows fastening the band along its entire length, so it always fits different wrist sizes (Fig. 150-153).

The snap back is die-stamped and turned. The material thickness is 0.50mm. Savings also had to be made on the movement caliber 27-460 M, so the small seconds hand was omitted. However, it could not be made with any more limitations, and the movement could well be the most valuable part of the entire watch. The "small Helvetia" is stamped on the case underside by the "9". On the snap back are, from the top, the company name "PATEK, PHILIPPE & Co", "-GENEVE-", and "SWISS". Vertically arranged below are, the casemaker's mark, the purity notation "18K/0.750" and the "large Helvetia",

Fig. 154 - The "Backwinder" series includes five References: 3563, 3569, 3573, 3585, and 3586. We show the penultimate model here. The case not only has a very elegant shape, but is also the first to be given a sapphire crystal instead of the usual plexiglas. The blue dial and hand display and index markers in white gold go well with the white gold case. The case middle, 36.0 x 42.0mm, was made from one piece, the back, as in Fig. 151, screws on with a ring nut.

followed by the case and Reference number "3565 1", the latter exceptionally crowded by the case number. Watchmaker's repair notations are carved into the fine bead-blasted inside back. The mark of the casemaker is of the collective trademark no. 5 with key no. 2, standing for the firm F. Baumgartner, SA, Geneva, which closed down in 1973.

Looking at this watch today, with its special Milanese bracelet, a trained expert will immediately notice that it does not meet the otherwise high standards of Patek Philippe. Here is a definite bargain watch, which only gets its very high quality from its fine movement. The continued popularity of this model is probably because of collectors who want to complete their collections. The Reference 3565 1 had a predecessor, which was also made for IOS. This model was delivered in a slightly different version. This manual watch Reference 3562 1 had a smaller case of 33mm diameter and the 23'''-300 PM, instead of the automatic caliber 27-460 M. Due to the lack of date display and the unrecessed crown, this model can be easily distinguished from its successor. The previously criticized Milanese bracelet was also used for the predecessor of the IOS watch shown here.

The IOS watch shown was sold by Henry's auction house in Mutterstadt on September 27, 2008, for €5846.15. The owner had not decided on a refurbishing, because of the very high cost, as of editorial deadline. The Reference 3565 and its predecessor 3562 1 are frequently offered at international auctions. On March 16, 2004, at Antiquorum in Geneva, a Reference 3562 1 with manual caliber 23'''-300 PM was auctioned for CHF 7800 (movement number 1,149,316, case number 2,676,028). On October 24, 2004, a Reference 3565 1 with automatic caliber and original box was offered at the same auction house in Geneva and sold for CHF 10,800. Patek Philippe also sold the model Reference 3565 1 through its the normal distribution channels without the IOS imprint. Such a watch was offered by Christie's in Geneva on May 15, 2006, where it sold for CHF 7800 (movement number 1,129,384, case number 2,674,304).

To Wear: + To Collect: + For Investment: -

Reference 3585 (Figs. 154-155)

We now present a very elegant piece from the "Backwinder" series: the blue dial and white gold case give this watch an elegance exclusive to Patek Philippe. There were a total of five References in the "Backwinder" series: References 3563 (Fig. 145), 3569, 3573, 3585 (Fig. 154), and 3586. There are also many sub-models of these five References in many styles. The Reference 3585 was launched in 1970 and offered primarily on the American and Far Eastern markets. The model presented here was chosen also because of some particular features and its printed archive extract (Fig. 155). This tells us

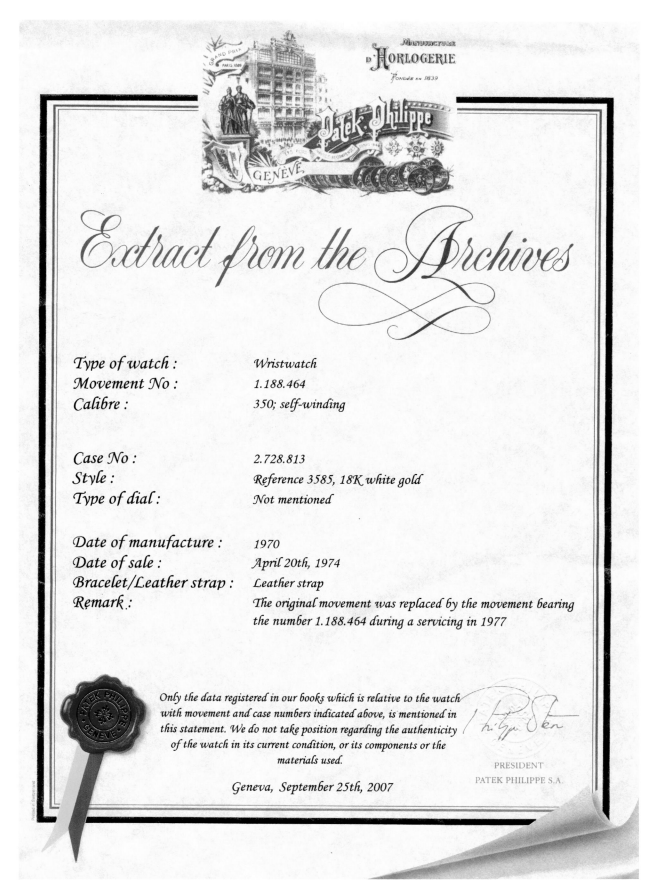

Extract from the Archives

Type of watch :	Wristwatch
Movement No :	1.188.464
Calibre :	350; self-winding
Case No :	2.728.813
Style :	Reference 3585, 18K white gold
Type of dial :	Not mentioned
Date of manufacture :	1970
Date of sale :	April 20th, 1974
Bracelet/Leather strap :	Leather strap
Remark :	The original movement was replaced by the movement bearing the number 1.188.464 during a servicing in 1977

Only the data registered in our books which is relative to the watch with movement and case numbers indicated above, is mentioned in this statement. We do not take position regarding the authenticity of the watch in its current condition, or its components or the materials used.

Geneva, September 25th, 2007

PRESIDENT
PATEK PHILIPPE S.A.

Fig. 155 - Full data on all manufactured watches are most carefully recorded at Patek Philippe, and can be requested at any time. The owner of the Reference 3585 at left sent the information about his watch to Patek Philippe in Geneva and received the "Extract from the archives" shown here. We learn from this extract that this watch was manufactured in 1970 and sold on April 20, 1974. More interesting, is the "Remark" that the watch was refurbished in Geneva after only three years of wear in 1977 and a new movement was installed.

that the watch is powered by the automatic caliber 350. The movement number is 1,188,464, with case number 2,728,813. The archive extract notes that the original automatic caliber was replaced with a new one during a customer servicing carried out in Geneva in 1977, when the caliber still in use today was installed. That a watch made in 1970, sold only on April 20, 1974, already required a new movement after only three years of wear, is hardly the high quality standard normally expected from Patek Philippe.

The watch dial is painted blue, as are the white gold index markers and baton hands. This is the first version to be fitted with a sapphire crystal.

The case housing, 36.0 x 42.0mm, is made from one piece, the back screwed on with a ring nut. The width of the band attachment measures exactly 20.2mm. We could not inspect either the movement or the inscriptions on the inside back, because the Ulm concessionaire would not open this watch.

Some comments on the "Backwinder" setting crown. With the crown in position 0, you can wind the movement; position 1 lets you adjust the time. The movement has no stop-second.

The back is opened in two steps. First, we must loosen the small cylinder head screw that holds the crown and remove it together with the crown. Using a special key, the ring nut can be loosened and, only then, the back, which is positioned by two notches at the "12" and "6", can be carefully removed.

This watch was purchased by a watch enthusiast for €3979 on the internet; because of the considerable costs it has not been decided whether to get the necessary Patek Philippe servicing.

Reference 3585 are rarely offered for sale. A Reference 3585 was auctioned at Antiquorum in Geneva on November 17, 2002, for CHF 6720. At Christie's in Rome on June 1, 2005, an identical model was sold for €6200.

To Wear: + To Collect: + For Investment: -

5.3 New cases and calibers – Not always an easy road to success (Reference group 3588-3700)

Reference 3588, the "Pope's watch" (Fig. 156)

We are now going to discuss a special watch with a somewhat mysterious history. Our description recounts what we were told by the owner of this rare piece.

In 1970, Hausmann & Co, Via del Corso 406, Rome, received a commission from the Vatican to deliver 12 Patek Philippe watches in a special design. The new, super-slim Automatic Reference 3588 was selected as a model. For this special design, the dial was to be painted in the Vatican's color, a special purple, rather than the normal style. The hour index markers were to be faceted, rather than printed Roman numerals. The distinctive faceting process lets the gold of the dial base show through, creating an almost mystical appearance for this watch.

Hausmann delivered the dozen watches to the Vatican in 1971, during the Pontificate of Paul VI, who, from 1963 to 1978, was the 261st Pope on the throne of St. Peter in Rome. At this time, Church prelates could receive one of these watches as a special honor, presented directly from the hands of His Holiness. An American cardinal, who was the great uncle of the current owner, was one of those who received this honor.

This watch is shown in Fig. 156, along with a complimentary ticket to the Papal mass celebrated on September 10, 2006, in Munich. The colors of both match exactly. That Sunday, Pope Benedict XVI celebrated the religious service that has become known in church history as the "Papal Mass in Munich", with more than 250,000 believers at the open grounds of the New Munich Trade Fair Centre.

The reader may certainly well ask, where the other eleven remaining watches are. Unfortunately, only the Vatican archives could answer that question.

Our "Pope's Watch", Reference 3588, is powered by the new automatic caliber 28-255. The movement bears the number 1,280,422 and the case is number 2,714,748. This watch was produced in 1970 and sold the following year. The dial is made of yellow gold. The surface of was galvanically silver-plated, given a sunburst finish, and finely painted.

The next step was to print the company name and national origin "SWISS". The dial was set on a dividing head and the 12 hour index markers faceted. In this case, the index markers are not faceted in V form, as the work was done on the Reference 3415 dial (Figs.88 & 91), but rather in a W form.

Technologically, it is simpler to facet a dial with a small seconds hand, because the hole for the small seconds can be used to fix the dial's position. This dial had no such bore, so it had to be clamped centrally, using the two dial feet, and under negative pressure. Only then can the engraver use the diamond tool to cut into the gold.

Our "Pope's watch" was analyzed under a stereo-microscope. This examination led us to the conjecture that the Vatican purple was applied as a second coating, over the first coating of the familiar blue color. The company name and the national origin were imprinted only after this second lacquering, which speaks again for the authenticity of the dial. The assumption is that, as only a small number of 12 dials were required, these were made from parts already in stock, then repainted in the color requested by the Vatican.

The case measures exactly 35.0mm in diameter, and despite the sapphire crystal, it is only 6.1mm thick. It has three parts: bezel, housing, and snap back. Presumably, the case housing, including the lugs, was stamped from one piece, turned, milled, and the surfaces finished.

The crown is slightly recessed, to protect it. The snap back is 0.5mm thick. The caliber 28-255 measures exactly 2.55mm in height, taking up only 42% of the total watch thickness. The rotor has a swing weight of 21-karat gold that moves in both directions.

A "small Helvetia" is printed on the snap back. The inscription on the bead-blasted inside back is arranged cleanly over the entire space. Stamped under each other are the "large Helvetia", the purity notation "18K/0.750", and the company name "PATEK-PHILIPPE & Cᵒ", "-GENEVE-", and "SWISS".

Below come Reference and case numbers and the casemaker's mark, collective trademark no. 5 with key no. 1. This stands for Ed. Wenger SA, Geneva, which shut down in 1992.

Our "Pope's Watch" was sent via Patek Philippe in Munich to Geneva for a servicing. The work cost €747.62 (invoice dated September 26, 2003). Patek Philippe at first refused to issue the requested archive extract, on the grounds that this watch movement and case number did not go together. Had

Fig. 156 - This picture shows not only the "Pope's watch", but also a ticket to the Papal Mass in Munich. According to the owner of this watch, his great-uncle, an American cardinal, received the watch as a special award from the hands of Pope Paul VI in Rome. The ticket, for the guests of honor to the Papal Mass celebrated on September 10, 2006, in Munich, has the same color as the dial of the "Pope's watch", the special Vatican purple.

the Holy See ensured that discretion would apply here, just as it is taken for granted in upper church circles?

To Wear: ? To Collect: +++ For Investment: ++

Reference 3588, a normal version (Figs. 157-158)

We have selected the following watch to give our readers a comparison of the "Pope's Watch" and a normal version of the Reference 3588. Here we must emphasize that Patek Philippe launched an entirely new generation of watches with the Reference 3588. The key point of this new generation is the flat design, which made it possible to compete with the new, widely produced quartz watches. At the same time, Patek Philippe adopted this new technology and launched not only the automatics with the super-slim mechanical calibers 28-255 and 28-255, but also watches with quartz caliber CEH beta-21. The design of these watches, such as the Reference 3597/1, was something that needed getting used to and they did not sell well at international auctions.

Fig. 158 - Comparison of Reference 3588, as the "Pope's Watch" (right) and as a commercial version. On closer inspection, we find that the lugs on the left watch are set slightly back on the case and no longer sharp-edged.

Fig. 157 - The Reference 3588 is the first watch with automatic winding mechanism, fitted with the super-slim caliber 28-255. With this Reference, Patek Philippe ushered in a whole new generation of watches. The most important point of this new line, was the flat design, to be able to stand up to the then-new, solid looking quartz watches. The watch shown here has a case diameter of 35.0mm and a thickness of just 6.1mm. The case has a snap back. The caliber 28 255 is impressive, with only 2.55mm height (movement no. 1,281,380, case no. 2,708,009).

Fig. 159 - With the Reference 3591, Patek Philippe continued a line newly launched in the late 1960s. This style includes simple shapes and flat cases. The white gold case has 33mm diameter and is closed with a snap back. The construction included the cylindrical design of this back, allowing integration of sealing ring, making the case watertight.

The automatic Reference 3588 here is from the U.S. and was acquired by a German watch lover for $4200. The movement has the number 1,281,380; the case number is 2,708,009. The dial was painted gold, and the company name, the Roman numerals, and the national origin "SWISS" were all printed. The golden baton hands were originally painted black. Due to the low height between the dial and sapphire crystal, no applied index markers were used. Some watches of this model came with enameled dials and fired Breguet numerals.

The movement, case, and hallmarks for this watch are identical to the previously described "Pope's Watch".

Models of the Reference 3588 frequently come up at auctions. On November 12, 2003, Antiquorum in Geneva offered one with a black dial and leather strap and sold it for CHF 8400. On October 16, 2008, a watch identical to the model presented here was offered by Antiquorum in New York and sold for $8400. Finally, on December 3, 2008, Christie's in Hong Kong offered a version with a soldered gold bracelet, which went for $12,151 (movement number 1,281,022, case number 2,713,435).

To Wear: ++ To Collect: + For Investment: +

Reference 3591, a new way (Figs. 159-161)

We can see a certain change in the design of Patek Philippe watches and cases at the end of the 1970s. Only a few models remained faithful to the classic style of the firm, sometimes with cost-saving changes. The Reference 3591 is one of these. It was manufactured with the designation 3591-1 with

soldered gold bracelet; as 3591-2 with a leather strap. The preferred markets were the USA and the Far East.

The Reference 3591-2 shown here is powered by the caliber 28-255 movement number 1,292,432. The case number is 522,745. The dial is made of white gold, has a sunburst finish, and is painted light blue. The Roman numerals, the company name and the national origin "0 SWISS 0" are printed cream. Patek Philippe could no longer explain why the designation usually used for gold index markers was printed on this piece. The white gold baton hands are also painted cream.

The two-part case measures 33.0mm in diameter. The case housing was manufactured as a turned part, the narrow lugs soldered on. The snap back is opened with a small lip. An O-ring set in the cylindrical part of the cup-shaped snap back makes the watch watertight. It takes some strength to open and close this back.

The caliber 28-255 is locked directly into the case with two brackets, and there is no separate movement retainer ring. On the outside of the case, the "small Helvetia" is stamped by the "9". On the upper inside back, printed in a row, appear the casemaker's mark (vertical), the purity notation "18K/0.750", and the "large Helvetia". Beneath come the company name "PATEK, PHILIPPE & Co" and "≡GENEVE≡". The national origin "SWISS" is missing. In the lower third come the case and Reference numbers. The inner surface is finely bead-blasted and the back is 0.5mm thick. The casemaker's mark is for the collective trademark no. 1, with hammer-head number 115. This stands for the company Manufacture Favre et Perret SA, La Chaux-de Fonds, which still exists today.

Fig. 161 - This nearly 15-fold magnification shows a detail of the caliber 28 255. In the foreground is the angular profiled rotor hoop, which runs on four vertically arranged ruby rollers. Also nice to see the are the balance cock with "KIF Antishock" shock absorber, Gyromax balance, and flat spiral. At the bottom left is the movement no. 1,292,432; to the right, the caliber designation 28-255 and, quite modest, the Geneva Seal. The very thin lugs are not soldered completely cleanly.

Fig. 160 - View of the Reference 3591 caliber 28-255 and inside back. The case originated as a turned part, the lugs are soldered. The rotor, consisting of an angular ring, the rotor carrier and a golden swing weight, catches the eye. Also clearly recognizable is the balance cock with Gyromax balance (movement no. 1,292,432, case no. 522,745). This example shows how expensive a rash internet adventure can be.

This watch is from Korea and was acquired by a German watch enthusiast for $2850 (approximately €2577.55) on February 24, 2003. Only after he received it did the collector realize that the movement was in rather bad condition. When the Korean seller was asked about these problems, which reduced the watch's value, he promised to pay for half of the repair costs. When the watch came back from Geneva six months later, the repair bill amounted to €3371.89. The restoration, at €1560, the movement plate (base plate) at €695, the exchange of the rotor for €410.50, and the replacement of the dial for €359 and the balance for €231.50 were the biggest items. The Korean seller did not respond to an e-mail informing him of the servicing costs, nor could he be reached by phone. A registered letter was subsequently returned marked "undeliverable". Thus, the German owner had to pay the full repair costs alone, meaning that purchase and repair of this watch had cost €5959.44.

Reference 3591-2 watches are not often for sale. A white gold version of our model was auctioned at Sotheby's in London on September 28, 2006, for £3840. At Antiquorum in New York on April 4, 2009, a yellow gold style with soldered gold bracelet was sold for $7200. A white gold Reference 3591-1, with integrated gold bracelet, was auctioned for CHF 7200 at Sotheby's in Geneva on May 12, 2003.

To Wear: + To Collect: + For Investment: +

Reference 3601 (Figs. 162-164)

We are presenting two interesting watches from the Reference group 3600, References 3601 and 3602. The latter watch was a small sensation, as we shall see later. Except for the dial and bezel, both watches are almost identical, yet these

Fig. 162 - The case design of the new generation of watches is well illustrated in this composite image of the References 3601 (right) and 3602 (left). We see on the opened back of the Reference 3601 the cylindrical part with its thin rubber gasket. The left case shows how the closed back fits. The small "lip" makes it possible to insert the small plastic spatula used as a lever when raising and opening the back.

two watches show completely different faces. First, however, the main data on these two watches. The Reference 3601 has the caliber 28-255 C with movement number 1,301,935 and case number 526,841. The Reference 3602 model has movement number 1,306,031 and case number 539,833. The movements are 4,096 numbers apart, the cases 12,992.

The 3601 dial is painted cream-white; the Roman numerals, the interval marks for the minutes, the company name and the national origin "SWISS" are printed. The penultimate "E" of "GENEVE" does not have a grave accent. The yellow gold baton hands are painted black. As with all newer Patek Philippe watches, sapphire crystals are standard.

This is a two-part case. The case housing with integrated bezel was stamped from a solid piece, turned, milled, diamondized, and satin-finished in some areas. For protection, the crown is half-recessed in the case. The case diameter is 33.0mm. The snap back design matches that of the Reference 3591 (Figs. 159-160) and is kept water tight with an O-ring.

As far as the case of this Reference 3601 is concerned, an unknown watchmaker made a complete botch of it. For some reason, when closed, the snap back threatened to rub against the rotor inside. Instead of looking to the cause, he set six granular points on the flange of the case back, creating an additional distance of just 0.05mm.

The movement is in excellent condition; this watch was exquisitely renovated by Patek Philippe. Although the movement cannot take a chronometer test, because the required small seconds hand is missing, the watch works spot-on. The hallmarks on this Reference correspond to those on the Reference 3591, since it comes from the same casemaker (Fig. 160).

This watch was acquired by a collector in the United States. The purchase price was $4609.99; shipping and import sales tax were additional. A complete servicing at Patek Philippe cost another €1868.06 (invoice dated May 19, 2003). The movement refurbishing at €813, the "Classic" buckle 14mm J at €231, and the barrel bridge at €136, were the biggest items.

Reference 3601 watches are frequently available for sale. At Antiquorum in New York, a yellow gold version was sold on June 22, 2000, for $4080. A yellow gold piece was sold on November 17, 2002, for CHF 7800 at the Geneva Antiquorum in Geneva. At Sotheby's in Geneva on May 12, 2003, a yellow gold Reference 3601 was auctioned for CHF 8160. In July 2010, an American antique watch dealer offered another yellow gold version for $14,000. Whether it was sold at that price could not be learned by our editorial deadline.

To Wear: ++ To Collect: ++ For Investment: +

Reference 3602 (Fig. 165)

The bezel and dial are the only external differences between the Reference 3602 and Reference 3601. The Reference 3602 bezel is decorated with the "*Clous de Paris*", or hobnail pattern. The Patek Philippe shown here does not have a normal dial, but a small work of art. The dial is made of two parts. Both inner surface and outer ring are decorated with "*Clous de Paris*". The basic dial is made of 18-karat gold, which was galvanically silver-plated. A yellow gold ring is applied, printed with the Roman numerals and the point markers for

Fig. 163 - The Reference 3602 dial is a work of art in itself. The lower hobnail-patterned area is gold and galvanically silver-plated. A gold circle holding the hour and minute display is set on this. The outer bezel is also in hobnail pattern. The golden Breguet hands emphasize the noble appearance of this watch (about 11-fold magnification).

Fig. 164 - Reference 3601 with the watch back in the foreground. The inside back is finely bead-blasted and is inscribed with the usual hallmarks and notations. The six points on the closing rim of the back are puzzling, however. It is likely that a watchmaker botched the job badly, wanting, for whatever reason, to increase the small case interior diameter by 0.05mm. We measured this precisely. The watch was made in production year 1974 (movement no. 1,301,935, case no. 526,841).

Fig. 165 - This Reference 3602 watch was manufactured in 1978 and sold on March 20, 1980, according to the archive extract. Something new on the watch back is the hallmark for the Vienna Convention of 1972 at the top. To facilitate the trade and export of precious metal goods, the then-EFTA countries agreed in 1972 to an international convention for examination and identification of precious metals, known as the Vienna Convention. This agreement went into force in Switzerland in 1975. This is also the reason that the new Reference 3601, manufactured in 1974, does not have the hallmark inscribed; back magnified approximately 3.3x; watch approximately 2.4x (movement no. 1,306,031, case no. 539,833).

the minutes. Breguet hands complete the noble appearance of this watch. You can admire this dial in all its glory in Fig. 162, 163 & 165. The case diameter is 33.0mm, the watch is 6.2mm thick and the material thickness of the snap back is 0.5mm.

This gem has been refurbished at Patek Philippe in Geneva, though the movement only needed a cleaning, lubricant replacement, and some adjustment. This servicing cost €680.34. The inscriptions on the bead-blasted inner back matches the previously described Reference 3601; the case was made by the same casemaker. What is new is the additional, post-1972 Vienna Convention gold hallmark: a symbolized scale with the number 750 (Fig. 37). This new hallmark is between the lower lugs with the "small Helvetia".

The watch is from the U.S. and was not previously known to the author. A German collector bought it on the internet on January 10, 2004, paying $5395 (approximately €4352.74). According to the archive extract before us, this watch was made in 1978 and sold on March 20, 1980. The special dial was noted there.

It is hard to find a Reference 3602 for sale. A version in yellow gold with white dial was sold on the internet on February 11, 2010, for exactly $7000. A white gold piece with a blue dial was auctioned on November 13, 2007, at Sotheby's in Geneva for CHF 13,750 (movement number 1,302,310, case number 530,344).

This information allows the owner of the special design Reference 3602 to estimate the value of his watch. It is certainly much higher than the two we described previously. There is a comparison of the two watches in Figs. 164 & 165. The snap backs display the respective inside inscriptions. On the Reference 3602, first comes the hallmark for 18K/0.750 gold introduced by the Vienna Convention of 1972. This agreement among the then-EFTA countries was signed in Vienna in November 1972 and came into force in 1975. This new hallmark (a symbolized scale printed with 750) took its rightful place on the Reference 3602 manufactured three years later. The Reference 3601, manufactured approximately four years earlier in 1974, still does not have this additional hallmark.

To Wear: + To Collect: ++ For Investment: ++

Reference 3700/1 Nautilus (Figs. 166-170)

The Nautilus is one of Patek Philippe's most spectacular watches. This sports watch was launched in 1976 and is still one of the most popular models. Patek Philippe did not originally plan this steel watch; its development reflects external initiatives. One such was the resounding success of the sports watch model "Royal Oak" made by competitors Audemar Piquet from Le Brassus. Another was the offer of "Royal Oak" designer Gerald Genta to create a classy sports watch for Patek Philippe. Although both watches were designed with half-shell cases, the "Royal Oak" initially received a better public reception because of its design. This was certainly due to the Royal Oak's clear lines and classic "porthole" face.

As to the Nautilus, even confirmed friends of the Geneva brand had difficulty getting used to its appearance and often opted for the competing product from Le Brassus. Today, however, the tide has turned in favor of Patek Philippe. You now have to dig a lot deeper into your pocket to buy a Nautilus Reference 3700/1

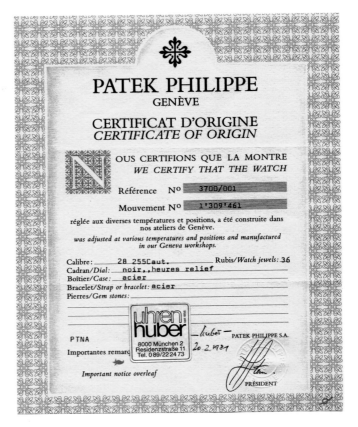

Fig. 166 - The Feb. 20, 1981, sales certificate for the 3700/1 "Nautilus" we describe here. It was issued by the Munich company Uhren Huber.

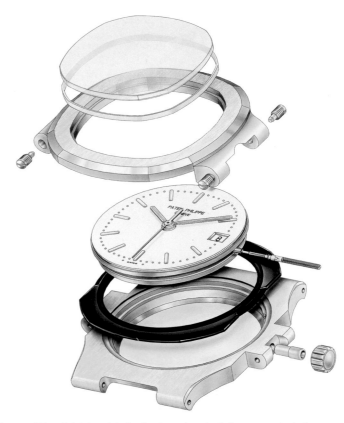

Fig. 167 - This exploded view of the Nautilus shows the entire design structure clearly. On page 191 we discuss the level of pressure the watch crystal had to withstand at 120 meters.

Fig. 168 - The Nautilus Reference 3700/1 has a mono-shell case with attached metal bracelet. The movement, fitted with the dial, is inserted from the top. You can see on the seal on the reverse bezel (movement no. 1,309,461; case no. 540,862).

from the 1970s and 1980s, also affectionately called "Jumbo", than for a Royal Oak from the same period.

At the very least, the Nautilus model let Patek Philippe appeal to those customers who sought a new, classy sports watch with its famous name.

The model Nautilus Reference 3700/1 was offered in steel, steel/gold, yellow and white gold, and, in limited numbers, in platinum. In addition to its futuristic look, the viewer's eye was immediately caught by its unusual case size. With a total width of a full 42mm (without the crown) the Nautilus was ahead of its time and an early pioneer in the lavish dimensions of today's watches.

The steel version presented here has movement number 1,309,461 and case number 540,862. It was purchased on February 20, 1981, at Uhren-Huber in Munich, Residenz Strasse 11, for exactly DM 5000.

The horizontally striped dial is anthracite. The index markers and both hands are made of luminous material applied by milling. The date display is by the "3".

The 42mm wide case almost looks like a porthole; some might say like a TV. It is made of stainless steel and has a very special design. There is an exploded image of the case and the watch in Fig. 167. The case was not optimally designed from the perspective of engineering mechanics and also of many

Fig. 169 - This detail of the Reference 3700/1 "Nautilus" shows the shape and surfaces of its somewhat unconventional design. The "Nautilus" was not envisaged in Patek Philippe product planning, but was proposed by watch designer Gerald Genta. He had previously created the famous sports watch "Royal Oak" for Audemars Piguet.

Fig. 170 - The "Nautilus" was launched in 1976 as a sports watch and is still one of the most popular models. Here, the Reference 3700/1 Nautilus is shown set on the cork box it came in when it was introduced. The sailing ship in the background excellently suits this particular watch.

watchmakers. A standard Patek Philippe real screw back would have been a better solution. The bezel is mechanically executed as a bridge in this mono-shell case. After the movement is installed, the bezel is mounted on the case and connected at both sides with two set screws. Cone-shaped screw heads have conical counterparts in the case to fix the bezel in position. The specially shaped seal guarantees the watch is waterproof to a depth of 120 meters. The tension on the four exactly aligned cones does not allow vertical pressure.

Therefore, the only thing that ensures water resistance is the flexibility of the special seal. Such a solution would likely only occur to a non-specialist designer, who only has an approximate understanding of technical mechanics.

With increasing external pressure, i.e., the greater the depth in the water, these noted design weaknesses tend to equalize, because the whole case is compressed from outside. The dial has to endure astounding forces at 120 meters below the water surface. At this depth the water puts 120 tons or 120,000 kg, of pressure on a square meter. That means, for the 6.7 cm² sapphire crystal surface, the weight is 6.7 x 12 = 80.4 kg.

The movement has the caliber number 28-255 C, which had been already installed in many Patek Philippe watches. The inscriptions on the finely bead-blasted inside back of the half-shell case are quite simple. Above is the manufacturer's name, "PATEK PHILIPPE", and "GENEVE". The case number is in the middle and the Reference number 3700/1 at the bottom.

The two case parts are made from one piece; the design is very labor intensive and expensive. This also goes for the upper part, which can be seen clearly in Fig. 168.

Now more than ever, the Nautilus is one of Patek Philippe's most successful models. The design of the case has been revised somewhat over the years and the two lateral extensions slightly rounded (Fig. 193). The range was extended to additional models, so that a full 16 pages is dedicated to this line in the 2001 Patek Philippe catalog.

The watch presented here belongs to a friend of the author. After 14 years he brought his beautiful piece back to the concessionaire Andreas Huber in Munich and commissioned a servicing. This customer service cost exactly DM 957, according to the service card no. 40467, dated May 10, 1995. The guarantee covers a period of six months.

The Nautilus Reference 3700/1 is often for sale at auctions. At Antiquorum in Geneva on November 15, 2005, a white-gold piece sold for CHF 78,000. At the same auction house in Geneva on November 11, 2007, the price for a stainless steel model attained CHF 36,000. On October 14, 2009, this auction house offered a golden yellow version, which changed hands for CHF 33,600.

From these auctions we can see that the steel "Jumbos" bring in sales prices similar to those for yellow gold models.

The Nautilus represents Patek Philippe's only watch line that has been on the program for around 35 years without a change in its outward appearance; therefore, we should also briefly mention the successor models here. The "Jumbo" Reference 3700/1 was followed by the somewhat smaller Reference 3800/1. Currently, again equipped with the manufacturer's own automatic movement caliber 335 with date display and sweep seconds hand, it is one of the its most famous "long distance runners". The successor Reference 3900/1 was initially fitted with a quartz movement and subsequently with the automatic caliber 330 SC. The 1991 price list shows the Nautilus Reference 3800/1 costing DM 9750 in steel, DM 35,300 in yellow gold, DM 37,550 in white gold, and DM 74,800 in platinum.

The current Nautilus is listed under the Reference number 5711/1. According to the 2009-2010 price list, the stainless steel model costs exactly €14,089. This price comparison demonstrates that a 30 year-old Nautilus Reference 3700/1 can command a price double that of a new model.

To Wear: +++ To Collect: ++ For Investment: ++

The description of the Nautilus completes the round up of wristwatches by the Geneva manufacturer which are worth collecting. It may have been desirable, here and there to present another model, but we attempted to pay attention to current taste and to the scope of this book. Chapter 6 is dedicated to the special rarities of Patek Philippe, which are extremely uncommon and equipped with complications. It can also be seen that the Patek Philippe watches are in demand far more than the models of other Swiss watch manufacturers and also command the highest growth in value and the highest prices.

6. Rarities and complications: Unprecedented record prices

Any involved watch enthusiast will have asked at least once, why Patek Philippe has achieved such a superior market position. And why it has taken this unsurpassable number-one position, with its apparently "uncomplicated" watches. Even the author cannot give any "correct" answer. After all, in the 1930s to the 1960s, next to Rolex and Vacheron & Constantin, there was no other renowned watchmaker on a par with Patek Philippe.

Had Vacheron & Constantin's former owner Georges Ketterer continued to work with the same determination and willpower as Patek Philippe's father Henri and son Philippe Stern, the Geneva-based brand today would be facing a serious contender for the top spot in the Swiss watch industry. But even before the change of ownership of Vacheron & Constantin in 1985, this story was ending in Patek Philippe's favor.

In this chapter, we are presenting eight watches with "small" and "major" complications. We consider "small" complications to be watches with special features, such as a chronograph. The "major" complications are watches with perpetual calendars and other special mechanical features. The hammer prices for these watches range from €148,000 to CHF 6,259,000.

After Patek Philippe's technical and stylistic detours in the late 1970s to early 1990s, the Geneva-based brand is today fully geared for success and has reached an outstanding level of advantage over other watch brands. Even Blancpain, resurrected and vigorously promoted with a lot of money, has not succeeded in even remotely competing in design and reputation. As evidence, we present two examples which occasion reflection about the watch scene. At Christie's in Geneva on May 10, 2010, a Blancpain manual minute repeater in yellow gold, was offered at auction and sold for CHF 25,000 (Reference 0033-1418-55, movement number XX/XXV, ca. 1988). The latest list price for this watch was €115,150.

A Blancpain perpetual calendar with minute repeater, automatic movement and platinum case, the finest of the fine, was sold at an auction by Christie's in New York on June 16, 2010, for $32,500, approximately €26,650 (Reference 5335-3427-58, movement number 0, ca. 1995). The latest list price of this model was precisely €150,540.

Reference 1527 (Fig. 171)

After this brief introduction, we shall now present the current record holder of this book. On May 10, 2010, at Christie's in Geneva, a Patek Philippe chronograph with perpetual calendar was auctioned. The watch was given the Reference number 1527, but this number was not inscribed in the inside back. The archive extract states that it was manufactured in 1943 and sold on August 27, 1946 (movement number 863,247, case number 634,687). An interesting feature of this watch is the inside back inscription, not discussed in the auction catalog. The "large Helvetia" and the purity notation "0.750" are in the upper quarter. On the bottom third are printed under each other, the company name "PATEK, PHILIPPE & Cº", "-GENEVE-", the case number, and the mark of casemaker, the collective trademark no. 5 with key no. 9. This stood for the company Emile Vichet SA, Geneva, which closed in 1960.

After a fierce bidding match, Arnaud Tellier, director of the Patek Philippe Museum in Geneva, won the two-bidder contest for his museum, paying exactly CHF 6,259,000.

To explain this Reference number 1527, it must be pointed out that a simple hand-wound watch was launched in 1942 under the identical Reference number. The watch was powered with the caliber 12'''-120. A year later, the model with center seconds hand and caliber 12''' SC followed.

Fig. 171 - The record holder of this book is the Reference 1527. This watch with perpetual calendar and chronograph was sold on May 10, 2010, for CHF. 6,259,000 Technically, this unique piece, made in 1943 is very close to the Reference 2499, also a perpetual calendar chronograph, shown in Fig. 173. In 1961, this Reference 2499 could be had for DM 3960, according to the price list. *Image Christie's.*

Fig. 172 - Reference 2438/1, a manually wound caliber 27 SC Q with "perpetual calendar." This model is one of the few watches with a screw back and six deep notches to open the back. The version shown here in pink gold was only manufactured in small numbers. It has a corresponding price: this watch changed hands on Nov. 12, 2007, for CHF 661,000. *Image Christie's*.

Of course, the auctioneer Aurel Bacs, out of discretion, would not tell us just who was the last underbidder for this lot. This chronograph with perpetual calendar is a unique piece, already well known for years, and was extensively discussed in the 1997 book with the original title *Patek Philippe: Orologi, Complicati da Polso*, on pages 102-105.

Reference 2438/1 (Fig. 172)

Whoever could freely spend DM 3555 in 1961, could buy a Patek Philippe Reference 2438/1 (in the inside back 2438-1). It was listed with this price on page 20 in the 1961 German Patek Philippe catalog.

At the Christie's auction in Geneva on November 12, 2007, this watch was sold for CHF 661,000. The dial and pink gold case are fantastically designed. When they are made by the Geneva brand to which this book is dedicated, such simply beautiful watches only succeed.

The Reference 2438/1 and its successor model 2497 were manufactured from 1952 to 1963, in all precisely 197 pieces were manufactured. The dials of these two References were identical, but not the cases. The case of the Reference 2438/1 has a diameter of 37.0mm and a screw back. The Reference 2497 is made with diameter of 37.8mm and has a snap back.

The hand-wound movement with perpetual calendar caliber 27 SC Q has the movement number 888,176 and case number 2,619,215. According to the archive extract, this rare piece was produced in 1959 and sold on March 21, 1964.

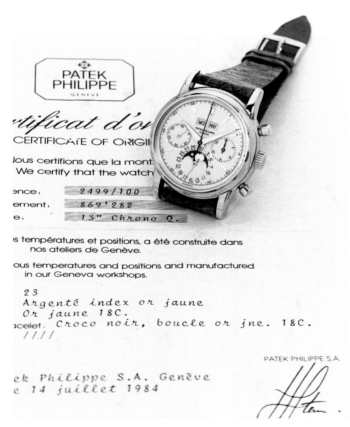

Fig. 173 - Only 379 copies of the Reference 2499 were manufactured from 1950 to 1985. You could buy this watch in Germany for DM 3960 in 1961. The guarantee certificate by the watch states that it was sold on July 14, 1984, the French national holiday, at the Geneva headquarters. This beautiful perpetual calendar with chronograph was auctioned on Dec. 12, 2008, at Christie's in New York and changed hands for $302,500. *Image Christie's*.

Most Reference 2438/1 models came with a yellow gold case. Only a minority, such as the piece shown here, were given cases of pink gold. This color difference is also reflected in auction prices, as can be seen by comparing with three examples of the yellow gold version. In Antiquorum in Geneva on April 23, 1995, a Reference 2448/1 was auctioned for CHF 85,000 (movement number 888,157, case number 2,619,196). On December 8, 2006, at Sotheby's in New York, a Reference 2438/1 was sold for $374,400 (movement number 888,099, case number 687,964). At Christie's in Geneva on May 10, 2010, a Reference 2438/1 attained CHF 327,000 at auction (movement number 888,105, case number 687,970).

One of the few pieces with a pink gold case came under the hammer on May 16, 2005, at Antiquorum in Geneva and changed hands for CHF 590,000 (movement number 888,174, case number 2,619,213).

All the Reference 2438/1 cases were delivered by the casemaker Ed. Wenger SA, Geneva. This company was registered under the collective trademark no. 5 with key no. 1, but closed down in 1992.

A final note on the Reference 2438/1. The literature and auction catalogs are haunted with the words "4th series with screwed back". This cannot be left unchallenged. All four series of Reference 2438/1 had the screw back case design shown here.

Reference 2499/100 (Fig. 173)

The Reference 2499 chronograph with perpetual calendar was launched in 1950 and remained in the program until 1985. Exactly 349 copies were manufactured; it was replaced by the successor model Reference 3970.

Reference 2499 was produced in four series. The cases for the first two series have square buttons; those of the other two series are round. The first series dials had a pulsation scale inside the minute circle; for the second series a tachymeter was inscribed outside the minute circle. The third and fourth series had the dial design shown here. The 1961 German Patek Philippe catalog showed a piece from the third series. The case diameter is listed there as 37.7mm and the price as DM 3960.

The model shown here is from the fourth series. It was produced in 1984 and sold on July 14 that year. The manually wound movement with chronograph and perpetual calendar has the designation 13''' Chrono Q, with movement number 869,282. The case bears the number 2,792,138.

The watch was auctioned on December 12, 2008 at Christie's in New York for $302,500. Demand was also high in 2009, as the following three examples demonstrate. A Reference 3499/100 in yellow gold attained CHF 260,000 on March 28, 2009, at Antiquorum in Geneva (movement number 869,398, case number 2,779,159, 4th series, production year 1980, and sold on June 30, 1980). At Christie's in Geneva on May 11, 2009, a piece in pink gold was offered at auction and sold for CHF 1,935,800 (movement number 868,752, case number 696,517; 2nd series, production year 1960; sold on October 30, 1963; made for concessionaire GOBBI MILAN). On December 14, 2009, at Patrizzi & Co. in New York, a yellow gold Reference 2499 was auctioned for $720,000 (movement number 868,598, case number 696,510; 2nd series, production year 1957; sold on June 18, 1960).

Fig. 174 - This somewhat unusual picture shows a yellow gold Reference 1518 from the back. The case measures 35mm in diameter, less than the Reference 2499, which is 37.7mm. The snap back can be seen from both outside and inside. The caliber 13''' Chrono Q is shown in full detail. A buyer was prepared to pay $272,500 for this watch with perpetual calendar and chronograph on Dec. 12, 2008. *Image Christie's.*

Reference 1518 (Figs. 174 & 175)

The first chronograph with perpetual calendar was launched by Patek Philippe in 1941 and given the Reference number 1518; exactly 281 pieces were manufactured up to 1954. The Reference 1518 was the predecessor model to the Reference 2499. Given the special importance of this model, but also because of the incomprehensibly large price difference, we are presenting two examples in this chapter.

In contrast to Reference 2499, the Reference 1518 case diameter is only 35mm. The dials are identical in design and dimensions, because both are powered by the same caliber. The case is made in three parts, consisting of snap-on bezel, case housing, and snap-on back. The case housing was stamped from one piece, turned, milled and given the appropriate surface finishes. In contrast, the successor Reference 2499

has a turned case middle and soldered on band lugs. In the watch shown in Fig. 174, the caliber 13''' Chrono Q with movement number 867,360 is at work. The gold case has the number 650,449. According to the archive extract, this watch was manufactured in 1948 and sold on November 23 the same year. As was standard in 1948, the Reference number 1518 was stamped on the inside back.

The first Reference 1518 shown here was auctioned on December 12, 2008, at Christie's in New York, selling for $272,500. The second Reference 1518 pictured in Fig. 175 was highlighted in the Christie's auction catalog, as one of the best-preserved specimens of this model. However, we have to take into consideration that generations of "polishers" have left their mark on the "small Helvetia" stamped on the case housing by the "9", because the hallmark is barely recognizable any more (see Figs. 92 & 93)). This watch

Fig. 175 - Perpetual calendar chronograph 1518 in yellow gold, produced in 1942. The Christie's Geneva auction catalog described this watch as one of the best preserved pieces of the Reference 1518; it was sold on Nov. 12, 2007, for CHF 945,000. The imprint *"Calendrier Perpetuel"* on the two day and month windows deserves special attention. *Image Christie's.*

Fig. 176 - The Reference 1463 was the first waterproof chronograph by Patek Philippe with round push pieces and a 34.5mm case diameter. This model, launched in 1940, was well received from the beginning and remained in production until the end of the 1960s. Stainless steel models often trade higher than those with gold cases. The upper version in pink gold was sold on Nov. 24, 2007, at Auktionen Dr. Crott for €150,000. The lower model in stainless steel with matching band was already mentioned in the Preface and attained CHF 529,000 at auction at Christie's in Geneva on Nov. 12, 2007. *Images Auktionen Dr. Crott and Christie's.*

has movement number 862,931 and the case number is 629,589. Also interesting is the dial marking *"CALANDRIER PERPÉTUEL"* above the two windows for day and month. According to the archive extract, the watch was made in 1942 and sold on April 21, 1943. There is also no Reference number imprinted on the inside back. On November 12, 2007, the watch was offered by Christie's in Geneva and sold for a substantial CHF 945,000.

Reference 1463 (Fig. 176)

The stainless steel Reference 1463 that we already discussed in the preface is shown in Fig. 176. Above, we present a pink gold model.

An importance piece of advance information for all those interested in this chronograph: in the literature and in the auction catalogs, the case diameter of this Reference is always given as 35mm. However, if you measure the diameter with calipers or a micrometer, you get exactly 34.5mm. This measurement is also listed in the Patek Philippe prospectus. If the chronograph you are looking at has a 34.5mm case

diameter, you can be reassured. This is not a watch that has had a lot of later reworking; it left the Patek Philippe factory with this diameter.

The chronograph Reference 1463 with manual winding and caliber 13''' was launched in 1940 and remained in production until the end of the 1960s. The case was made in yellow and pink gold and steel. According to the German price list for 1961, a yellow gold design cost DM 1915 and the stainless steel model cost DM 1350.

The chronograph Reference 1463 features a two-part case and screw back. The movement also has a dust cover. The case housing with integrated bezel is stamped from one piece, turned, milled, and given the specified surface finishes. The screw back is turned, milled, and fitted with a decagonal closure. The hallmarks on the inside back match those previously described, but the Reference numbers can only be found since 1948.

The first-pictured stainless steel piece has the movement number 868,840 and the case number 660,184. It was manufactured in 1955 with the dial marked "FRECCERO", and sold on March 14, 1957. FRECCERO S.A., AV Mayo,

Fig. 177 - The first watch with perpetual calendar and automatic winding mechanism was given the Reference number 3448; it was launched in 1962 and remained in the program until 1984. The white gold version presented here was sold at Auktionen Dr. Crott on July 5, 2008 for €148,000. *Image Auktionen Dr. Crott.*

561 563, Montevideo, Uruguay, has been a Patek Philippe concessionaire for over 70 years. The watch described here was auctioned on November 12, 2007, at Christie's in Geneva for CHF 529,000.

The pink gold version shown above has the movement number 868,532 and case number 672,788. It was produced in 1953. It was auctioned at Auktionen Dr. Crott on November 24, 2007, for €150,000.

Reference 1463 chronographs have interesting, but highly variable potential to increase their value. A steel version of this reference was auctioned at Antiquorum in Geneva on April 10, 2009, for CHF 180,000 (movement number 862,997, case number 625,762, produced in 1942 and sold on July 19, 1944). Christie's in Geneva auctioned a steel version on November 16, for CHF 459,000 (movement number 863,724, case number 640,561, produced in 1945). At Antiquorum in Geneva on April 10, 2009, a Reference 1463 in pink gold was auctioned for CHF 372,000 (movement number 863,918, case number 644,760 produced in 1946 and sold on July 9,1947).

Reference 3448 (Fig. 177)

This model with perpetual calendar and automatic movement was launched in 1962 and stayed in production for over 20 years. It is powered by the caliber 27-460 Q. It was indirectly intended to replace the models 2438/1 and 2497, which were being terminated in 1963. Exactly 586 Reference 3448 pieces were manufactured.

The Reference 3448 case is designed in three parts. The *snap-on* bezel is a turned part. The case housing was stamped from a solid piece, turned, milled, and given the specified surface finish. The inside back was turned and snapped on.

The case diameter is exactly 37.5mm and there is no explanation as to why 37mm is generally cited in the literature and in auction catalogs. In their time, these watches soon became known as slow movers and were, according to Martin Huber in Munich, difficult to sell.

Some Reference 3448 "exotics" were also manufactured. These included an estimated six pieces with no moon-phase; one version had a leap year display instead of the moon-phase.

The Reference 3448 attains good, but often varying results at auctions. The white gold Reference 3448 reproduced in Fig.

177 was auctioned on May 7, 2008, at Auktionen Dr. Crott in Frankfurt, selling for €148,000 (movement number 1,119,121, case number 322,471). On March 4, 2005, Antiquorum in New York offered a yellow gold version of the Reference 3448 with concessionaire mark "CARTIER", which sold for $230,000 (movement number, 1,119,087, case number 320,312).

Christie's in Geneva on November 17, 2008, auctioned a Reference 3448 in yellow gold for CHF 219,000 (movement number 1,119,088, case number 320,313). On March 29, 2009, at Antiquorum in Geneva, another yellow golden version was auctioned for CHF 95,000 (movement number 1,119,529, case number 332,897, produced in 1978 and sold on May 23 that year).

These eight watches and their auction results demonstrate both the opportunities and the risks that Patek Philippe's "large" and "small" complications present. The widely varying auction results for comparable watches are difficult to understand. Perhaps these different results can be explained on one side by the objective condition of the respective watch and the current demand on the other. Even the reputation of an auction house can play a role.

For this reason, a potential buyer should personally examine the desired watch before an auction, and go through our often-cited checklist in this book (see Chapter 8). With a consistent approach and systematic application of the knowledge this book provides, an investor can realize far better yields than from standard assets such as stocks, bonds, and securities. Perhaps reading dry stock market reports is less enjoyable than making a thorough study of this book.

This is because bonds and stocks are basically only fictitious values. In comparison with these, a fine wristwatch by Patek Philippe represents a tangible value. Of course, a collector's piece by Patek Philippe can experience major fluctuations in value over the years, but it never loses its real value.

Nevertheless, start first with small stakes, trying your luck with the References 570, 2508 and 2509, for example (see Figs. 41, 42, 62, & 65). Small gains are also enjoyable, especially as in 2010 the interest rate for fixed deposits fell to just 1%. You should only venture into the expensive "small" and "large" complications, if you really know the watch auction scene and can support your trading there on solid experience.

7. Watches from the current collection: Continuity and highest quality

Gisbert L. Brunner

New Patek Philippe wristwatches:
Always a worthwhile investment

Even if the competition does not want to hear it: when it comes to luxury watches today, for those who can afford it, there is only one name and that is Patek Philippe. This manufacturer has continuously built up an outstanding reputation over the course of 172 years and retained it with great care. For connoisseurs, this signature epitomizes not only the equivalent of real estate of an ideal position, it is, in this case, a whole that is far more than the sum of its parts.

Since 2010, without exception, the finest mechanisms of their own manufacture have been ticking in every Patek Philippe watch. In addition, the vertical range of manufacture of the Geneva luxury label is significantly more than 90 percent. Every watch movement, whether mechanical or electronic, presents a unique degree of technical perfection. The staff in the various workshops, with their years of watch making training and craftsmanship, refine each individual part based on strict quality standards. Edges are beveled at a 45 degree angle and steel parts polished many times and, partially satin-finished. Even seemingly mundane components, such as gear wheels, must also undergo these time-consuming procedures, with no ifs, ands, or buts. It goes without saying that all this expenditure of effort explains why so few pieces are manufactured at the House of Patek Philippe.

Best of all, the future purchaser never sees many of the parts finished in this careful manner. Whoever decides to buy a Patek Philippe watch, knows that he will not be getting a slick piece of deceptive packaging. This is guaranteed both by this image-conscious product signature and by the Patek Philippe seal on every movement. It is self-evident that the watch movement design also represents the "state of the art".

As owners and managers of a purely family business, Philippe Stern and his son Thierry are fully aware of their total responsibility for their heritage. Of course, even Patek Philippe must think economically. But profit maximization is not an objective to be pursued at all costs. Quite the contrary: Patek Philippe would prefer to refuse to deliver a watch, rather than letting it possibly get into the wrong hands. The company has a very consistent policy aimed at prohibiting any kind of "grey market" transactions. Patek Philippe watches can be found exclusively at hand-picked concessionaires or at a few of their own boutiques. The sales women and men working there are trained by Patek Philippe to be able to provide product-specific advice. After the sale, they are obliged to conscientiously fill out the warranty document, including the customer's name, since without this, the global warranty is no longer valid.

Patek Philippe will only deliver a complicated timepiece to one of its concessionaires if the name of the prospective customer is already known in advance. Patek Philippe would ruthlessly deal with any trickery or machinations, by withdrawing the concession. These facts and the fact that a Patek Philippe long in the future, when it has passed through the hands of several generations, will always be maintained and repaired, guarantees its unusually high sustained value. In collectors' circles, many models, including those such as the in-high-demand Reference 3970 manually wound, perpetual calendar chronograph, or the Reference 5170 chronograph, already cost more than the official price listing, even before the latest pieces are ready for delivery.

Fig. 178 - Chronograph with manual winding mechanism Reference 5170 in yellow gold. This model, introduced at the Basel World 2010, is kept on time by the manufacturer's own chronograph caliber CH 29-535 PS.

Fig. 179 - "Calatrava" Reference 5120 in 750 white gold. The dial and its back both gleam with
a restrained elegance one can find only at Patek Philippe.

Fig. 180 - The "Calatrava" Reference 5127 (right), compared to its predecessor model Reference 3998 from the 1990s. Both watches demonstrate a timeless beauty.

In general, the prices of special mechanical pieces continue to rise over the years. That has been the situation in the past and there is not the slightest doubt that it will continue to be so. A watch's sustained or even enhanced value is a pleasant side effect, but it should not be the decisive criterion for buying a Patek Philippe. Far more important is the purchaser's awareness of owning a largely handmade and exquisitely wrought masterpiece, which documents that, even in our fast-paced world, the good old values still exist. Whoever buys a Patek Philippe from the current collection to wear on their own wrist, is always well dressed. This watch will also equally impress the lucky heirs, since fine watch making never goes out of style.

Of course, Patek Philippe watches are not cheap, nor is there any desire to make them so, because what would ultimately suffer would be what the customer receives after their purchase. In this sense, a Patek Philippe is worth every dollar and cent of the price paid.

Uncompromising, from our own manufacture.

The Reference 5170 (Fig. 178)

With its first semi-industrially manufactured manual wound chronograph caliber CH 29-535 PS, Patek Philippe gave precedence to the gentler sex. The manufacturer dedicated this cushion-shaped Reference 7071 to them. But, at least since the Basel World 2010, the lords of creation are no longer excluded. They can enjoy the elegant retro Reference 5071J. This yellow gold model with a high potential for understatement, refers with its design to classic models from the 1940s and 1950s and with its Reference number to the legendary 5070, so fiercely sought by connoisseurs. The most significant features of this wonderfully nostalgic, 39-millimeter newcomer is the pulsometer scale, calibrated to 15 pulse rate. The installed movement, with "time-writing" function, shines with all its many innovations, as described elsewhere in great detail, despite its deliberate superficially conservative appearance.

Classic elegance: Patek Philippe's "Calatrava" Reference 5120 (Fig. 179)

We do not have to use many words describing the case, dial, and hands of this thoroughly classic white gold wristwatch with the memorable Reference number 5120. The design qualities simply speak for themselves. This starts with the bezel with "*Clous de Paris*" or, in plain English, hobnail pattern decoration and continues to the overall height of just 6.7mm, which is due to the automatic caliber 240. Since 1977, it has been gleaming in its height of just 2.40mm; with its micro-rotor, it is 2.53mm. With regular wear the 22-karat gold oscillating weight develops a power reserve of 48 hours. The winding and setting crown bears the "Calatrava Cross", which Patek Philippe adopted as a decorative hallmark at the beginning of the 20th century. Over many decades, however, its usage was rather irregular, and without closer association with the manufacturer's products. It was not until the 1980s that this symbol, which goes back to the four Spanish Military Orders of Alcantara, Calatrava, Montesa, and Santiago, acquired its comprehensive importance for Patek Philippe and its unique timepieces.

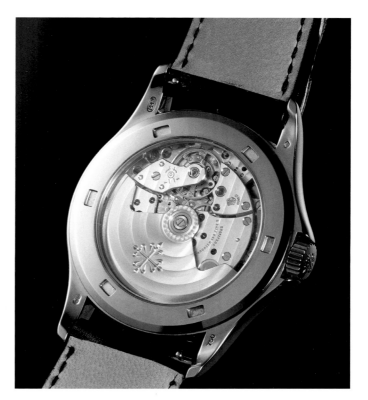

Fig. 181 - Reference 5127 seen from the rear. Its screw back with sapphire crystal has six die-stamped notches for opening the case. The caliber 315 SC has a Gyromax balance and gold rotor.

Plain and simple: The Reference 5127 (Figs. 180-181)

The Reference 5127 also bears the evocative name of "Calatrava" and it pays homage to the perception of the French poet Antoine de saint-exupéry, that perfection is achieved, not when there is nothing more to add, but when there is nothing left to take away.

Reducing the exterior to the essential is accompanied by a tremendous wearability, only made possible by the hand-made leather strap. Beyond that, the hand polished case fits snugly, without damaging your cuffs. The automatic movement 315 SC with solid gold rotor is made of 316 individual parts. As to gold, the price of this watch also comes from the sheer quantity of the yellow gold used to make it. Patek Philippe gladly leaves a cost-cutting approach to materials to other makers.

Patek Philippe "Travel Time": From cosmopolitans for cosmopolitans (Figs. 182-183)

Patek Philippe watches are traditionally worn by people around the globe. The manufacturer's cosmopolitan thinking created numerous pioneering achievements for world-time wristwatches. The "Calatrava Travel Time" combines the clarity and the easy handling of the classic Reference 2597 HS (*heure sautante* or jumping hour hand) with a second, independently adjustable hour hand. Inside the Reference 5134 case, Patek Philippe uses the 3.35mm high, hand-wound movement 215 PS FUS 24H. Two years of intensive development work were needed to equip the existing *oeuvre* with a total of 48 additional parts. These are set under the dial and require just 0.8 millimeters of additional height. At home the "travel watch", if desired, shows just one time, because both hour hands overlap

Fig. 182 - World travelers can have no better companion than the two-time-zones Reference 5134 watch. The black second hour hand can be adjusted to the respective local time using the push piece. The 24-hour display tells the wearer whether the time is day or night.

and move forward simultaneously. When you leave your home time-zone, the respective local time, represented by the dark hour hand, can be moved backwards or forwards in one-hour increments by using the corrective push pieces. A small 24-hour dial at the "12" shows whether it is day or night afar. Finally, a sophisticated protective mechanism prevents damage to the switching mechanism in the event that both push pieces are operated simultaneously.

All twelve months at once: Patek Philippe's "Gondolo Calendario" (Figs. 184-185)

The fine-sounding name "Gondolo" comes from Gondolo & Labouriau, a top Brazilian concessionaire, based in Rio de Janeiro. Between 1902 and 1935, the firm received no fewer than 22,264 timepieces from Patek Philippe. In addition to the classic three-hand "Gondolos" in different sizes, there were also pieces with 24-hour dial and chronograph.

Fig. 183 - Detail of the case with push piece to adjust the second zone time. The snap-on bezel, the case housing, and the two push pieces express the high level of craftsmanship.

Fig. 184 - Partial view of the "annual calendar" Reference 5135. Every detail is perfect; you could not make anything more beautifully.

Fig. 185 - Reference 5135 with annual calendar and white gold case. Behind the sapphire crystal screw back you can see the caliber 324 S QA LU 24H with gold rotor.

In those days, the Reference 5135 complications were still beyond the horizon. The Swiss Patent Number CH 685585 G for the intelligent annual calendar dates from March 1, 1996. This calendar takes into account and indicates the lengths of the month from March 1 to the end of February the following year. Three small windows in the upper half of the dial provide this information. A 24-hour hand rotates at the "6", facilitating calendar adjustment. Then there is the lunar disk, which will only diverge from the astronomical standard by one day after a good 122 years. The manufacturer's caliber 324, which is denoted 324 S QA LU 24 H in combination with this calendar, has a 45 hour power reserve. The Gyromax balance, with four spokes and Masselotte weights generates 28,800 oscillations per hour. The cushion-shaped, somewhat nostalgic white gold case has, of course, a sapphire crystal display back.

Fig. 186 - The Patek classics include the self-winding perpetual calendar. Below is the latest model Reference 5140 in yellow gold; above the previous model 3940, launched in 1985, also in yellow gold. The difference can be recognized by the different lengths of the index markers at "3" and "9". The expanded case diameter, from 36 to 37.2mm, made this possible.

Classic *par excellence*: The Patek Philippe Reference 5140 (Figs. 186-187)

Patek Philippe can and may count as the undisputed pioneer of watches with perpetual calendars. The debut of the first time piece of this complex genre was in 1925. The calendar-switching mechanism of the model sold in 1927 featured jumping indicators. From 1941, Patek Philippe offered small series of watches with perpetual calendars. In the beginning, these were with chronographs and later without. In 1962, Patek Philippe presented the world's first self-winding wristwatch with perpetual calendar (see Fig. 177). By 1985, the movement blanks for the central rotor-caliber 27-460 Q were used up. Because customers meanwhile were demanding significantly flatter models, Patek Philippe presented the new Reference 3940 in 1985. In the meantime, this, too, has found a worthy successor in the 37.2mm wide 5140 with the same caliber 240 Q. The calendar switch mechanism increases the height of the basic 240 caliber by just 1.35mm, to 3.88mm in total. In contrast to their opulent predecessors, the References 3940 and 5140 also have a 24-hour display which considerably eases the adjustment of the perpetual calendar. It is almost self-evident that this watch has leap year and moon-phase indicators, quality seals, and careful finishing of the approximately 280 components, all at the highest level.

Reference 5146: Patek Philippe's annual calendar in a larger guise (Fig. 188)

At this point, we do not have to say much about Patek Philippe's annual calendar. This wristwatch, which presents the days of the week and months in analog form with a hand, and the date digitally in a small window, has long been one of the modern classics. As attitudes have changed, men are increasingly demanding larger watch cases. Patek Philippe introduced the Reference 5146, among other pieces, at the Basel World 2005. Its red gold case, waterproof down to 25 meters and with snug-fitting qualities, now puts an astonishing 39 millimeters between the points of a caliper. The diameter increase, substantial as it is for Patek Philippe, is certainly not everything. It is accompanied by two new indicators. In addition to the known and proven, the red gold Reference

Fig. 187 - The Reference 5140 in nearly three-fold magnification, from the dial and back side. The sapphire crystal back reveals the various components of the caliber 240 Q. With the module for the perpetual calendar, this movement has an overall height of only 3.88mm.

Fig. 188 - Annual calendar Reference 5146 in a larger guise, bringing the whole case diameter to 39mm. The moon-phase also suits the watch very well.

Fig. 189 - The Aquanaut Reference 5165 in stainless steel with waterproof "tropical" band. The clasp design is especially interesting.

5146 presents the moon strikingly by the "6" and the power reserve below the "12". The latter is rather more discreet, because the automatic movement 324 S IRM QA LU with gold central rotor works very efficiently with regular wear.

For the Aquanaut's 10th anniversary: The Reference 5165 (Fig. 189)

Back in 1997, the year of its international debut, the steel Aquanaut, with its surprisingly modern design, created a sensation in the spectrum of the Patek Philippe collection. The eight-sided case with rounded corners neither can nor would deny the influence of the Nautilus model. Also notable are the black dial and the "tropical" strap of equally durable and water resistant composite material. This sporty wristwatch opened the door to the world of Patek Philippe for younger customers.

For the Aquanaut's ten-year anniversary in 2007, the basic model design was given a thorough refurbishing. A new feature of the anthracite dial was its embossed groove structure. The strap was changed to make it more comfortable to wear and was fitted with a new clasp with double safeguard. The "Large" version, Reference 5165, has the same diameter of 38mm as its largest predecessor. For good reasons, Patek Philippe did not change features such as the screw lock crown, waterproof to 120 meters, luminescent hands and index markers, "tropical" strap, and the automatic caliber 315 SC.

Fig. 190 - Annual calendar Reference 5396 R in 750 white gold. The design of the dial recalls the 1930s. References 96, 130, 419 and 437 watches also had dials in this style.

Fig. 191 - The Reference 5396 R with annual calendar features a three-part case with snap-on bezel and screw back. In keeping with tradition, the case housing is stamped from a flat piece of 750 white gold, turned, milled and given the intended surface. A masterful piece indeed.

Always the end of February: The Patek Philippe annual calendar Reference 5396 (Figs. 190-191)

Technically, Patek Philippe's mechanical annual calendars have long been considered modern classics. Just once a year, always at the end of February, it urgently demands the attention of its owner, who must re-set the sophisticated calendar mechanism manually to March 1. Because the times have changed even for Patek Philippe, the new Reference 5396R has a case diameter of 38 millimeters. But that is not enough. The calendar indicators also have a new form, but one which reflects the history books. As with the manufacturer's traditional calendar watches, the windows for day and month are close to each other. The date numbers move through a dial cutout by the "6". In addition, this gold wristwatch provides a 24-hour hand which rotates over the moon-phase display. The automatic movement is once again 324 S QA LU 24 H and consists of 347 components. Patek Philippe took its inspiration for the dial from a design from 1934.

Fig. 192 - Even from the Reference number 5196, you can guess the origin of this watch. It is the current successor to the Reference 96, launched in late 1934 (Fig. 39). The original 30.5mm case diameter has grown to a contemporary 37mm.

Fig. 193 - After 30 years, the striking Nautilus has lost none of its fascination. Above, we see the Reference 3700 /1, already presented in Fig. 170; below it is the Jubilee model Ref. 5711/1A, launched in 2006. Besides the sweep seconds hand, the new version has slightly rounded sides and, in lieu of the mono-shell, a three-part case. The constructively critical combination of the three case parts with four conic-topped set screws was retained (see Figs. 167 & 168).

Greetings to the Reference 96: Patek Philippe Reference 5196 (Fig. 192)

The mother of all Calatrava models from Patek Philippe was not particularly large, with its diameter of 30.5mm. In the green Patek Philippe archive books, this wristwatch, introduced in December 1934, is presented compactly as the Reference 96 (see Fig. 39). It was available with a variety of different dials. A small seconds hand rotated by the "6". The cases were made of yellow and red gold, platinum and steel. But it can no longer be said that the new, Retro-Reference 5196 with hand-wound movement 215 PS is small. Its case measures a modern 37mm. Nonetheless, Patek Philippe has not wavered from the classic design. Even the case materials have remained largely the same, except that now, instead of stainless steel, the even finer white gold is used.

Reference 5711: For the 30 Anniversary of the Nautilus (Fig. 193)

Philippe Stern described the development of the Nautilus in the mid-1970s, without much emotion. "Then we asked designer Gérald Genta to make a sports watch for Patek Philippe. We had a waterproof watch in mind". A long process followed. It took more than two years until the Nautilus was finished, and, even then, there was no resounding success in 1976. Maybe it was the price of the debut watches, which cost more in steel than a traditional gold watch. But it could also be that the misery was due to the *zeitgeist* of the era. Of course, the family firm did not give up without a fight. Finally, in 1998, the large steel models broke things open. Almost "overnight", demand exceeded the supply. The premiere model, with its two-piece, waterproof to 120 meters,

Fig. 194 - Annual calendar with chronograph Ref. 5960 P in a platinum case. This model got the first Patek-Philippe-manufactured self-winding chronograph caliber CH 28-520 IRM QA 24H.

"*monocoque*" steel case, 42mm diameter and 3.15mm high, was fitted with a Jaeger-LeCoultre automatic movement and bore the Reference number 3700/1. In 2006, on its 30th birthday, the classic Reference 5711/1A grew to 43mm in diameter. Its case, now three-piece, was given a sapphire crystal back, which could, at last, now adequately display the manufacturer's proven caliber 315 SC, self-winding movement with the 21-karat central rotor.

Long awaited: Patek Philippe's annual calendar chronograph Ref. 5960 P (Figs. 194-197)

"Good things come to those who wait", could be the motto of the genesis of the first automatic chronograph from the Patek Philippe factory. The caliber CH 28-520 IRM QA 24H has a ratchet-wheel control and "flyback" function. Four hertz balance frequency lets the chronograph hands move in eighth-of-a-second increments. A modern disc clutch accomplished the traction connection between the fourth wheel and chronograph hands. Due to the lack of gears, the hand does not jump at the start of the chronograph. Since the drop of the balance amplitude is likewise averted when the stop-mechanism is activated, this allows the chronograph to run constantly. This compensates for the absence of the small seconds hand. The restart of the chronograph is done simply via the flyback push button. Totalizers for the minutes and hours are concentrically arranged by the "6". The power reserve indicator and annual calendar, along with day/night indicators, are also there. A unidirectional gold rotor with zirconium ball bearing winds the 7.68mm high, 456-part movement (diameter 33mm). The power reserve is 55 hours. For the case of the first edition, Patek Philippe used discreet platinum. In the meantime, the case is also available in red gold.

Fig. 195 - Reference 5960 P as seen by the wearer. Three-part case with snap-on bezel, stable case housing, and twelve-sided screw back with sapphire crystal inset.

Fig. 196 - The platinum version 5960 P followed a model with red gold case Ref. 5960 R.

Fig. 197 - Annual calendar with chronograph Reference 5960 R from the front and back. The new Gyromax balance is interesting; it now has four shanks, but still only four Masselotte weights

Back in flight: The Nautilus flyback chronograph
(Figs. 198 & 199)

If a wristwatch remains almost unchanged for 30 years, that is a major achievement. In 2006, Patek Philippe celebrated the birthday of its sport classic Nautilus. On this occasion, the case had to undergo some technically radical measures. Though with similar features, it is, henceforth, not only a three-piece case, but semi-transparent, which means that the sapphire display back allows curious glances at the equally new chronograph caliber 28-250 C with self-winding, ratchet control, friction clutch, and concentrically arranged totalizers that go up to twelve hours and then return to zero, known by experts as "flyback". Its date window jumps promptly at midnight to the next day, within a tenth of a second. Manual corrections are required during months with less than 31 days. The Reference 5980/1A's robust stainless steel shell is a stately 44mm in size. No previous Nautilus was so opulent.

Fig. 198 - The Nautilus chronograph Ref 5980/1A has a 44mm case diameter.

Fig. 199 - The Nautilus chronograph Ref 5980/1A impresses not only by its great performance, but also by the new three-piece designed case. Bezel and case back are connected to the case housing by four set screws.

8. Buying a vintage
Patek Philippe wristwatch

Opportunities and risks

8.1 Checklist for buying a watch

Anyone ready to invest a five-or six-figure amount in a wristwatch, should plan his strategy carefully. That is why the following checklist was created. If a potential seller does not want to deal with these questions, he may not consider it necessary or he may have something to hide. In such a situation, it is up to the buyer to always take some time and consistently work through the checklist. A watch is bought quickly, but often difficult to sell again. The reason is obvious: the next potential buyer will probably proceed according to this checklist.

Here are the questions and criteria:

I. The dial
- Is the surface lacquered, gold-plated, solid gold, enamel, etc.?
- Design: index markers, Roman or Arabic numerals, Breguet numerals, etc.?
- Original condition, an original replacement, or refurbished? When refurbished, by the manufacturer (with certificate) or a third-party company?
- If it is a replacement dial, when was this done, and was it part of the manufacturer's servicing?

II. Movement (hand-wound and automatic)
- Are the caliber designation and movement number notation comparable to the watches listed in this book?
- Does the movement appear in mint condition?

- What is the movement's state of wear? Are screws holding the movement or other screws missing, are pinions and gear wheels run down, is the rotor bearing worn out, are there marks from the rotor on the plate or case back?
- Are the oil and lubricant levels too low?
- Is the rhodium plating partially worn off the plates and bridges, and can you see the brass underneath?
- Are there rust patches or traces of water damage anywhere?
- How are the performance values (Witschi-time scales)?

III. Case (two-or three-piece, with snap or screw back)
- Are Reference and case numbers correct according to the examples in this book and in the right places?
- Do the diameter and other measurements correspond to the original examples and dimensions listed in this book?
- Does the inside back contain the correct hallmarks and other information, according to the examples in this book?
- If there are repair notations on the case back, how many are there and how can they be interpreted?
- Is the inside back sanded down or re-turned, to remove any possible repair signs?
- Is the material thickness still correct, or was the outside back trimmed?
- Are all the case edges still keen or are they rounded off?

IV. Functions
- Can the crown be pulled into the various setting positions?
- Can the time and date be adjusted exactly?
- Does the crown still have well-defined edges, meaning it was little used or is it worn?

Fig. 200 - Comparison of a genuine snap back and one which has been tampered with. The snap back below comes from the pink gold Reference 1491, Fig. 39, and is original. All information was printed with various stamps. The yellow gold snap back has been tampered with. Letters, numbers and other markings are engraved, that is, machine processed. Except for the lower case "i" in "SWiSS" and some other variations, almost everything was copied correctly. Only an expert would see the difference. The layman can, however, detect these manipulations with aid of a stereo microscope or by X-ray. This tampered with or faked back was sold on eBay on Jan. 26, 2010, for $531 (€390.15).

V. Model
- Is this model one of the classics listed here?
- Is the model design in contemporary style?
- Was this model manufactured in large or small numbers?
- For modern watches: is this model one of the new, limited styles, such as the annual calendar "Wempe 125th anniversary"?

VI. Papers and other documents
- Are the sales and warranty papers available, and are they issued and stamped by the concessionaire?
- Is there an archive extract from Patek Philippe? Was this issued for this watch model or are just the Reference, movement and case numbers included? The first is the only way to be able to verify that all information is correct and complete (see page 216).
- Are there any other proofs of purchase from antique watch dealers, repair and service invoices from the manufacturer, or other documents that allow making a reliable assessment of the condition and upkeep of this watch?
- Was the watch purchased at a public auction?

VII. Band and clasp
- Is the watch band original or a replacement from a secondary supplier?
- If the band is still original, is it little worn and does it still have a good appearance?
- For a gold watch with leather strap, are the golden spring bars still there (look with a fine wooden stick or toothpick by the spring bar on the side with the "pin")?
- For a leather strap, does it still have the original (golden) buckle?
- It is a fact, that a clasp of newer design is good and expensive (store price around €1800-€1900)

VIII. From the first owner or many previous owners
- Can you determine how many people owned this watch?
- For old watches, can you find out information about their origin and history?

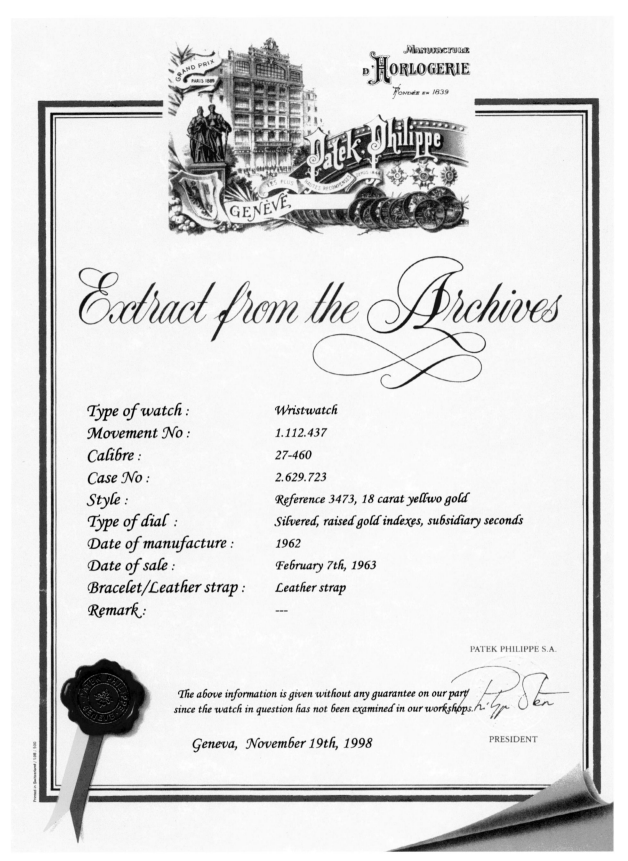

Fig. 201 - An archive extract includes all the relevant data for a watch. All production data is recorded in the Patek Philippe archives. Here, the watch was sent to Geneva and the extract requested as part of the servicing. On the dial (Type of Dial), the styling is described accurately and as appropriate for this watch. This document was dated Nov. 19, 1998 (watch in Fig. 121).

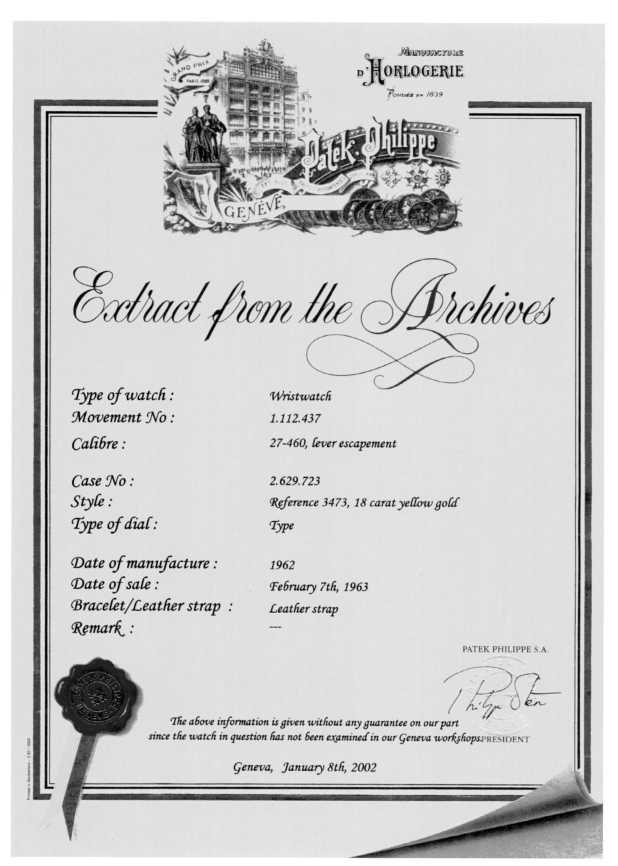

MANUFACTURE
D'HORLOGERIE
FONDÉE EN 1839

Patek Philippe
GENÈVE

Extract from the Archives

Type of watch :	Wristwatch
Movement No :	1.112.437
Calibre :	27-460, lever escapement
Case No :	2.629.723
Style :	Reference 3473, 18 carat yellow gold
Type of dial :	Type
Date of manufacture :	1962
Date of sale :	February 7th, 1963
Bracelet/Leather strap :	Leather strap
Remark :	---

PATEK PHILIPPE S.A.

The above information is given without any guarantee on our part
since the watch in question has not been examined in our Geneva workshops. PRESIDENT

Geneva, January 8th, 2002

Fig. 202 - Another archive extract obtained for the same watch some four years later. Instead of the watch itself, only the movement and case numbers were sent to Geneva. In the certificate dated Jan. 8, 2002, at the dial (Type of Dial) just "Type" listed. The document is signed by Philippe Stern, President.

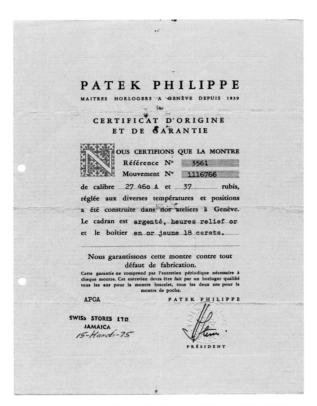

Fig 203 - The warranty certificate of the Reference 3561 shown in Fig. 143. It was sold by Swiss Stores Ltd, Jamaica, on March 15, 1975.

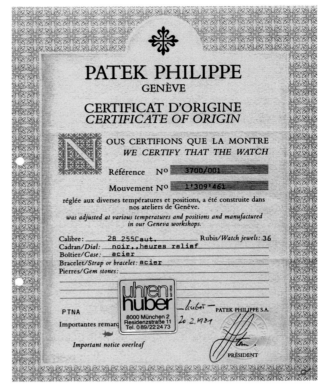

Fig. 204 - The warranty certificate for a Nautilus Ref. 3700/001, issued by Uhren Huber in Munich and signed personally by the owner, Martin Huber, on Feb. 20, 1991. This document is also signed by Henri Stern, the father of Philippe Stern.

IX. Accuracy, an important statement

– Is there a current Witschi measuring instrument log, which shows, from five or six positions, data on rate, rate deviation, balance amplitude, and the symmetry of the oscillation system (drop or symmetry)

– If this information is not available, can these measurements be obtained from or performed by a concessionaire with the right equipment?

– Is there information on previous servicing and related rate checks?

– Are there measurements of the case waterproof quality (measurement log)?

The measurement log illustrated here shows the accuracy of different watches. First, the mean rate is listed in six positions over 24 hours. The second position ascertains the mean amplitude. At the far right, the drop, i.e., the symmetry of the oscillating system, is listed. The first log comes from the Reference 2481 in yellow gold pictured in Fig. 57 (caliber 27 SC, lift angle 48°). The daily average rate (x) was close to +0.4 seconds and thus almost precisely accurate, whereas the average daily rate deviation (D) at 92.4 seconds is beyond the pale. The amplitudes in the four vertical columns are the only half the Reference value. This watch urgently need refurbishing.

The second log belongs to the Reference 570 in red gold in Fig. 41 (caliber 12'''-400, lift angle 46°). This watch loses 4.7 seconds a day. The mean rate deviation of 34.5 seconds is not acceptable. The amplitudes in the vertical area are too low. The drop of 3.6 demonstrates the lack of symmetry of the oscillation system. This watch must be serviced immediately.

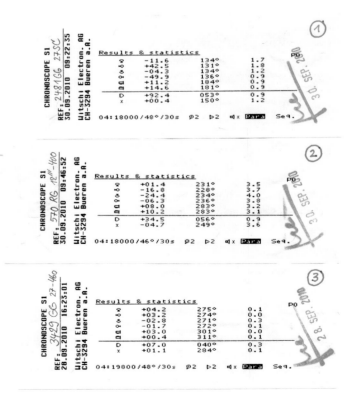

Fig. 205 - A test on the electronic Witschi rate test instrument is always the moment of truth for a watch. According to the measurement record at top, the watch urgently needed a refurbishing. The rate performance of the watch in the center measurement log is not bad, but certainly at no chronometer value. Here also, the watch should be taken to a good watchmaker. The rate values on the bottom measurement record correspond to chronometer specifications and are a testament to the best craftsmanship.

The third example shows the measurements of the Reference 3425 (caliber 27-460, lift angle 48°), shown in Fig. 101 (bottom). This watch was refurbished at Patek Philippe in Munich in 2003 and spent the following years in the safe. Despite this long period, this watch still attained chronometer values when this measurement was done. It gains about a second per day, reaches a delta of 7.0 seconds and amplitudes are in order. Also, the vibration system symmetry value is still correct.

A Patek Philippe guaranteed chronometer quality should not be more than 8 seconds day in the mean rate deviation in six positions. The amplitude should be in the vertical positions about 280° or above and in the horizontal position, approximately 260°. The drop for a refurbished watch should be around 0.1 to 0.2.

X. Legal considerations
- For private purchases, is the watch
  free from any third-party claims?
- Is the status of the watch in compliance with
  national customs and tax requirements?
- If the watch is shipped from abroad, have customs duties and
  import VAT been paid? If so, is the corresponding official
  documentation available?

XI. Purchase contract
- Did the seller offer an (informal) sales contract?
- Is all the relevant information about the seller listed in this
  contract, such as address, item, tax status, etc.?
- Is all the technical data, sales price, and the age
  of the watch listed in this sales contract?
- Does the seller give a warranty and a right of return
  within a stated deadline, in the contract?
- Does the seller guarantee the generally original
  condition in the sales contract?

XII. General information in conclusion
- Does the buyer or watch enthusiast really have a long-term
  affinity and special predilection for the model in question?
- Has the prospective buyer studied the market situation,
  and has he inquired about sales or prices of
  comparable models from other suppliers?
- Has the purchaser, before completing the deal, informed
  himself about market position, potential value appreciation, and
  brand recognition of the selected model?

The potential buyer should not accept any compromise, because he is paying the asking price without any ifs, ands, or buts.

8.2 Buying from antique watch dealers
One of the most obvious possibilities for acquiring a vintage Patek Philippe wristwatch, is to purchase one from an antique watch dealer. However, rules have to be observed here as well, and we list them below.

About 20 years ago, a watch lover was looking for a vintage watch, and bought one at an antique watch dealer in downtown Munich for exactly DM 11,000. This was a Patek Philippe Reference 3514 in yellow gold (movement number 1,123,062, case number 317,598; for examples, see Fig. 125).

The following text was handwritten on the dealer's invoice: "1 men's watch Patek Philippe 18 ct. automatic with leather strap and gold clasp. 1960s". Neither the Reference was noted, nor were the movement and case numbers listed. About three months later, the same watch enthusiast bought another automatic Patek Philippe from the same dealer and decided this time on a Reference 2552 in yellow gold (movement number 763,871, case number 697,802, see Fig. 82). On the invoice, again for over DM 11,000, the following text was handwritten, as before: "1 men's watch. Patek Philippe 18 ct. autom". Again the most important information was omitted and that is exactly what should be included for the purchase of such an expensive timepiece. In both instances, the watch dealer, himself a watchmaker by trade, emphasized with the deepest conviction that the watches were in excellent mechanical condition and the dials are still original.

To quote Lenin loosely, "Trust is good, verification is better". The proud watch owner, a few weeks after buying the second watch, visited Patek Philippe Customer Service in Geneva. There he presented the two watches and asked if they needed refurbishing. The Patek Philippe service staff person on duty was willing to take the two automatic watches to the workshop and seek the advice of his colleagues, only after a prolonged discussion with the watch owner.

After more than an hour's wait, Christophe Harsch, the service staff member, returned with the two now-open watches, and his colleagues' tidings. These were devastating. On both pieces, the dials had been renovated, but not according to the correct style. In the Reference 3514, production year 1965, the rotor was scraping on the screw back. The service staff had found eight repair notations, a testament to good wear.

As to the Reference 2552, production year 1957, the automatic movement 12'''-600 AT was in very bad condition. The replacement of the dial, refurbishing the movement, and correct renovation of the case for both pieces, cost about CHF 1200-1500. Lacking an alternative, the watches were left at the Patek Philippe in Geneva, with a commission for servicing.

Five months later, they were ready to be picked up in Geneva. For the automatic Reference 3514, the total costs were CHF 1260, with the movement refurbishing CHF 750 and the dial replacement CHF 465. The Reference 2552 servicing costs were even higher, at CHF 1530, with the movement refurbishing costing CHF 980 and the "best possible restoration of the dial", CHF 490. After this experience, the owner's joy in these two watches was no longer overwhelming. The Reference 3514 was valued at DM 12,000 and taken in part payment for the purchase of a much more valuable Patek Philippe. The antique Reference 2552, which after its visit to Geneva looked like new again, was sold to a Dutch ocean-going fisherman for DM 12,500.

This limited the damages for the Munich watch lover, and the new owners of these watches were actually satisfied with their purchases.

The Munich watch lover described here was, incidentally, the author of this book. Had he, 20 years ago, attended to everything in our checklist in this book, he would probably never had bought these two watches.

All in all, however, there are some clear advantages in buying from a dealer. You can take the watch in question in hand, examine the inner workings and pose all the relevant questions. There are grounds for the fact that comparable watches are often more expensive when bought from a dealer than on the internet. If these are not goods on consignment, the dealer must pay to buy the watches himself. The increased price is also due to operating costs, debt service, and the profit margin the dealer requires for his commercial success.

If you have found your dream watch at a dealer, the first issue for discussion should not be the price, but the watch's qualities. This is just where it would be a big advantage to take our checklist and go through it, item by item. When a five- or six-figure dollar/euro amount is under discussion, the dealer should certainly also be willing take the time necessary to take care of this potential business. Other customers are often quite willing to wait, if they can follow an informative sales discussion and even can learn something from it. Finally, this process means reaching a business deal that will be satisfactory for both sides – the best precondition for the next purchase. Anyone who has once caught the Patek Philippe bug, will not be satisfied in the future with just buying a single watch.

8.3 Buying at national and international auctions

The well-known auction houses offering valuable watches with international status, include Christie's, Sotheby's and Antiquorum, Patrizzi in Geneva, Ineichen in Zurich, and Bonhams in London, Edinburgh, Los Angeles, New York, and many other cities. There are also the Heritage auctioneers in the United States, as well as Dr. Crott in Mannheim and Henry's in Mutterstadt, both in Germany.

For the watch collector, the regular appearance of the auction catalogs is a real treat, especially since these catalogs contain excellent photos and the occasional in-depth information, and can be viewed via the internet. These insights allow for timely decisions about the intended purchases. Those who are on-site, can personally examine the watches before the auction and ask probing questions. Anyone who can only bid by telephone or on the internet, must rely on the descriptions in the catalogs. If the respective descriptions of the watches' condition, often formulated in specialized terminology, do not prove accurate after the purchase, the cards are stacked against the buyer.

In particular, this is because the auction house always sells watches for third parties, and thus is only acting as an intermediary. Once a watch is bought and the purchase price paid, it can become difficult to lodge any complaints about, and get recognition of, possible defects and associated problems that have only been identified after the sale. When the author himself was collecting high-quality, self-winding watches from Patek Philippe and Vacheron & Constantin more than 20 years ago, he attended in many Christie's, Sotheby's, and Antiquorum auctions in Geneva, London, New York, and Hong Kong. Being present on such occasions, a professionally trained eye can determine the differences between the actual state of a watch and its description in the catalog. It can never be fully established, just what a vintage wristwatch had experienced over 40 or 50 years.

If you want to bid for a certain watch at an auction by phone or over the internet, you should send the auction house a list of relevant questions about that watch, in good time. If the auction house only responds with the routinely created "Condition Report", you should insist emphatically on receiving the answers. A telephone conversation with the responsible "watch expert" has been established as a helpful measure. In such a dialogue, the competent expert will have the watch in question in hand and can answer the questions fully. It does not hurt to include the key statements in a caller record. When so much money is at stake, such as for a watch costing $20,000 or $30,000, you have every right to make demands on the relevant auction house; in no case should you be satisfied with blanket statements.

When your dream watch has been located, checked out, and bought at auction, what remains is the payment of the bill and the next appropriate steps. After payment, the watch will be sent to the bidder by insured high-value-item shipping. For international auctions, the auction houses often use specialist companies that take care of shipping and customs clearance. Charges for such additional services often amount to $150 to $250. In Germany, the customs duties are levied on the invoice value and the delivery costs; on delivery or pick-up these are billed and collected immediately. These charges currently include 19% import VAT and customs duties from €0.30 to €0.80. If a watch lover personally bought a watch at foreign auction, he must declare the watch at customs and pay the duty. If you fail to comply with these legal requirements, you are committing tax evasion.

We should briefly mention a special situation here. If a buyer bought his watch at Sotheby's in New York, for example, and took it to Germany just for testing and evaluation. Then, six months later, if he sent this watch to Christie's in Geneva, he could also decide to import this valuable piece just temporarily. For such a transaction, he needs an authorized forwarding agent, who specializes in the carrying out such business and is recognized by the Customs authorities. Fees for such transactions are not negligible.

8.4 Buying at a watch fair

The Munich Uhren-Technik-Börse (Watch Fair) has now become the biggest trading center for buying, selling, and exchanging wristwatches. It takes place at regular intervals at the Hotel Westin Grand Arabellapark. You can find exact dates for these events and information on other events and watch markets on the internet at www.trustedwatch.de. It is the author's view that watch auctions and watch exchanges complement each other very well.

At auctions, a broad public can choose among a wealth of previously tested watches. Prices are often correspondingly high. At watch fairs, rare pieces can turn up, which will only be discovered or recognized by an expert or specialist enthusiast. Unfortunately, these opportunities are becoming less and less frequent. The wide amount of information in the literature and media, and the growing interest in vintage watches, have ensured that such "lucky chances" now happen only rarely.

Fig. 206 - The regulator, that is, the entire vibration system, of a hand-wound movement caliber 27 SC in about 17-fold magnification. The fine adjustment of the regulator with a micrometer screw and swan neck spring, the "KIF" shock absorber, the Breguet spring, and screw balance wheel can be seen in full detail. This is also true of the caliber designation 27 SC and the Geneva Seal.

Nevertheless, watch markets provide many benefits for collectors of fine timepieces. You can examine the watch you want personally, compare price and condition of the Reference in question between multiple offerings, and finally make your decision. In some essential points, buying at a watch fair has clear advantages compared to buying at an auction. In contrast with the auction house, at the watch fair, you can negotiate the price and possibly make an exchange with another watch in payment. This is especially true if your current budget for your new dream watch is not large enough and you would like to use another, no longer so highly regarded, timepiece for payment. However, the risk of getting a "glamorized" or "faked" watch is several times greater at a watch fair than at an auction. Here also, you should use the checklist provided without any compromise, and go through it item by item, before making any decision. Should the seller you are dealing not accept this process, he will certainly have his reasons for that. Today, nobody has to anything to give away, least of all antique watch dealers.

8.5 Buying on the internet

If we take seriously the statement by the relevant department head at the Munich police headquarters that currently 40% of all fraud incidents happen on the internet, then special care is imperative. Despite this advance warning, we should not overlook that there is no other way of buying that presents both opportunities and risks so close together as buying online. This applies as much to the offerings on eBay (www.ebay.com) as for those you can find via Google (www.google.com). You might also find the collector's piece you are looking for on the already mentioned watch website www.chrono24.com.

As a test, we looked for a Patek Philippe Reference 2526 on those internet addresses in a time span of a few hours. No watch was listed on eBay worldwide. The Google search, on the other hand, was much more successful and we ended our test after finding four buying opportunities. The most interesting Reference 2526 specimen was found on the online auction house LIFEAUCTIONEERS website (www.lifeauctioneers.com). This was a model made for "Tiffany & Co", with movement number 760,001 and case number 674,917; it was sold on June 30, 1953. The movement number 760,001 tells us that we are dealing here with the second movement produced for this famous caliber. This watch was sold for $42,000.

There were six versions of the Reference 2526 offered on www.chrono24.com at this time, five of them in yellow gold, one in platinum. While the prices for the yellow gold versions ranged between €21,972 and €24,500, the Roman dealer with the platinum watch had only posted the note "price on request". When buying on the internet, the same rules apply in principle, as for other purchase methods. However, buying on the internet generally requires greater expertise. Anyone who does not wants to avoid a bad experience with Patek Philippe watches, should read this book very book carefully and only make their decision after making comparative assessments.

For a successful conclusion for your purchase attempt, it is best to carefully follow the following recommendations:

I.   If the seller's offer does not include all relevant information, send the seller an email requesting answers for all your remaining questions.

II.   When a very expensive watch is at stake, ask the seller to send you the movement and case numbers and compare the data with the Patek Philippe archive in Geneva.

III.   In any doubtful case, the best way to ascertain that this watch exists is by requiring the seller to send you a picture showing the watch lying on the headlines of a current newspaper.

IV.   In any case, before completing the purchase, you should communicate with the seller by phone, exchange addresses and phone numbers, and clarify how packaging and shipping are to be done. You should also ask on the telephone, if the buyer can pick up the watch personally.

V.   In countries posing higher risks, such as Indonesia, it is better not to buy anything.

VI.   If you made your bid on eBay at the last moment and got the sale, you should immediately contact the seller to get confirmation of the agreed terms.

VII.   Only use PayPal, a subsidiary of eBay, to make your payment. This payment method makes it possible for you to lodge a complaint if the purchased watch does not correspond to the description or has not arrived, for whatever reason. You have 30 days to clarify any issues or conflicts, and receive a refund if necessary. This way, you will not lose your money if this was a bad buy. You have to become a PayPal member, which is easy to do. It is also important that both partners are certified PayPal members. At all costs avoid making any payment by bank transfer or Western Union.

VIII.   Before payment and shipping, you should agree about the shipping method, costs, and customs declarations. Although significantly more expensive, FedEx, UPS, and DPD (German Parcel Service) offer shipping alternatives to the Post Office. These three named firms also take care of importation and customs clearances for foreign shipments, and, as commercial service companies, are usually much faster than the good old Post Office. There are also companies that specialize in high-value shipments. These can be found on the internet.

IX. Customs duties and import sales tax are payable when the item is imported. For example, if a watch is sent from the U.S. via USPS (United States Postal Service), it can often take weeks before you get a notice from the nearest Postal Customs office about the arrival of the expected shipment. Usually, you must pick up the shipment in person and pay the import duties based on the invoice issued by the seller. To avoid cheating, the Customs now require proof of payment such as PayPal, to calculate the import charges. Honesty is the best policy.

X. If the shipment has arrived and the watch has been unpacked in the presence of witnesses, you should then make a thorough examination; for an expensive watch with the help of an expert. In case of serious doubts about the authenticity or condition of the watch you should immediately contact Patek Philippe and make an appointment for an inspection.

XI. When paying via PayPal, you have 30 days to resolve conflicts. In the worst case, send the watch back to the vendor and have the purchase price refunded from his PayPal account.

XII. If the purchase of a newly acquired watch is completed successfully, you should let the seller know. On eBay, give a positive rating; for other purchase methods, send a friendly e-mail.

For purchases at a very high price range, for example, over $10,000 or $20,000, you should always arrange a personal handover date, such as at a local bank or at the nearest Patek Philippe concessionaire. This also gives you the opportunity to handle this purchase on a "cash for goods" principle, and so eliminate unnecessary risks. A "cheap ticket" overseas may cost $1000-$1500, but that is still much cheaper than taking a big loss on what was supposed to be a good business deal.

9. The professional refurbishing

(Servicing)

Anyone who drives an automobile and values reliability and a good state of repair will have no objection to following the maintenance guidelines recommended by the manufacturer. This principle applies both for the fuel-efficient four cylinder cars from Wolfsburg (VW) and the powerful eight cylinder cars from Untertürkheim (Mercedes-Benz).

If a car motor operated with an average rate of 3,000 rpms, that would mean a full 180,000 revolutions per hour. Operating three hours a day, 365 days per year, this all adds up to exactly 157.1 million revolutions.

When a watch operates at 28,800 vibrations per hour (vph), per day the total is 691,200 – a watch never stops; per year, there are a total of 252,288,000 vibrations. Various oils and grease ensure proper lubrication and keep the wear in check. In addition the watch should be handled carefully to prevent any unnecessary strain on the case and the mechanism. The watch should be taken off before bathing and put in a safe place, even if the manufacturer guarantees it to be waterproof to 120 meters depth. A far-sighted golfer takes off his watch before playing. If it is wrapped in a wool or silk cloth and safely stowed in a side pocket of the golf bag, a valuable watch will survive all 18 holes undamaged. But anyone who keeps his watch on, even if it is a sports model, is risking that, with every swing of his golf club, the balance staff and other sensitive components, will experience a shock-like, unacceptable level of stress.

Finally, a word about temperature. Of course, a good wristwatch can cope with several degrees below 0 (C) and even with desert heat. But a Patek Philippe wristwatch is not intended for, nor was it made for, these extreme conditions. These fine-quality Genevan watches are made to let their owners enjoy wearing them and tell the exact time in the most beautiful way. These small micro-mechanical miracles should be given a complete refurbishing every five to six years, even with only occasional wear, so that their special qualities can be maintained over decades. If, however, the watch gets regular wear, service-cycles of four to five years are recommended. A trained eye can see at a glance the oil level in the upper shock absorber of the balance shaft in an opened watch. If the lubricants are too low there, the same is true in other watch parts. A refurbishing is therefore imperative.

9.1 A refurbishing at Patek Philippe

The German branch of Patek Philippe is located in the heart of Munich (address: German Patek Philippe GmbH, Briennerstr. 12, 80333 Munich, Tel: 089 28 67 62-0). It has been open to the public since 2005. This branch's primary concern is supporting and supplying the concessionaires in Germany, and it has primary responsibility for the German side of the business. Anyone wanting to entrust his watch to this branch, but who lives too far away, can send it via insured post. The customer will immediately be sent a receipt, and a few days later an estimate for the desired or required work. Today, most Patek watches in Germany are serviced in the Munich workshop. Only a few complications and older watches are still sent on to Geneva for refurbishing.

Customers can personally take their watches in for refurbishing and repair to the Geneva headquarters (address: Salon Patek Philippe, Rue du Rhône 41, CH-1204 Geneva, tel. +41 22 809 50 50), now in full new glory after the total renovation in 2006. A watchmaker is always available for consultation and technical questions. Other service centers, located in around the world, can be found on the internet (www.patek.com). Patek Philippe certifies these centers up to a certain qualification level, beyond which the work will be

Fig. 207 - German Service chief Birte Zweiniger of Patek Philippe GmbH in Munich, surrounded by her team (in half-circle from left to right): Peter Luck, Johannes Joos, Stefan Huber, Harald Schmid and Michael Schlör. All members of the worrkshop team are qualified watchmakers. The three other team members, not shown, were not at the department that day.

done in Geneva. For example, anyone in Munich wishing to entrust his beloved wristwatch to a concessionaire, can do so at the jeweler Bucherer, formerly Huber, at Residenz Strasse 11, opposite the State Opera. A Bucherer workshop staff member is trained to work on Patek Philippe watches and can refurbish these valuable watches in-house, up to level 2.

Just what are the advantages giving a watch a refurbishing at Patek Philippe? There are two primary arguments that are not easy to refute. For one thing, Patek Philippe watchmakers work always and only with the products of their firm. Each move is repeated many times a day and can almost be done blindfolded. At the same time, if movement parts have to be replaced, there are no bureaucratic complexities or hurdles. There is no need for extensive study of descriptions of the caliber or laborious planning to get all the replacement parts. At Patek Philippe, the watchmakers go to the relevant cabinet and take out everything required, needing just a few minutes for this step. Many functional parts, that often are still in full working order, can be replaced simply on a preventive basis.

Finally, there is former President Philippe Stern's word of honor, which states that every watch, including those manufactured earlier, must meet the highest standards for precision and accuracy.

What more could any wearer of a beautiful Patek Philippe watch want?

After the issue of quality, the questions of costs and delivery time are also relevant for Patek Philippe customers. We can answer the first question from numerous, well-documented examples of repair work done, which allow interesting and detailed insights into such work.

With regard to the second question, it is not easy for Patek Philippe to give a satisfactory answer. Depending on the watch type and extent of the service work needed, delivery times usually range from five to eight months. If a dial has to be restored and there is no suitable spare part in stock, the waiting time can take even longer.

In conclusion, it is a matter of maintaining value. If a Patek Philippe wristwatch is renovated in their own workshop and the invoice on this work is available, this influences the watch's resale value quite significantly. In this case, even the equally qualified work of a concessionaire or its licensed workshop, counts only as second rank.

Fig. 208 - Watchmaker John Joos at his workplace.

9.2 Refurbishing at the concessionaire

Patek Philippe has defined several levels for watch servicing. These take into account both the watch's age and complexity the movement. These criteria also apply for Patek Philippe's own establishments, where many, but not nearly all, the References can be renovated.

There are, nevertheless, certain advantages in going to a concessionaire and having the refurbishing done there. First, the location is convenient even for such professional work, since the in-house workshop is usually located in the same building as the store. You can see the respective expert directly and ask for advice. The watchmaker knows the special aspects of the caliber and can competently provide the requested information. During the servicing, he usually has the most important spare parts on site and must order only special or rare components from Geneva. Depending on the size of workshop, one or two employees are specially trained to work on Patek Philippe watches, but, of necessity, also do refurbishments of watches from other manufacturers.

In this, a Patek Philippe watch has a lot in common with a fast, rear-engine powered car from Zuffenhausen (Porsche). With such a demand for high-grade work, only particularly qualified expert hands can achieve the required brand quality level without compromise.

This challenge can create a special opportunity for the concessionaire. If he has one or two talented watchmakers in his workshop and allows them receive ongoing training at Patek Philippe in Geneva, he can build up over time the same competence that Patek Philippe itself offers. This calls for some strategic planning by the concessionaire.

For comparable work, the concessionaire can ensure shorter delivery time. Service costs can be kept lower, if the concessionaire does not bill his client according to pre-set charges, but rather based on the actual time required. Another benefit for the concessionaire is marketing. With direct channels and personal contact with the customer, he can develop a relationship level that goes far beyond demonstrated competence and exact timing results. A customer satisfied with the servicing his watch received is likely to be on the lookout for a new watch; why not right there? A customer will definitely continue to do business where he feels comfortable.

RECHNUNG

PATEK PHILIPPE

U / Zeichen 04-03-0072

I / Zeichen

Rechnungs-Nr. G674

München, den 26. September 2003

Referenz: 3588J   **Werknummer: 1280422**   **Gehäusenummer: 2714748**

Leistungen:

Komplette Revision   453,00 €

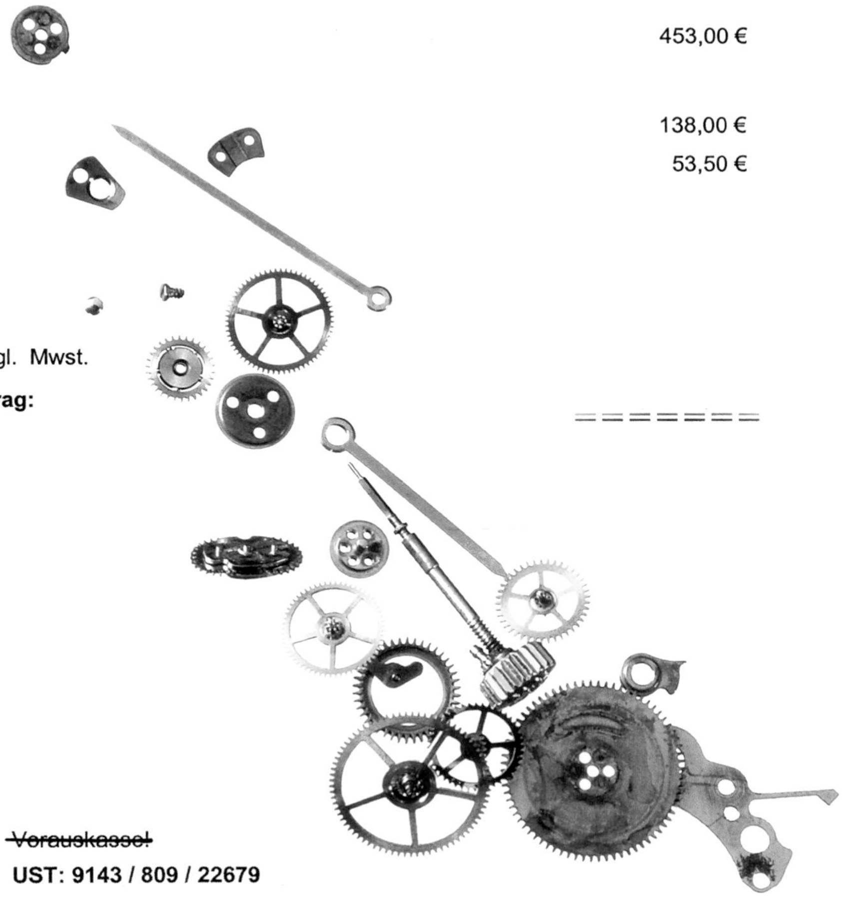

Ersatz:

    Federhausbrücke   138,00 €

    Zeigerspiel   53,50 €

Nettopreis

      zzgl. Mwst.

Gesamtrechnungsbetrag: =======

Zahlungsbedingungen: ~~Vorauskasse!~~

UST: 9143 / 809 / 22679

Auf obige Arbeiten gewähren wir 12 Monate Garantie

DEUTSCHE PATEK PHILIPPE GmbH
BRIENNERSTRASSE 12A D-80333 MÜNCHEN TEL. (089) 28 67 62 - 0 FAX (089) 28 67 62 - 20
GESCHÄFTSFÜHRER YANNICK MICHOT - REGISTERGERICHT MÜNCHEN HRB 121293 - DE 113837919
BANKVERBINDUNG: DEUTSCHE BANK MÜNCHEN - KTO.-NR: 4 176 806 - BLZ: 700 700 10 - www.patek.com

Fig. 209 - Renovation invoice including all the replaced parts of the refurbished movement.

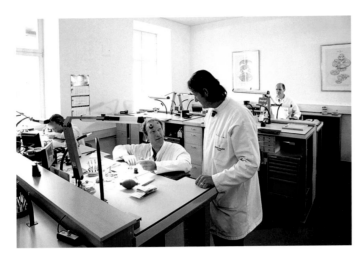

Fig. 210 - A view of the workshop at the German Patek Philippe GmbH in Munich.

Fig. 211 - A tableau of a watch maker's tools.

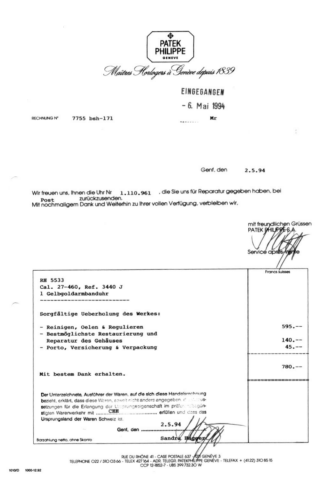

Fig. 212 - Refurbishment invoice from Patek Philippe in Geneva of May 2, 1994. The service was for an automatic Ref. 3440 J, costing CHF. 780

Fig. 213 - Refurbishment invoice for a Reference 3445 dated Jan. 22, 2003, carried out at the German Patek Philippe GmbH in Munich. Note the single item "rotor exchange" for €196.

9.3 Refurbishing at a trusted watchmaker

For a watchmaker, knowing a customer personally can be the secret of success and can often be considered a special marketing strategy. Anyone who not only has the technical skills and good work performance, but can also find time for a personal discussion, will be very accommodating to the special needs of a watch lover. The prerequisite for a long-

term customer relationship is always based on good and accountable performance as a watchmaker.

One collector, who also made watches available for this book, has had some watches serviced at a Munich antique watch dealer. However, after the work was done and paid for, when these watches were checked at Patek Philippe on a timing machine and a Witschi-gauge the results were very disappointing. Although the average rates were generally acceptable, the average daily

Fig. 214 - We can see total concentration in master watchmaker Peter Luck's gaze.

Fig. 215 - Master watchmaker Michael Schlör installing the center wheel of a hand-wound movement.

rate deviation and the amplitude and drop in six positions were in no way acceptable (see Fig. 209). On the other hand, a watchmaker near Pforzheim has successfully been renovating watches of outstanding brands like Rolex, Patek Philippe, and Vacheron & Constantin for years. This watchmaker has done excellent service work on some of the watches shown in this book and demonstrated his special competence.

Your trusted watchmaker must live with a small handicap. If the watch movement does not have any damaged parts and only needs a normal servicing, this watchmaker can deliver good work. If parts are required, which can be obtained from general suppliers (e.g., screws, springs, etc.), that is also no problem for him. However, when genuine spare parts are required, then things can get difficult. In Germany, only concessionaires can order spare parts from Patek Philippe, and even these are differentiated. What matters here, is which training level the responsible worker has already passed at Patek Philippe in Geneva, as we discussed in the previous chapter.

Essentially, what counts is the knowledge and the ability of each watchmaker, because the Gaussian distribution is as relevant for our watchmakers, as it is for doctors and engineers: Only about 10% of all participants make the grade.

What do we learn from this? If a vintage Patek Philippe wristwatch has not been seen by an expert for decades and work is necessary on the dial, movement, and case, the author would only entrust this beautiful piece directly to Patek Philippe. This is because the same professional groups who work together to manufacture a watch, also cooperate to carry out such an extensive renovation. The watchmaker is responsible for the movement and assembly of the watch. The casemaker takes care of manufacturing the case, and repairing it. The polisher ensures the correct case finish is

created, as well as well-defined edges. In Switzerland, every representative of these three professional groups must complete the company's own training, which takes a full three to four years at Patek Philippe. The strict division of labor among these three work areas is absolutely respected for service work at Patek Philippe, so that the company's same high quality standards are met for renovating a wristwatch as for the production of new watches.

When a normal servicing is due and you personally know the workshop manager at the nearest concessionaire, you can entrust your watch to him in good faith. If a watch needs work that does not require any replacement parts and watchmaking performance is paramount, your trusted watchmaker is the right choice. And because most vintage watch stores are operated by watchmakers and often have a wide range of older watches available, things can often move to buying another watch.

As we have seen, each of these three possibilities provide opportunities and risks.

A word in conclusion.

If a case is very battered or has deep scratches and other damage, some watchmakers tend to simply polish them off with a buffing wheel. This is the completely wrong thing to do, because such a "rape" of the case changes its original form and removes much valuable precious metal. In the example of Reference 3425 (Fig. 102) the responsible casemaker convincingly demonstrated how to repair the damage and bring the watch back to its original condition. This applies not only to correcting the shape, but also to restoring the original well-defined case edges. Unprofessional polishing with a buffing wheel gives a superficial gloss, but always with the drawbacks of rounded edges and a large loss of material (see Figs. 92 & 93). Of the three ways to have your watch serviced that we described, the laser method discussed on page 113, followed by correct contouring, is what should be used. The technique of lasering the material, turning, milling and diamondizing, is something mastered by only a few companies, which are found either near Pforzheim or the watchmaking strongholds of French-speaking Switzerland.

10. Value and value appreciation potential

In our preface, we presented the example of a simple chronograph Reference 1463 in stainless steel. According to the 1961 German sales catalog, this modest looking time recorder could be had for just DM 1350. At a Christie's auction in Geneva on November 12, 2007, a buyer paid a full CHF 529,000 for one of these watches (lot 35, movement number 868,840, case number 660,184, produced in 1955, seller's signature "FRECCERO", with steel bracelet; Fig. 176). At the same Geneva auction house, another version of this watch was sold on November 19, 2009, for CHF 459,813 (lot 85, movement number 863,724, case number 640,561, stainless steel, vendor signature "WALSER WALD", produced in 1945).

In both instances, if you had a savings account with 5% annual interest or an investment portfolio with a guaranteed annual return of 10%, with an initial capital of DM 1350, according to the Leibniz compound interest formula: $K_n = K_0 (1 + p/100)^n = K_0 q^n$ these two investments will earn the following (K_n = new principal, K_0 = initial capital, n = years, p = interest rate):

Example 1
Purchase from FRECCERO
(5% return on the savings account
or a 10% return for the portfolio)
$K_n = K_0 (1 + p/100)^n = 1,350 (1 + 5/100)^{46} = DM 12,736.25$
$K_n = K_0 (1 + p/100)^n = 1,350 (1 + 10/100)^{46} = DM 108,242.34$

Example 2
Purchase from WALSER WALD
$K_n = K_0 (1 + p/100)^n = 1,350 (1 + 5\ 100)^{48} = DM 14,041.71$
$K_n = K_0 (1 + p/100)^n = 1,350 (1 + 10\ 100)^{48} = DM 130,973.27$

In Example 1, the capital has increased by factors of 9.43 and 80.18. In Example 2, the factor values are 10.4 and 97.02. What would an investment advisor say about these figures?

If we take as another example the Reference 2585 in stainless steel, this time even the bankers would be awed (see Fig. 85). This watch was sold at Sotheby's in New York on October 28, 1996, for $11,500. On May 16, 2005, the same watch showed up at Christie's in Geneva, was offered for CHF 40,000 and finally sold for CHF 104,400 (approximately $85,195). Subtracting from this amount the commission and the premium, the seller still gained some CHF 73,080 or $59,636.50. Minus the previous investment of $11,500 in New York, the net profit came to $48,136.50. This means a 4.2-fold capital increase in barely nine years.

10.1 Watches from auction houses

We already listed the major auction houses at the beginning of Chapter 8.3 (see page 220). The price a watch can command depends on several criteria. First a word about the trend of the times, which depends on both the overall economic situation and the particular watch model. The supply of valuable watches only rose significantly in the mid-1980s. Prices for special wristwatches hit their peak around 1990 and fell by half during the economic slump of 1993. Subsequently, prices have been rising slowly but steadily.

Anyone wanting to buy watches at auctions, Patek Philippe watches in this case, must really know the specific piece offered and be able to estimate what the demand will be for the watch he intends to purchase. Auction participants come from various interest groups. Some are dealers wanting to increase their stock and resell the auctioned watch as quickly as possible. Then there are the collectors who want to expand their collections. There are also the rarity hunters, who want to track down and buy generally unknown, but valuable

Fig. 216 - A Christie's auction in Geneva. A rare unique piece was auctioned there on Nov. 13, 2006. The double chronograph with one push piece was made in 1925 for a left-handed person, and sold on Jan. 4, 1927. Chief auctioneer Aurel Bacs is looking at the scoreboard, which shows the watch and the current level of bidding, at CHF 1,000,000. In the end, this collector's piece, also shown at left, went for CHF 2,372,000. *Image Christie's.*

watches. Finally there is the group of bidders acting for third parties, who must follow their client's directives exactly. This includes the bidders sent by museums. At such auctions, a collector cannot expect any bargains, just cost- and value-oriented purchases for his collection. Such items are generally not suitable for prompt resale, since the other bidders at the auction would have made a slightly higher bid to gain the sale, if they had wanted that piece.

Final advice:

– For expensive watches, go to the auction a day early and use the opportunity for previewing the items.
– Take the checklist in this book with you and go through your most important questions with the auction house experts. You should bid only on that lot when you are convinced that you have found the right watch.
– Draw up a table of figures for the watches to be offered, showing what you want to be your last three to four bids (including buyer's premium) from left to right.
– Complete the bidding table using the following three bidding levels and highlight these in red; then, if you want to bid more at the last moment, you already know the full price.

Lot 242 (+ 20% buyer's premium)						
without premium	2,000	2,200	2,400	2,600	2,800	3,000
with premium	2,400	2,640	2,880	3,120	3,360	3,600
planned highest bid						

– Wait to make your last bid until just before the hammer falls.
– If you do not want to take the auctioned piece with you directly after the auction, arrange for shipping and insurance when you are making your payment. This way, you can save additional correspondence.
– The watch cannot be returned unless it turns out to be a "*marriage*" or fake. Any subsequent repairs are charged to the buyer, because pieces are bought as seen.

These steps can make buying vintage watches at auction houses somewhat more secure, but not necessarily very profitable. If you want to re-auction a watch purchased two or three years later, a consignment fee of some 20% will be deducted from the hammer price. Furthermore, the new owner must pay roughly a 20% premium. This means there is a difference of 40% between the sum you receive and what the new owner has to pay. A good example of this is the Reference 3454 (see Fig. 113).

10.2 Watches from watch fairs

Buying at an international watch fair can often be a good opportunity both to acquire a rare watch at a favorable price and with considerable value enhancement potential. A good example would be the Reference 3433 (see Fig. 105). A collector purchased this watch at the Munich Uhren-Technik-Börse (Watch Fair) for €4800. A critical aspect was that an incompetent "manipulator" had mounted a dial without a small seconds hand on this Patek Philippe, and the watch could be identified only by the inscriptions on the inside back. Patek Philippe charged exactly €3031.20 for the masterful restoration of this beautiful piece. With a total investment of €7831.20, the collector did not make a bad investment; on the open market, you cannot find Reference 3433 pieces for less than €10,000.

Shortly before this book's editorial deadline, a dealer offered an un-renovated Reference 3433 for €12,588. After prolonged negotiations, he parted from it for €11,000. There are no other models of the Reference 3433 on offer worldwide.

Nevertheless, our repeatedly-discussed checklist applies when buying watches with great appreciation potential. What use is a good buy, if, due to unseen technical defects, the watch cannot be resold for a profit, but only at a loss?

10.3 Watches on the internet

One thing first: Where the highest returns beckon, the greatest risks also lurk. A Munich watch enthusiast purchased a Patek Philippe Reference 2438 in yellow gold in Australia and paid $36,000. The apparently same Reference in pink gold can be found in Chapter 6, "Rarities and Complications", Fig. 172. After he had paid for the watch via PayPal in four part-payments, it arrived one week later. The supposed bargain hunter had his first doubts. Seeking help, he turned to the author and asked him for advice. Even a first glance showed that this watch was a mediocre "marriage". Only the caliber 27 SC was genuine; the module for the perpetual calendar had been taken from the watch of another maker. The case and the dial had been copied and in the cheapest possible way. Despite these findings, the watch had to be sent to Patek Philippe in Geneva for an evaluation, since PayPal would only allow a reverse transaction if there was neutral evidence. After returning the watch and waiting about 20 days, the Munich collector received refund in his PayPal account.

There was a small tragedy behind this story, as we learned later. A Korean engineer working in Australia had purchased this watch from a dealer during a visit to Los Angeles. In his complete ignorance, he had been persuaded that this piece was a rarity and he was getting a "bargain price" for a collector's piece at $25,000. However, in the meantime, he had become unsure about the purchase, and also needed money for his upcoming wedding. He wanted to get rid of this "marriage", unfortunately without success, as we have seen here.

We have already discussed how to proceed with internet purchases, in detail in Chapter 8.5, "Buying on the internet". Now, two examples of how one can indeed generate modest but, in terms of percentage, interesting gains.

A collector bought a Reference 2508 in yellow gold in the U.S. With an eBay price of about €6077.06 and €1155 customs duties, this watch had cost some €7232 (see Fig. 64). On www.chrono24.com, shortly before editorial deadline, two additional copies of this Reference were offered in Europe, for €18,000 and €19,000. If the collector, after the 12-month speculation period expires, wants to re-sell the watch with a markup of about 50%, he only has to generate an income of €11,000 in a direct sale. This should not be that difficult, because three Reference 2508 watches were on offer on eBay in the U.S., in addition to what is on www.chrono24.com. Two of these had yellow gold cases and one was in white gold. The immediate prices were $19,800, $18,950, and $40,000, of course, without the costs for repair and import duties.

Fig. 217 - An internet offering on the eBay portal. The Reference 3445 in 750 white gold shown in Figure 111, exactly matches the watch offered here. The initial offer of the seller from Taipei, Taiwan, was $12,500. We have not pursued whether or how this watch was sold. *Image eBay.*

Fig. 218 - Vintage automobile and watch enthusiast Hanns-Peter K. can have a good laugh. Both the beautiful Cabriolet 250 SE and the remarkable Patek Philippe Ref. 3445 can be considered good value investments. In a resale, these two cult status pieces from 1966 could bring in more than double their acquisition prices.

The hand-wound model Reference 570 is one of the current cult watches. A collector from Heidelberg purchased a pink gold Reference 570 with a small seconds hand for $6766 (about €5100) on eBay in the U.S. (see Fig. 41). Including shipping and import charges, he had to pay about to pay some €6136 for this piece.

In summer 2010, only one pink gold version of the Reference 570 was listed on www.chrono24.com. The vendor, Interwatches from Miami, Florida, USA, wanted $18,500 for this piece without shipping costs and customs duties. The next offer of a Reference 570 in pink gold, listed as "price on request", had already exceeded the last price entry of €23,500; it is exactly like the model shown Fig. 41. This offer came from a seller in Lugano.

At the same time on eBay, only one Reference 570 in pink gold with a small seconds hand could be found. This offer, also from the dealer Interwatches, was on www.chrono24.com. The purchase price was also $18,500. If our watch collector reckons in another €1600 for a servicing at Patek Philippe, his total investment for this watch will come to around €7736. If he wants to pass on this renovated piece after the 12-month speculation holding period, with a 50% markup, he would only have to demand €11,600 for a direct sale of this beautiful piece. Shortly before the editorial deadline for this book, the dealers Bachmann & Scher offered a white gold Reference 570 with caliber 27 SC for €23,500, and the company PrimeTimeWatches offered a yellow gold piece for €12,800. In neither case had the watches been refurbished at Patek Philippe.

10.4 Watches from private sales

Buying a watch privately can be problematic. However, should a valuable Patek Philippe emerge as part of an inheritance and the liquidator's asking price meets your budget, go ahead immediately. With many watches, the liquidator first goes to a dealer and has him appraise the watch collection. As a rule, the trustees will not agree to an immediate sale because there have to be at least two offers when a higher sum is at stake.

Other rules apply for transactions with acquaintances or friends. Accept an offer if the price is clear and understandable and you do not get the impression that your counterpart wants to make lucrative business deal for himself at your expense. Among friends and acquaintances, you do not make deals, but rather pass along a reasonable price, 1 to 1. Trust strengthens friendship.

If an acquaintance has to part with some valuable watches for financial reasons, you should not take advantage of this situation. Ask some dealers about the current purchase prices for these watches and make an offer to your friend based on that price. If he agrees to your asking price, you need not have a guilty conscience. The friend has a prompt and fair price for his timepiece and can extricate himself from his temporary financial hole, while the buyer has obtained watches at prices that he can realize on a later sales or exchange. You should consistently go through our frequently-cited checklist for such purchases.

11. References with commentary - Models from the 1930s to the 1980s

Compiled by Gisbert L. Brunner, revised and expanded by J. Michael Mehltretter

REFERENCE	FIRST MF'D	CASE/SHAPE/MATERIAL	CALIBER/FEATURES/SPECIALTIES
96	1934	ro YG, RG, PT, ST, WG/RG	C 12'''120, very large numbers
96 NC	1938	ro YG, RG, ST, PT	C 12 SC
96 SC	1936	ro WG, PT	C 11, normal calendar, rare
96 PC	1937	ro YG	C 11, perpetual calendar, retrograde date display, rare
96 HU	1939	ro YG	C 12''' HU, world time indicator
96 DD	1939	ro RG	C 12'''120, weekday/date display, rare
96 PO	1950	ro YG	C 12'''120, *Observatory Exemplar* special balance, rare
106		re YG, WG, K	9'''90, "Reverso", rare
130	1934	ro YG, RG, ST, PT, ST/RG	13''', chronograph
130 NC	1937	ro WG	13''', chronograph with normal calendar, rare
404	1935	re YG	C 9'''90, curved case, rare
405	1935	re YG	C 9'''90
406	1935	re YG	C 9'''90
409	1935	re YG	C 9'''90
410	1935	re PT	C 9'''90, rare
416	1935	ro YG, RG	C 12'''120
417	1934	re YG, PT, ST	C 9'''90
419	1935	ro YG	C 12'''120
420	1934	re ST/YG, YG	C 9'''90
425	1934	re YG, RG, PT	C 9'''90, large numbers
429	1935	re ST/YG	C 9'''90, rare
430	1935	re YG	C 9'''90, rare
431	1946	re YG	C 10'''200
433	1935	re YG	C 9'''90

REFERENCE	FIRST MF'D	CASE/SHAPE/MATERIAL	CALIBER/FEATURES/SPECIALTIES
436	1935	re YG	C 9'''90
437	1935	ro ST	C 10'''110 and 10'''200
438	1935	ro YG, RG, ST	C 10'''200, waterproof
439	1935	sq YG	C 9''' LeCoultre, rare
448	1935	ro YG, RG, ST	relatively large numbers
450	1935	re ST	C 9'''90
452	1935	re YG	C 9'''90
453	1935	ro PT/RG	center band lugs
461	1936	re YG	C 9'''90
462	1936	re YG	C 9'''90
467	1936	re YG, PT	C 9'''90
466	1936	re ST, ST/RG	C 9'''90
469	1936	re YG, PT	C 9'''90
470	1936	re YG, PT	C 9'''90
471	1936	re YG	C 9'''90
477	1936	re YG, PT	C 9'''90
478	1936	re YG	C 9'''90
482	1936	sq YG/PT	C 9''', LeCoultre., sapphire dial, rare
485	1936	ro YG	C 12'''120, adjustable band lugs
487	1936	re YG	C 9'''90, rare
490	1936	re ST	C 9'''90
491	1936	re YG	C 9'''90, rare
492	1936	re YG, RG, ST	C 9'''90
494	1936	re YG	C 9'''90, rare
498	1937	re YG	C 9'''90
499	1937	ro YG, PT	9''' LeCoultre, rare
506	1937	sq YG	10''', rare
514	1937	re YG, ST	C 9'''90
515	1937	re YG	10''' HU, world time indicator, rare
516	1939	re YG, YG/PT	C 9'''90
519	1937	re YG, ST	C 9'''90
520	1937	re YG	C 9'''90, rare
521	1937	re YG, PT, ST	C 9'''90, rare
524		re RG, RG/WG	C 9'''90, asymmetrical
525	1937	re YG	C 9'''90
526	1937	re YG	C 9'''90, rare
527	1937	re YG	C 9'''90, rare
528	1937	re YG	C 9'''90, rare
530	1937	ro YG, RG, ST	13''', chronograph
530	1938	ro YG, RG, ST	C 12'''120
531	1937	ro YG	C 12'''120
533	1937	ro YG, RG, ST	13''', chronograph
534	1937	ro YG, RG, ST	C 12'''120
534	1937	ro YG, RG, ST	C 12 SC
537	1937	ro YG	C 10''', rare
538	1937	ro YG	13''', chronograph
540	1937	ro YG	C 12'''120
541	1937	ro YG, RG/ST, PT	C 12'''120, rare, one piece with date display and moon-phase in PT
542	1937	ro YG	C 10''' HU, world time, rare 448
543	1937	re YG	C 9'''90, rare
545	1937	ro YG	C 9''' LeCoultre, rare
547	1937	ro YG	C 12'''120

REFERENCE	FIRST MF'D	CASE/SHAPE/MATERIAL	CALIBER/FEATURES/SPECIALTIES
551	1937	re YG	C 9'''90
556	1938	sq YG	C 8'''85
560	1938	sq YG	C 8'''85
562	1938	sq YG	C 9'''90, rare
564	1938	sq YG	C 12'''120
565	1938	ro YG, RG, ST	C 12'''120, waterproof
565	1942	ro YG, RG, ST	C 12 SC
570	1938	ro YG, RG, ST, PT	C 12'''120
570	1939	ro YG, RG, ST	C 12 SC
570	1939	ro YG, RG, ST	13''', chronograph, rare
572	1938	ro YG	C 12'''120, center band lugs
576	1938	sq YG	C 8'''85, motorist, rare
579	1938	ov YG	C 9'''90
584	1938	ro YG, RG	C 12'''120
588	1938	re YG	C 8'''85, rare
590	1938	ro YG, RG	C 10'''105, 10'''200
591	1938	ro YG, RG	13''', chronograph
592	1938	ro YG, ST	C 12'''120, rare
596	1938	sq YG	C 9'''90
597	1938	ov YG	C 9''' LeCoultre
598	1938	re YG	C 8.85, motorist, rare
1400	1938	re YG	C 9'''90, rare
1401	1938	re YG	C 9'''90, rare
1402	1938	re YG	C 9'''90, rare
1404	1938	sq YG	C 10'''105, rare
1406	1939	sq YG	C 10'''105, rare
1407	1939	re YG	C 9'''90, rare
1408	1939	sq ST, ST/YG	C 10'''110, hooded band lugs
1409	1939	sq YG	C 10'''105, rare
1410	1939	sq YG	C 10'''105, hooded band lugs, rare
1411	1939	sq YG	C 10'''105, rare
1412	1939	sq YG	C 10'''105, rare
1413	1939	ro YG	C 10'''105, rare
1414	1939	ro YG	C 10'''105, rare
1415	1939	ro YG, RG	C 12''' HU, world time, drop-shaped lugs
1415/1	1940	ro WG	13''', chronograph with manual HU, rare
1416	1939	ro YG, RG	C 12''' HU, world time, straight lugs., rare
1417	1939	sq YG, RG	C 9'''90, hooded band lugs
1418	1939	sq YG	C 9'''90, hooded band lugs, no second
1419	1939	sq YG	C 10'''105, center lugs, rare
1420	1939	re YG	C 9'''90, center lugs, rare
1421	1939	re YG	C 8.85, one movable lug, rare
1422	1939	re YG	C 9'''90, rare
1423	1939	re YG	C 9'''90, rare
1424	1939	re YG	C 9'''90, rare
1426	1939	sq YG	C 10'''105, center band lugs, rare
1428	1939	ro YG	C 10'''110
1430	1939	re YG	C 9'''90, rare
1431	1939	sq YG, RG, PT, ST, ST/YG,	C 10'''105, 10'''110, 10'''200
1432	1939	sq YG, RG, ST, ST/YG	C 10'''105, 10'''110, 10'''200
1434	1939	re YG	C 9'''90, rare
1435	1939	ro YG	C 12'''120, rare

REFERENCE	FIRST MF'D	CASE/SHAPE/MATERIAL	CALIBER/FEATURES/SPECIALTIES
1436	1938	ro YG, RG, ST	13''', Double chrono, until 1971
1436 PC	1952	ro YG	13''', *Rattrapante,* PC
1437	1939	sq YG	C 9'''90, hooded band lugs
1438	1939	sq YG, RG	C 9'''90, hooded band lugs
1439	1939	re ST	C 9'''90
1440	1939	re ST	C 9'''90
1441	1939	re ST/YG	C 9'''90
1442	1940	re YG, RG	C 9'''90
1443	1939	re YG, RG	C 9'''90
1444	1939	re YG, ST	C 9'''90
1445	1940	sq YG, RG	C 9'''90, no seconds hand
1445/1	1940	sq YG, RG	C 9'''90
1446	1939	ro YG	C 12'''120, rare
1447	1939	re YG	C 9'''90, rare
1448	1940	ro YG	C 10'''200
1449	1940	sq YG	C 9'''90
1450	1940	re YG, RG, PT	C 9'''90, large numbers
1451	1940	sq YG, RG	C 9'''90, rare
1452	1940	sq YG, RG	C 8.85, rare
1453	1940	sq YG, RG	C 10'''200
1454	1940	sq YG, RG	C 10'''200, rare
1455	1940	sq YG, RG	C 10'''200
1456	1940	re YG, RG	C 9'''90, rare
1457	1940	re YG, RG	C 9'''90, rare
1458	1940	sq YG, RG	C 10'''200, round lugs
1459	1940	sq YG, RG	C 10'''200, straight lugs, rare
1460	1940	re YG, RG	C 9'''90, hooded band lugs, rare
1461	1940	ro YG, RG, ST, ST/YG	10'''200
1463	1940	ro YG, RG, ST	13''', chronograph, waterproof
1464	1940	re YG	C 9'''90, rare
1465	1940	re RG	C 8'''85, rect. cross, rare
1466	1940	ro RG	C 10'''105, rare
1467	1940	re RG	C 9'''90, rare
1468	1940	re RG	C 9'''90
1469	1940	ro WG/RG	C 10'''110, hooded band lugs, rare
1470	1940	re YG, RG	C 9'''90
1471	1940	ro YG, RG	C 10'''200
1472	1940	ro YG, RG	C 10''', rare
1473	1940	ro ST, ST/YG	C 10'''200, 10'''-110
1474	1940	re YG, RG	C 8'''85
1475	1940	sq YG, RG	C 8'''85
1476	1940	re YG	C 8'''85
1477	1940	ro RG	C 10'''200
1478	1940	sq RG	C 8.85, rare
1479	1940	sq RG, ST	C 8.85, rare
1480	1940	re YG, RG	C 9'''90
1481	1940	sq YG	C 8'''85
1482	1940	re RG	C 9'''90, three-pt lugs
1483	1940	re YG, RG	C 9'''90
1484	1940	sq YG, RG	C 8'''85
1485	1940	sq ST	C 10'''200
1486	1940	sq YG/RG	C 10'''200, hooded band lugs, waterproof

REFERENCE	FIRST MF'D	CASE/SHAPE/MATERIAL	CALIBER/FEATURES/SPECIALTIES
1487	1940	re YG, RG	C 9'''90, rare
1488	1940	re YG	C 9'''90
1489	1940	sq RG	C 10'''200, C 10'''110
1490	1941	sq YG	C 8.85 C, date/month display via lug drums
1491	1940	ro YG, RG	C 12'''120, large numbers
1491	1943	ro YG, RG	C 12 SC, large numbers
1492	1940	ro YG, RG	C 12'''120
1493	1940	re YG, RG	C 9'''90
1494	1940	re YG	C 9'''90, rare
1495	1940	ro YG	C 12'''120
1496	1940	re RG	C 9'''90, rare
1497	1941	ro YG	C 12'''120 and 12 SC, rare
1499	1941	re RG	C 9'''90, rare
1500	1941	re RG	C 9'''90, rare
1502	1941	ro YG	C 12'''120, rare
1503	1941	ro RG, ST, ST/YG	C 12'''120
1504	1941	ro YG, ST	C 12'''120
1505	1941	ro RG	C 12'''120, calendar w/date, weekday, month, rare
1506	1941	ro YG, RG	13''', chronograph
1507	1941	sq YG	C 9'''90
1509	1941	ro YG, RG, ST	C 12'''120
1509	1941	ro YG, RG	C 12 SC
1510	1941	ro YG	C 12'''120, hooded band lugs, rare
1511	1941	re RG	C 9'''90, rare
1512	1941	re RG	C 9'''90, rare
1513	1941	ro RG, ST, ST/YG	C 12'''120
1513	1945	ro ST, ST/YG	C 12 SC
1514	1941	ro YG	C 12'''120, rare
1516	1941	ro YG, RG	C 12'''120
1516	1941	ro YG, RG	C 12 SC, rare
1517	1941	ro YG, RG	C 12'''120
1518	1941	ro YG, RG, ST	13''', chronograph PC, 281 pieces
1519	1941	sq YG	C 10'''200
1522	1941	sq ST	C 10'''110
1523	1941	sq ST	C 10'''110
1524	1941	re RG	C 9'''90, rare
1525	1941	sq YG	C 10'''110
1526	1941	ro YG, RG. ST	C 12'''120 PC, 210 pieces
1527	1942	ro YG, RG, PT, ST	C 12'''120
1527	1943	ro YG, RG, ST	C 12 SC
1527	1943	ro YG	13''', chronograph PC, one piece
1528	1942	ro YG, RG, ST/YG	C 12'''120, center band lugs
1529	1942	sq YG, RG	C 9'''90
1530	1942	re YG, RG, ST, ST/YG	C 9'''90
1531	1942	re YG, RG, ST, ST/YG	C 9'''90
1532	1942	re YG, RG, ST, ST/YG	C 9'''90, hooded band lugs
1533	1942	ro YG	C 10'''110, adjustable band lugs
1534	1942	ro YG, RG	C 12'''120, adjustable band lugs
1535	1942	sq YG, RG, ST, ST/YG	C 10'''200, 10'''105
1536	1942	ro YG, RG	C 12 SC, special drop-shape lugs
1537	1942	ro YG, RG	C 10'''110
1538	1942	ro YG, RG	C 10'''110

REFERENCE	FIRST MF'D	CASE/SHAPE/MATERIAL	CALIBER/FEATURES/SPECIALTIES
1539	1942	ro YG, RG	C 10'''110
1540	1942	ro YG	C 10'''110, hooded band lugs, rare
1541	1942	ro YG	C 10'''110
1542	1942	ro RG	C 10'''110, special curved lugs
1543	1942	ro YG, RG	C 12'''120
1544	1942	re ST	C 9'''90, rare
1546	1942	ro YG	C 12'''120, rare
1547	1942	ro YG	C 12'''120
1548	1942	ro YG	C 10'''110, rare
1549	1942	ro RG	C 10'''110, hooded band lugs, rare
1550	1942	ro YG	C 10'''110, hooded band lugs, rare
1551	1942	ro RG	C 10'''110, hooded band lugs, rare
1552	1942	ro ST	C 12 SC, with calendar
1553	1942	re YG	C 9'''90, rare
1554	1942	ro RG	13''', chronograph, movable lugs
1555	1942	sq YG	C 10'''110, rare
1557	1942	sq RG	C 10'''200, rare
1558	1942	re YG, RG	C 9'''90
1559	1942	re YG, RG	C 9'''90
1560	1942	re YG, RG	C 9'''90
1560/1	1942	re YG, RG	C 9'''90
1561	1942	ro RG	C 12'''120, rare
1561	1942	ro RG	13''', chronograph, rare waterproof
1564	1942	re YG, RG	C 9'''90
1565	1943	ro YG, RG	C 12'''120, hooded band lugs
1566	1943	sq YG, RG	C 10'''200
1567	1943	sq YG, RG	C 10'''200, 10'''110, 10'''105
1568	1943	re YG, RG	C 9'''90, rare
1569	1943	ro YG, RG	C 12'''120, large numbers
1570	1943	re YG, RG	C 9'''90
1571	1943	ro YG, RG	C 12'''120
1572	1943	sq YG, RG	C 10'''200, 10'''110, rare
1573	1943	re RG	C 9'''90, rare
1574(/1)	1943	sq YG, RG, PT	C 10'''200, 10'''110, 10'''105
1575	1943	sq YG, RG	C 10'''200
1576	1943	re YG, RG	C 9'''90
1577	1943	re YG, RG	C 9'''90
1578	1943	ro YG, RG	C 12'''120, 27 SC
1579	1943	ro YG, RG, PT, ST, ST/YG	13''', chrono.
1580	1943	re YG, RG	C 9'''90
1582	1944	ro YG, RG	C 12'''120
1583	1944	ro YG	C 12'''120, very distinctive lugs, rare
1584	1944	ro YG, RG, ST/YG	C 12'''120
1585	1944	ro YG, RG	C 12'''120, hooded band lugs
1586	1944	ro YG	C 12'''120, rare
1587	1944	ro YG, RG	C 12'''120
1588	1944	re YG, RG	C 9'''90, large numbers
1589	1944	ro YG, RG	C 12'''120
1590	1944	ro YG, RG	C 12'''120, large numbers
1591	1944	ro YG, RG, ST	C 12 SC, w/ PC, 12 pieces, waterproof
1592	1944	re YG, RG	C 9'''90, hooded band lugs
1593	1944	re YG, RG, PT	C 9'''90, large numbers

REFERENCE	FIRST MF'D	CASE/SHAPE/MATERIAL	CALIBER/FEATURES/SPECIALTIES
1594	1944	ro YG, RG	C 12'''120
1595	1944	ro YG, RG	C 12'''120, 12 SC
1596	1944	ro YG, RG	C 12'''120
1597	1944	ro YG, RG	C 12'''120
1598	1944	ro YG, RG	C 12'''120
2400	1944	re YG, RG	C 9'''90, rare
2401	1944	ro YG, RG	C 12'''120
2402	1945	re YG, RG	C 9'''90
2403	1945	re YG, RG	C 9'''90
2404	1945	re YG, RG	C 9'''90, large numbers 1539
2405	1945	ro YG, RG	C 12'''120
2406	1945	ro YG, RG	C 12'''120, 12'''400, (12 SC rare)
2407	1945	ro YG, RG	C 10'''200, 10'''110, 10'''105
2408	1945	sq PT	C 10'''200, rare
2409	1945	sq YG, RG, PT	C 10'''200
2410	1946	ro ST	C 10'''200
2411	1946	sq YG, RG	C 10'''200
2412	1946	sq YG, RG	C 10'''200
2413	1946	re YG, RG	C 9'''90
2414	1946	re YG, RG	C 9'''90 1549
2415	1946	re YG, RG, PT	C 9'''90, stepped case
2416	1946	re YG, RG	C 9'''90
2417	1946	re YG, RG	C 9'''90
2418	1946	ro YG, RG	C 12'''120
2419	1946	ro YG, RG	C 10'''200
2420	1946	ro YG, RG	C 10'''200
2421	1946	ro YG	14, minute repeater, rare
2422	1946	sq YG, RG, PT	C 10'''200
2423	1946	sq YG, RG	C 10'''200
2424	1946	sq YG, RG	C 10'''200, large numbers
2425	1947	sq YG, RG	C 10'''200
2426	1947	ro YG, RG	C 12'''120,1560
2427	1948	re YG, RG	C 9'''90
2428	1948	ro YG, RG	C 10'''200, large numbers
2429	1948	ro YG, RG	C 10'''200
2430	1948	ro YG, RG	C 12'''120
2431	1948	ro YG, RG	C 12'''120, large numbers
2432	1948	ro YG, RG	C 10'''200
2433	1948	sq YG, RG	C 10'''200
2434	1948	re YG, RG	C 9'''90
2435	1948	sq YG, RG	C 10'''200
2436	1948	sq YG, RG	C 10'''200, large numbers
2437	1948	sq YG, RG	C 10'''200, large numbers
2438	1948	ro YG	C 12'''120, with PC, rare
2438/1	1952	ro YG	C 27 SC, with PC, 179 pieces, with 2497, waterproof
2439	1948	ro YG, RG	C 12'''120, rare
2440	1948	re YG, RG	C 10'''200, large numbers
2441	1948	re YG, RG	C 9'''90, large numbers
2442	1948	re YG, RG, PT	C 9'''90
2443	1948	re YG, RG, PT	C 9'''90, large numbers
2444	1948	sq YG, RG, PT	C 10'''200, large numbers
2445	1948	sq YG, RG	C 10'''200

REFERENCE	FIRST MF'D	CASE/SHAPE/MATERIAL	CALIBER/FEATURES/SPECIALTIES
2446	1948	sq YG, RG	C 10'''200
2447	1949	sq YG	C 12'''120, 12 SC
2448	1948	ro YG	C 12'''120
2449	1948	ro YG	C 12'''120, large numbers
2450	1948	ro YG	C 12'''120, 12'''400, large numbers
2451	1949	ro YG, ST	C 10'''200, waterproof
2452	1949	m YG	C 10'''200
2453	1950	ro YG	C 10'''200
2454	1950	ro YG	C 12'''120
2455	1950	ro YG	C 12'''120
2456	1950	re YG	C 9'''90
2457	1950	ro YG, ST	C 27 SC, successor to Ref. 96 C
2458	1950	ro YG	C 12'''120
2459	1950	ro YG	C 12'''120
2460	1950	ro YG	C 27 SC
2461	1950	re YG, PT	C 9'''90, successor to Ref. 425, large numbers
2462	1950	ro G	C 10'''200
2463	1950	ro G	C 10'''200
2464	1950	ro G	C 10'''200
2465	1951	re G	C 9'''90, rare
2466	1950	ro G	C 27 SC
2467	1950	sq PT	C 27 SC, rare
2468	1950	re G	C 9'''90
2469	1950	to G	C 9'''90
2470	1950	to G	C 9'''90
2471	1950	re G	C 9'''90, cloisonné dial
2472	1950	sq G	C 10'''200, large numbers
2473	1950	sq G	C 10'''200, large numbers
2474	1950	sq G	C 10'''200, large numbers
2475	1950	sq G	C 10'''200
2476	1950	re G	C 9'''90, large numbers
2477	1950	re G	C 9'''90
2478	1950	ro G	C 12'''120, rare
2479	1950	re G	C 9'''90
2480	1950	re G	C 9'''90, hooded band lugs
2481	1950	ro	C 27 SC, rare, also w/ Cloisonne dial
2482	1950	ro	C 27 SC, also w/ Cloisonne dial
2483	1950	ro YG, RG, ST	C 12'''120, 27 SC, waterproof
2484	1950	ro G	C 10'''200
2485	1950	sq G	C 10'''200, rare
2486	1950	sq YG	C 10'''200, bezel RG
2487	1951	sq YG, PT	C 10'''200
2488	1951	sq YG, RG, WG, PT	C 10'''200, also diamond bezel
2489	1951	re G	C 9'''90, rare
2490	1951	sq G	C 10'''200
2491	1951	sq G	C 10'''200
2492	1951	sq G	C 10'''200
2493	1951	sq G	C 10'''200
2494	1951	ro G	C 12'''120, 12'''400
2496	1951	sq YG, WG, PT	C 10'''200, hobnail case, rare
2497	1951	ro YG, WG, PT	C 27 SC, w/ PC, 179 pieces w/ 2438/1
2498	1951	ro YG	C 12'''120, w/ PC, ex. Ref. 1526

REFERENCE	FIRST MF'D	CASE/SHAPE/MATERIAL	CALIBER/FEATURES/SPECIALTIES
2499	1951	ro YG	13''', chronograph w/ PC, 349 pieces
2499	~1980	ro YG	13''', double chronograph, rare
2500	1951	ro YG	C 12'''120
2501	1951	ro YG	C 10'''200
2502	1951	to G	C 9'''90
2503	1951	re YG	C 9'''90
2505	1951	ro YG	C 10'''200
2506	1951	ro YG	C 10'''200
2507	1951	ro YG	C 10'''200
2508	1950	ro YG, RG, ST	C 27 SC, waterproof
2509	1950	ro YG, RG, ST	C 12'''120, 12'''400, waterproof
2510	1952	ro YG	C 12'''120
2511	1952	ro YG	C 12'''400
2512	1952	ro YG	13''', chronograph-double large case
2512/1	1952	ro YG	C 27 SC, large case
2513	1953	sq G	C 10'''200
2514	1952	sq YG	C 27 SC
2516	1953	sq G	C 10'''200
2517	1952	re YG	C 9'''90, hooded band lugs
2517/1	1962	re YG	C 9'''90
2518	1952	re YG	C 9'''90
2519	1952	sq	C 9'''90
2520	1952	re YG	C 9'''90
2523	1953	ro YG, RG, WG	C 12''' HU, two crowns
2524	1952	ro YG	12''', minute repeater, rare
2524/1	1955	ro YG, RG, PT	12''', minute repeater, rare
2524/2	1958	ro YG	12''', minute repeater, rare
2525	1952	ro YG	C 10'''200
2525/1	1956	ro YG, RG, WG	C 12'''120
2526	1953	ro YG, RG, WG, PT	C 12'''600, automatic, waterproof, usually with enameled dial
2527	1953	sq G	C 10'''200
2528	1953	sq G	C 10'''200
2529	1953	sq G	C 10'''200
2530	1953	re G	C 10'''200
2531	1952	re G	C 9'''90
2532		ro YG, RG	C 12'''120, waterproof
2533		ro YG, RG	C 27 SC, waterproof
2534	1958	ro YG	14''', minute repeater, rare
2536	1958	ro	C 12'''400
2537		ro YG, RG	C 12'''400
2540	1954	sq YG, RG	C 12'''600, automatic
2541	1954	ro G	C 12'''400, waterproof
2543	1954	ro G	C 12'''400
2544	1954	ro G	C 12'''400
2545	1954	ro YG, WG, PT	C 12'''400, waterproof
2546	1954	ro G	C 10'''200
2547	1954	ro/to G	C 10'''200
2548	1954	ro G	C 10'''200
2549	1954	ro YG	C 10'''200
2550	1954	ro YG	C 10'''200
2551	1954	ro YG, RG, WG	C 12'''600, automatic, waterproof
2552	1955	ro YG, PT	C 12'''600, automatic, waterproof

REFERENCE	FIRST MF'D	CASE/SHAPE/MATERIAL	CALIBER/FEATURES/SPECIALTIES
2553	1954	re G	C 9'''90, extremely rare
2554	1952	re/to G	C 9'''90
2555	1954	ro YG, WG, PT	C 27 SC, waterproof
2556		ro YG	Lepine caliber 30, Bulletin de marche
2557	1954	ro YG	C 10'''200
2558	1954	ro G	C 12'''400, hooded band lugs
2559	1954	ro G	C 12'''400, hooded band lugs
2560	1954	ro G	C 12'''400, hooded band lugs
2561	1954	ro G	C 8'''85
2562	1954	sq G	C 8'''85
2563	1954	sq G	C 10'''200
2564	1954	sq G	C 9'''90, rounded edges
2567	1954	re G	C 9'''90
2568	1955	ro YG	C 12'''400
2569	1955	ro YG	C 12'''400
2570(/1)	1958	ro YG	C 27 AM 400, Amagnetic
2571	1955	ro YG	13''', Chronograph-*Rattrapante* w/ PC, (1930 –1938 movements installed)
2572	1955	ro YG	C 10'''200
2573/2		ro YG, WG, RG	C 10-200
2574	1958	re G	C 9'''90, rounded edges
2577	1958	ro G	C 10'''200 (2577 R-SCI w/ enameled dial)
2578	1958	ro G	C 12'''400
2579	1958	ro G	C 12'''400
2580(/1)	1958	re G	C 9'''90
2581	1958	ro YG	C 10'''200
2582	1958	ro G	27 SC
2583	1958	ro G	C 12'''600, automatic
2584	1958	ro G	C 12'''600, automatic
2585	1958	ro ST	C 12'''600, automatic, waterproof, extremely rare (3 watches known)
2586	1958	ro G	C 27 SC
2587	1958	ro G	C 27 SC
2588	1957	ro G	C 23-300
2589	1957	ro G	C 23-300
2590	1957	ro G	C 23-300
2591	1957	ro YG, WG, PT	C 23-300
2592	1957	ro YG, WG, PT	C 23-300
2593	1958	ro YG, WG, PT	C 23-300, waterproof
2594	1959	ro G	C 23-300, flat bezel
2594/1	1959	ro G	C 23-300, guilloche bezel, until 2594/11
2594/11	1959	ro G	C 23-300, guilloche bezel
2595	1958	ro YG, WG	C 23-300
2596	1958	ro YG	C 10'''200
2597	1958	ro G	C 12'''400
2597 HS	1958	ro YG, RG	C 12'''400 HS, one or two adjustable seconds hands
2599	1958	ro RG	C 10'''200
3400	1958	ro PT	C 23-300, diamond trim
3401	1958	ro PT	C 10'''200, diamond bezel
3403	1958	ro YG	C 12'''600, automatic, waterproof
3404	1958	sq G	C 23-300
3405	1958	sq G	C 23-300
3406	1959	sq G	C 23-300

REFERENCE	FIRST MF'D	CASE/SHAPE/ MATERIAL	CALIBER/FEATURES/SPECIALTIES
3407	1959	ro G	C 10'''200
3408	1959	sq G	C 23-300
3409	1958	sq YG	C 9'''90
3410	1959	ro YG	C 12'''400
3411	1958	ro YG	C 27 SC
3412	1959	fa YG	C 23-300
3413	1959	fa YG	C 23-300
3414	1959	sq YG	C 9'''90, prototype, linear time display
3415	1959	ro YG, RG	C 12'''600, 27-460, automatic, waterproof
3416	1959	ro YG	C 23-200
3417	1958	ro ST	C 27-AM 400, Amagnetic, waterproof
3418	1958	ro ST	C 27-AM 400, Amagnetic, waterproof, changeable bands
3419	1960	ro ST	C 27-AM 400, Amagnetic, waterproof, changeable bands
3420	1959	ro G	C 27-AM 400
3421		ro PL	C 27 SC, jewelry watch
3422	1960	fa YG	C 99 P
3423	1960	ro YG	C 27 SC
3424	1959	fa YG	C 99 P, 8'''85
3425	1960	ro YG	C 12'''600, 27-460, automatic, waterproof
3426	1960	ro YG	C 23-300
3428	1960	ro YG, RG, PT	C 27-460, automatic, waterproof, usually w/enameled dial
3429	1960	ro YG, WG, RG	C 27-460, automatic, waterproof
3430	1960	sq YG	C 23-300, versions from 3430/1 to 3430/14
3433	1960	ro YG, RG	C 27-460, automatic, waterproof
3434AM	1960	ro YG	C 12'''400
3435	1960	ro YG, RG, PT	C 27-460, automatic, waterproof, snap back
3436	1960	sq YG	C 23-300
3437	1960	fa YG	C 23-300
3438	1960	ro YG	C 27-460, automatic
3439	1960	ro YG	C 27-460, automatic, waterproof
3439/1	1965	ro YG	C 27-460, automatic, waterproof, first HAU worldwide with sapphire display back
3440	1961	ro YG	C 27-460, automatic, waterproof
3441	1961	ro PT	C 27-460, automatic, diamond bezel
3442	1961	ro G	C 23-300
3443	1961	ro G	C 23-300
3444	1961	ro YG	C 27-460, automatic, waterproof
3445	1961	ro YG, WG, RG, PT	C 27-460 M, automatic, date hand, waterproof
3447	1961	ro G	C 99 P
3448	1962	ro YG	C 27-460 C, automatic, PC, 586 pieces.
3449	1961	ro YG	C 23-300 C, PC, 3 pieces
3450	1981	ro YG	C 27-460 C, PC + leap year, 244 pieces
3452(/1)	1961	ro YG, WG	C 27-460, 2 time zones on two separate dials and hands, rare
3453	1961	ro G	C 23-300
3454	1961	ro YG	C 27-460 automatic, waterproof, rare (6 watches known)
3459	1961	ro G	C 23-300
3460	1961	ro YG	C 27 AM, Amagnetic
3461	1961	re YG	C 23-300
3462	1961	re YG	C 23-300, rect. cross
3463	1962	sq YG	C 23-300
3464	1962	ro G	C 23-300
3465	1962	sq PT	C 23-300
3466		ro ST	C 27-460, automatic, waterproof, rare

REFERENCE	FIRST MF'D	CASE/SHAPE/ MATERIAL	CALIBER/FEATURES/SPECIALTIES
3467	1962	sq YG	C 23-300
3468	1962	ro YG	C 23-300
3470		ro YG	C 175
3471	1962	ro G	C 23-300
3472	1962	ro YG	C 23-300, crown at 12
3473	1962	ro YG	C 27-460, automatic, waterproof, rare
3474	1962	sq PT	C 23-30
3475	1962	sq YG, PT	C 23-300
3477	1962	ro YG	C 23-300
3479	1962	sq YG	C 23-300
3483	1963	ro ST	C 27 SC, waterproof, rare
3484	1963	ro YG	C 23-300
3485	1963	sq YG, WG	C 27-460, automatic, rare
3486	1963	ov YG	C 23-300
3487	1963	ov YG	C 23-300
3488	1963	sq G	C 175
3490	1963	sq YG, WG	C 175
3491	1963	sq G	C 175
3492	1963	sq G	C 175
3493	1963	sq G	C 175
3494	1963	sq G	C 175
3495	1963	ro G	C 10'''200
3496	1963	sq PT	C 10'''200
3497	1963	PT	C 99 P, special case
3498	1963	ro G	C 175
3499	1964	PT	C 99 P, special case
3500	1964	ro YG	C 27 SC
3502	1964	sq G	C 10'''200
3503	1964	sq G	C 175
3504	1964	ro G	C 27 SC
3506	1964	sq WG	C 175
3509	1964	ro G, ST	C 23-300
3510	1965	ro G	C 175
3512	1965	ro G	C 175
3513	1965	ro PT	C 175
3514	1965	ro YG, WG, RG, PT	C 27-460 M, automatic, waterproof
3516	1965	ro G	C 23-300
3518	1965	sq G	C 23-300
3519	1965	sq G	C 23-300
3520	1965	ro G	C 23-300
3522	1966	sq G	C 175
3523	1966	sq WG	C 175
3525	1966	sq YG, WG	C 27-460 automatic, waterproof
3526	1966	sq G	C 175
3527	1966	sq G	C 175
3528	1966	sq G	C 175
3536	1966	ro G	C 175
3537	1966	sq G	C 23-300
3538	1966	ro WG	C 23-300
3540/2	1966	sq WG	C 175
3541	1967	ro YG, WG	C 27-460 M, automatic, waterproof
3542		ro YG, WG	C 27-460, automatic, waterproof
3543	1967	ro G	C 23-300

REFERENCE	FIRST MF'D	CASE/SHAPE/ MATERIAL	CALIBER/FEATURES/SPECIALTIES
3544	1967	to G	C 23-300
3545	1967	ov G	C 23-300
3546	1967	to G	C 23-300
3548		elypt.YG	C 28-255 C, automatic
3549	1967	sq G	C 175
3550	1967	re YG	C 10'''200
3553	1967	sq G	C 177
3555	1967	sq WG	C 175
3557	1967	sq WG	C 23-300
3558	1967	ro YG, WG	C 27-460 M, automatic, waterproof
3561	(1968)	ro YG	C 27-460 M, automatic, waterproof, successor model to 3439/1, sapphire display back, rare
3562/1		ro YG	C 175, IOS watch
3563 PC	1981	ro YG	C 27-460 C, automatic, PC
3563	1969	ro YG, WG	C 350, automatic (later version)
3565/1		ro YG	C 27-460 M, automatic, IOS watch
3566	1968	to G	C 175
3567	1968	to G	C 175
3569		ro YG, WG	C 350, automatic
3570	1969	sq G	C 175
3571	1969	re G	C 175
3572	1969	sq G	C 175
3573		to YG, WG	C 350, automatic
3574	1969	ro ST	C 23-300
3577	1969	sq WG	C 175
3578	1969	sq G	C 175
3579	1969	ro ST	C 23-300
3581	1970	ov G	C 23-300
3582	1970	sq G	C 23-300
3583	1970	ov G	C 175
3584	1970	ov G	C 23-300
3585	1970	to WG	C 350, later C 1-350 automatic
3586	1970	ro G	C 350, automatic
3588		ro YG, WG	C 28-255, automatic
3589	1971	ov G	C 28-255, automatic
3590	1971	ro G	C 28-255, automatic
3591		ro YG, WG	C 28-255, automatic
3593		ro YG, WG	C 28-255 C, automatic
3594	1971	ov G	C 28-255, automatic
3597		to YG	quartz movement with date
3598	1972	ov G	C 16-250
3599	1972	sq WG	C 16-250
3600	1972	ro WG	C 28-255, automatic
3601		ro YG, WG	C 28-255 C, automatic
3602		ro G	C 28-255 C, automatic
3603		ro G	quartz movement with date
3604		to YG, WG	quartz movement with date
3605		ov G	C 28-255 C, automatic
3606		ro G	C 28-255 C, automatic
3615	1986	ro YG	C, PC and minute repeater
3700/1	1976	to ST, ST/YG, YG, WG, PT	C 28-255 C, automatic, waterproof

The above catalog includes almost all Patek Philippe References from the period covered in this book. However, we make no claims of completeness. This includes case materials, caliber and complications. There are also gaps in the Reference numbers. This happens when a new model is planned, but then not manufactured. If any reader has information which would help complete this catalog, the author would much appreciate a message. If the number of pieces made is fewer than 20, according to the available information, we used the term "rare". The term "large numbers" refers to production numbers over 1000.

Explanation of abbreviations and terms used:

CASE SHAPES:

fa	fantasy case
ov	oval
re	rectangular
ro	round
sq	square
to	tonneau or barrel-shaped

CASE MATERIALS:

G	no specific information on the type of gold
RG	red or pink gold
WG	white gold
YG	yellow gold
PT	platinum
ST	steel and steel combinations. i.e., ST/YG steel/ yellow gold

OTHER ABBREVIATIONS

PC	perpetual calendar
C	normal calendar
SC	sweep seconds hand

12. Summary list of watches

by Reference number with all relevant information

No.	Ref.	Material	Caliber	Movement no.	Case no.	Production year	Page
1	96	Pink gold	12'''-120	922,367	997.660,	1942	46
2	96	Yellow gold	12'''-120	968,921	303,990	1951	46
3	130	Yellow gold	13'''Chrono	867,227		1947	18
4	565	Yellow gold	12'''-120	938,562	667,674	1952	48
5	570	Pink gold	12'''-400	723,856	306,726	ca. 1954	51
6	570	Yellow gold	27 SC	708,105	4,178,999	1960	50
7	592	Steel	12'''-120	829,746	506,760	1939	52
8	1450	Yellow gold	9'''-90	970,304	651,174	1948	54
9	1463	Steel	13'''Chrono	868,840	660,184	1955	190
10	1463	Pink gold	13'''Chrono	868,532	672,788	1953	190
11	1491	Pink gold	12'''-120	968,379	664,108	ca. 1951	54
12	1491	Yellow gold	12'''SC	864,993	645,221	1947	54

No.	Ref.	Material	Caliber	Movement no.	Case no.	Production year	Page
13	1516	Yellow gold	12'''-120	965,722	332,339	1950	56
14	1518	Yellow gold	13'''Chrono	867,360	650,449	1948	59, 188
15	1518	Yellow gold	13'''Chrono	862,931	629,589	1942	190
16	1527	Yellow gold	13'''Chrono	863,247	634,687	1943	184
17	1563	Yellow gold	13'''*Rattrapante* or double chronograph	863,791	630,551	1946	13
18	1566	Pink gold	12'''-200	965,371	642,317	1946	60
19	2438/1	Pink gold	27 SC Q	888,176	2,619,215	1959	187
20	2449	Pink gold	12'''-400	726,775	670,660	1955	61
21	2451	Yellow gold	10'''-200	958,667	668,790	1952	62
22	2469	Yellow gold	9'''-90	974,777	668,045	1952	63
23	2469	Pink gold	9'''-91	976,035	682,468	1954	63
24	2481	Yellow gold	27 SC	707,885	2,607,824	1958	64
25	2481	Yellow gold	27 SC	707,656	2,607,790	1958	67
26	2483	Pink gold	12'''-120	968,697	661,631	ca. 1951	68
27	2499/100	Yellow gold	13'''Chrono Q	869,282	2,792,138	1984	187
28	2501/1	Yellow gold	10'''-200	958,784	672,412	1952	70
29	2508	Steel	27 SC	708.505	2.614.125	1960	70
30	2508	Yellow gold	27 SC	703,890	680,970	1954	74
31	2509	Yellow gold	12'''-120	938,783	673,731	1953	74
32	2509	Pink gold	12'''-400	726,820	693,707	1955	74
33	2523 HU	Pink gold	12'''-400 *Heures Universelles*	722,706	306,205	1953	21
34	2526	Yellow gold	12'''-600 AT	760,951	683,698	1953	22
35	2526	Yellow gold	12'''-600 AT	763,637	696,013	1956	75

No.	Ref.	Material	Caliber	Movement no.	Case no.	Production year	Page
36	2526	Yellow gold	12'''-600 AT	764,601	2,613,030	1957	78
37	2526	Yellow gold	12'''-600 AT	761,484	684,544	1954	76
38	2533	Yellow gold	27 SC	705,194	691,533	1956	82
39	2537	Pink gold	12'''-400	728,086	424,446	1957	83
40	2540	Pink gold	12'''-600 AT 1	764,811	699,844	1957	85
41	2551	Yellow gold	12'''-600 AT	766,071	2,608,560	1958	88
42	2551	Yellow gold	12'''-600 AT	766,216	2,608,524	1958	88
43	2552	Yellow gold	12'''-600 AT	762,058	688,312	1955	88
44	2552	Yellow gold	12'''-600 AT	762,428	689,767	1955	88
45	2554	Yellow gold	9'''-90	976,999	696,927	1956	92
46	2573/2	Yellow gold	10'''-200	748,484	424,900	ca. 1961	92
47	2583	Yellow gold	12'''-600 AT	763,399	697,241	1956	94
48	2584	Yellow gold	12'''-600 AT	765,654	2,606,355	1958	96
49	2585	Steel	12'''-600 AT	765.932	694,414	1958	96
50	3403	Yellow gold	12'''-600 AT	764,061	309,891	1956	97
51	3415	Pink gold	12'''-600 AT	766,091	2,608,806	1958	103
52	3415	Yellow gold	12'''-600 AT	766,095	2,608,696	1958	103
53	3417	Steel	27-AM 400	732,829	2,633,182	1963	104
54	3419	Steel	27-AM 400	730,715	2,619,877	1962	106
55	3420	Yellow gold	27-AM 400	734,094	432,458	1967	107
56	3425	Yellow gold	27-460	1,114,454	2,639,270	ca. 1965	110
57	3425	Yellow gold	27-460	1,114,987	2,666,201	ca. 1965	110
58	3429	Yellow gold	27-460	1,113,233	2,631,702	ca. 1964	113
59	3429	Yellow gold	27-460	1,113,443	2,644,656	ca. 1964	113

No.	Ref.	Material	Caliber	Movement no.	Case no.	Production year	Page
60	3433	Yellow gold	27-460	1,112,899	2,626,193	1962	114
61	3444	Yellow gold	27-460	1,111,024	2,619,254	1961	116
62	3445	Yellow gold	27-460 M	1,118,030	328,637	1970	119
63	3445	White gold	27-460 M PM	1,230,402	329,656	1971	121
64	3445	White gold	27-460 M PM	1,230,663	318,158	1971	120
65	3445	Yellow gold	27-460 M PM	1,230,981	329,328	1971	121
66	3448	Yellow gold	27-460 Q	1,119,121	322,471	1970	191
67	3454	Yellow gold	27-460	1,112,614	312,558	1962	124
68	3466	Steel	27-460	1,116,171	2,664,436	ca. 1969	128
69	3470	White gold	175	1,130,984	316,240	1964	128
70	3473	Yellow gold	27-460	1,112,437	2,629,723	ca. 1962	134
71	3483	Steel	27 SC	710,826	2,632,453	1963	134
72	3514	Yellow gold	27-460 M	1,123,252	319,417	1965	140
73	3514	Yellow gold	27-460 M	1,123 ,956	320,650	1965	140
74	3514	Yellow gold	27-460 M	1,124,557	319,469	1966	140
75	3514	White gold	27-460 M	1,126,585	322,943	1967	140
76	3541	Yellow gold	27-460 M	1,124,874	320,933	1966	140
77	3542	Yellow gold	27-460	1,115,027	321,169	ca. 1967	148
78	–	Steel	10'''-200	959,100	675,442	–	147
79	3558	Yellow gold	27-460 M	1,118,342	2,689,535	1970	148
80	3558	Yellow gold	27-460 M PM	1,230,449	2,695,315	1971	148
81	3561	Yellow gold	27-460	1,116,766	2,681,327	1970	152
82	3563/2	White gold	350	1,185,655	2,727,909	1974	155
83	3563 3	Yellow gold	1-350	1,499,198	2,698,334	1980	157

No.	Ref.	Material	Caliber	Movement no.	Case no.	Production year	Page
84	3565/1	Yellow gold	27-460 M	1,127,995	2,673,809	1968	158
85	3585	White gold	350	1,188,464	2,728,813	1970	160
86	3588	Yellow gold	28-255	1,280,422	2,714,748	1970	162
87	3588	Yellow gold	28-255	1,281,380	2,708,009	1970	167
88	3591	White gold	28-255	1,292,432	522,745	ca. 1972	167
89	3601	Yellow gold	28-255 C	1,301,935	526,841	1974	171
90	3602	Yellow gold	28-255 C	1,306,031	539,833	1978	176
91	3700/1	Steel	28-255 C	1,309,461	540,862	1980	176
92	3940	Yellow gold	240 Q				202
93	3998	Yellow gold	315 SC				196
94	5170	Yellow gold	CH 29-535 PS				197
95	5120	White gold	240				197
96	5127	White gold	315 SC				197
97	5134	Red gold	215 PS FUS 24 H				198
98	5135	White gold	324 S QA LU 24 H				200
99	5140	White gold	240 Q				202
100	5146	Red gold	324 S IRM QA LU				204
101	5165	Steel	315 SC				205
102	5396 R	White gold	324 S QA LU 24 H				207
103	5196	White gold	215 PS FUS 24 H				209
104	5711/1A	Steel	315 SC				209
105	5960 P	Platinum	CH 28-520 IRM QA 24 H				210
106	5960 R	Red gold	CH 28-520 IRM QA 24 H				211
107	5980/1A		CH 28-250 C				213

13. Index